THE CHURCH IN HISTORY

THE CHURCH'S TEACHING SERIES

Prepared at the request of the Executive Council of the
General Convention of the Episcopal Church

THE
CHURCH
IN HISTORY

Written by John E. Booty
with the assistance of a group of
editorial advisors under the direction of the
Church's Teaching Series Committee

THE SEABURY PRESS / NEW YORK

Second Printing

1979
The Seabury Press
815 Second Avenue
New York, N. Y. 10017

Printed in the United States of America

Library of Congress Cataloging in Publication Data

Booty, John E   The church in history.

(The church's teaching series; v. 3)
Includes bibliographical references and index.
1. Church history.
BR145.2.B66   270   78-26014
ISBN 0-8164-0420-8   ISBN 0-8164-2216-8 pbk.

Grateful acknowledgment is made to the following people
and institutions for permission to use the materials listed:

Robert Manz—photographs of Thomas Cranmer and
F. D. Maurice from St. John's Chapel,
Episcopal Divinity School, Cambridge, Massachusetts.

The Metropolitan Museum of Art—photograph
of sculpture of Ignatius of Antioch,
The Cloisters Collection, 1925.

Royal Rhodes—the map work which follows page 283.

The World Council of Churches—photograph of
Charles Henry Brent.

David Siegenthaler—Suggestions for Further Reading.

Foreword

The series of books published for the most part in the 1950s and known as the Church's Teaching Series has had a profound effect on the life and work of the Episcopal Church during the past twenty years. It is a monumental credit to that original series and to the authors and editors of those volumes that the Church has seen fit to produce a new set of books to be known by the same name. Though the volumes will be different in style and content, the concern for quality education that prompts the issuing of the new series is the same, for the need of Church members for knowledge in areas of scripture, theology, liturgy, history, and ethics is a need that continues from age to age.

I commend this new Church's Teaching Series to all who seek to know the Lord Jesus and to know the great tradition that he has commended to us.

John M. Allin
PRESIDING BISHOP

THE CHURCH'S TEACHING SERIES

Introduction

This is one of a series of volumes in the new Church's Teaching Series. The project has been both challenging and exciting. Not only is there a wide variety of opinions regarding the substance of the teaching of the Church, there are also varying and conflicting views with regard to the methods of communicating this teaching to others. That is why we have tried to pay close attention to the various movements within the Church, and to address them. The development of this new series, therefore, has involved hundreds of men and women throughout the Episcopal Church and is offered as one resource among many for the purposes of Christian education.

While it is neither possible nor perhaps even desirable today to produce a definitive series of books setting forth the specific teachings of a particular denomination, we have tried to emphasize the element of continuity between this new series and the old. Continuity, however, implies movement, and we believe that the new series breaks fresh ground in a creative and positive way.

The new series makes modest claims. It speaks not so much *for* the Episcopal Church as *to* it, and not to this Church only but to Christians of other traditions, and to those who wait expectantly at the edge of the Church.

Two words have been in constant use to describe this project from its inception: affirmation and exploration. The writers have affirmed the great insights of the Christian tradition and have also explored new possibilities for the future in the confidence that the future is God's.

Alan Jones
CHAIRMAN OF THE
CHURCH'S TEACHING SERIES
COMMITTEE

THE CHURCH IN HISTORY

Contents

· 1 ·

The Importance of Church History for Ourselves and for the Community

---

Why Study History?

We study history because we must if we are to be fully human.

How can such a sweeping claim be understood? We begin by confronting the fact that we are social beings. Aristotle, in the fourth century before Christ, wrote of the origins of the political community, the state. It all began with the necessary union of male and female for the perpetuation of humanity. There followed the association of people in families, in villages, in cities, and in nations. Thus the history of humanity began.

That which is true of our origins is emphatically true of our present condition. John Donne, writing in the seventeenth century as Dean of St. Paul's Cathedral, London, affirmed:

> No man is an island, entire of itself; every man is a piece of the continent, a part of the main. If a clod be washed away by the sea, Europe is the less, as well as if a promontory were, as well as if a man of thy friend's or of thine own were: any man's death diminishes me, because I am involved in mankind, and therefore do not send to me to know for whom the bell tolls; it tolls for thee.[1]

1

This involvement in mankind is not limited to space. It embraces time as well. Thus if Donne were living now he might, possibly, write:

"No man is a moment or a lifetime, entire of itself; everyone is a part of the whole, of time past, time present, and time yet to come. What Galileo saw and understood as he looked through his telescope—Alaric the Goth's sack of Rome, Lee Harvey Oswald's assassination of a President—all impinge on my life: Anyone's death, now, in time past, in time to come, diminishes me, because I am involved in mankind, and therefore do not send to me to know for whom the bell tolls; it tolls for thee."

Galileo's discoveries concerning the nature of the universe involved the death of a world view which had dominated human perceptions for centuries. Because he seemed to be turning the truth upside down, his discoveries aroused the ire of the church hierarchy. Alaric's sack of Rome is a symbol of the end of the Roman peace and of Roman domination of the Mediterranean world. But the event is also symbolic of the release of new possibilities, prospects which led to the development of Western Europe with its achievements and failures. Lee Harvey Oswald's fatal shooting of President Kennedy involved the death of hope for many people and a reassessment of ourselves and our corporate life in the latter half of the twentieth century. Such events in time past impinge on us now. We are involved in mankind through the ages. If we are to know who we are we must self-consciously relate ourselves to the past.

We are here engaged in understanding time and our relationship to time. We are probing the mystery of time. In such probing we may expect to discover something about our human nature which we might otherwise ignore. Indeed, because consideration of things past involves work and pain as well as entertainment and fulfillment we are inclined to deny the significance of the past. That we must not, cannot do so was the conviction of Charles Henry Brent, modern missionary, bishop, and statesman of the Episcopal Church. He once referred to a Scottish philosopher, whom he did not name, who asserted that the chief characteristic of time was "its togetherness."[2] Past, present, and future are interrelated. It is true of the individual whose personal history is involved in what we will and do at present. It is also true of society whose corporate history through centuries of human experience is involved in our present social policies and in their application.

Furthermore, if we ignore history we deteriorate, becoming less than fully human. If we refuse to study the past, we abdicate from the power and authority, which we rightly possess, over the historical forces that impinge upon us, and we are in grave danger of being led like dumb oxen into the future. There are strong tendencies within us, as individuals and as groups, to conform to the dominant intellectual, moral, and cultural trends of the present age, without thought, without criticism, and without control.

As humans we are gifted with that which Ortega y Gasset, the Spanish philosopher, has called the historical sense. This is the "sense" by which we perceive the past, and traveling away from ourselves into that past we gain necessary perspective on the present. If we exercise this sense we will gain the leverage needed to break away from the forces of this age which seek to control us, and we will regain our lost humanity. We will also be better prepared to move creatively into the future.

Some people might protest that the study of history often involves an irresponsible flight from present responsibilities. The study of history has also been used to buttress unwarranted, destructive authority in government, religion, art, and science. There is no denying the fact that historical studies can and will be used and abused in the service of base and dehumanizing motives. Historical study needs to be examined critically in order to discern the prejudices and presuppositions of its practitioners. When historical investigation is pursued with the utmost seriousness, the historical sense with which we are endowed works against all abuse and is a means by which we are protected against tyrannical power. Historical study as a rigorous, critical discipline exercised on behalf of humanity, its dignity and freedom, is essential to our well-being and indeed to our survival. This is a fact attested to by the psychiatrist who assists patients to recover their pasts in order that they may find themselves. It is a fact understood by the wise world leader who, for the sake of sanity and survival, will not let anyone forget the horrors of the Nazi death camps, the tragic nightmare of Hiroshima, and the napalm deaths in Vietnam.

Why Study Church History?

We study church history because we are human beings and possess an historical sense. We are involved in mankind. The church as a part of society shares history with those who stand apart from the church. But there is more to the answer than this.

Christianity by its very nature is concerned for history. Unlike others of the world religions, its roots are in historical events which are of the greatest significance. It is composed of the followers of Jesus Christ who we affirm was

> born of the Virgin Mary.
> He suffered under Pontius Pilate,
>   was crucified, died, and was buried.
> He descended to the dead.
> On the third day he rose again.

To be a Christian is to remember the historical Jesus and that which God did through him here on earth, among particular women and children and men. This remembering is not antiquarian in nature, nor is it meant to bolster present church authority. It is not static or passive. The remembering involves experiencing the presence of Christ *now* by the power of the Holy Spirit. As Scripture is read and the Word of God preached, as the Creed is said and the faithful join in Holy Communion, Christians participate in Christ. This is what is meant by the Eternal Present and it has roots in the Hebrew mode of remembering.

In the Book of Deuteronomy (26:5–8) a liturgy is given for the presentation of the firstfruits at the central sanctuary of Israel. Here God's mercies are recounted, and as they are, that which was past is present, the "he" becomes "us":

And you shall make response before the Lord your God, "A wandering Aramean was my father; and he went down into Egypt and sojourned there, few in number; and there he became a nation, great, mighty, and populous. And the Egyptians treated us harshly, and afflicted us, and laid upon us hard bondage. Then we cried to the Lord the God of our fathers . . . and the Lord brought us out of Egypt. . . .

In a similar manner, as Christians remembered their Lord he was in the midst of them. The barrier of time was overcome in the act of thanksgiving which is remembering.

To be a Christian is to remember events on both sides of the central events of God in Christ on earth. God worked through his chosen people, Israel. God works through his chosen people, the New Israel, the Christian community. We remember thus because faith affirms that God the Creator has been God the Redeemer of his marred and fallen creation from the beginning of time. The temporal reality—under Pontius Pilate—is Eternal Fact. Thus twentieth-century Christians understand that they are involved in the Old Israel: it is their history. Anti-Semitism is rejected. Twentieth-century Christians are also involved in the centuries of triumph and tragedy of the church: it is their history. Remembering the course of events from the beginning until now, with the center of history in the historic Jesus illuminating that which went before and that which followed after, Christians derive wisdom and power and inspiration to carry on. They are enabled to carry on that which makes effective the mission of Christ and to break loose from the past as it inhibits that mission of salvation for all peoples.

Remembering, in the dynamic manner which we have been considering, constitutes the primary vocation of the church. Remembering is the chief activity of Christians, for remembering involves action guided and empowered by the Holy Spirit. Remembering is a mode of worship which impels the worshiper to represent Christ in the world as the agent of justice and love.

Even this is not all that must be said. The study of church history is important not only for the reasons given above, but also because such study arouses a sense of the distance and the difference between past and present. This understanding of distance and difference has been of very great importance since, as some scholars believe, it was first introduced by humanists of the fourteenth and fifteenth centuries in Western Europe. It was among the roots of the Reformation of the sixteenth century. Martin Luther and others perceived how different the church they knew in the sixteenth century was from the church of the Apostles and their followers in the first and second centuries. Observing the difference, they sought to reform their decadent and corrupt church according to the example of the earliest church. This understanding of distance and difference can also be found at the roots of the nineteenth-century Anglo-Catholic objection to the Reformation. Hurrell Froude, the friend of John Henry Newman, was most vehement in his denunciation of the reformers, sensing the distance between them and the Middle Ages which he so much admired. A sense of distance and difference from the past, whether expressed through admiration or disgust, is vital for the most fruitful and honest study of history.

Some students of history resist awareness of distance and difference. They demand that everything be put in their own terms so that they may immediately understand and dominate the past. They prefer those who simply recite facts or those who fictionalize history, dressing it up with modern language and attitudes. The differences between past and present are glossed over or obliterated. Even those who understand the importance of remembering may be inclined to this error. To remember Jesus is not to make him one of us. A distance remains; there is a difference between him and us. Likewise, church history is not composed of an endless series of stories which can be used to embellish otherwise dull sermons, pointing out how Augustine or Calvin or Niebuhr thought as we do about this or that. A part of the community of saints, Augustine of Hippo remains a fifth-century bishop of a North African church. There is great distance and difference, in time, space, and basic attitudes, between Augustine and ourselves. To be a student of history in the best sense is to be conscious of historical distances and differences.

It is important, for instance, to realize that the way a person in ancient Rome perceived reality differs greatly from our own perceptions. We take for granted many things which would be incomprehensible to someone in the ancient world. Sigmund Freud's recovery of the unconscious, Charles Darwin's exposition of the evolution of species by means of natural selection, and the discovery of the place of planet earth not at the center of the universe but as a tiny speck rotating around a star which is one among countless numbers of stars—these commonplaces of the modern perception of reality were unknown in sixteenth-century England and in first-century Rome.

Consider for a moment the fact that early Christians viewed the world and humanity at the center of the universe surrounded by spheres at the outer limit of which there was located heaven, where God and the saints dwelt. This is not how we understand the universe, nor can it be, although we cannot say that the way we view it is final in the sense that it will never be modified. Nevertheless, we act on the basis of our understanding of earth as a planet of the sun, the sun as one among millions, the universe limitless.

This difference of perception has, as might be expected, ramifications. For one thing, under the old view God inhabited a place—up there! Now there are serious discussions concerning where God is, if he is anywhere. The modern understanding of God's location is inclined to be abstract and to seek for God, for instance, in the depth of being. Then, too, under the old view the way of salvation was likened to an ascent up a ladder. It has been pictured in terms of a ladder extending up from earth through the rotating spheres to God's heaven. Along the way evil spirits retard while angels assist the pilgrim up the ladder of perfection. The Christian life was thus a pilgrimage, involving the gradual perfection of the saints through prayers and good deeds. Our perception of reality influences our understanding of the Christian life. It is vitally important that we be aware of differing perceptions, realizing the distance which separates us from the past. Being thus sensitive to the differences we shall be better able to study, to criticize, to evaluate, and to learn. We shall also be better equipped to remember that which ought to be remembered and to forget that which ought to be forgotten.

For this reason—that the reader may have some sense of historical distance—there will be words and ideas in the following chapters which seem strange and are at first difficult to understand. You may ask why there are so many quotations, why some of them are so long, and why they aren't put into the author's words instead. The answer is that I want the reader to be constantly reminded of the distance and thus be enabled time and again to encounter the past, not as we would have it but as it was. You are asked, therefore, to *work* through this book, not skipping the quotations because they are difficult, letting them and the interpretations of them sink in until you feel the distance between then and now. Once the distance is sensed, the encounter with the past begins and you will find yourself passing beyond the differences to experience that lively remembering which enriches humanity and faith.

The effort required in reading church history brings rewards as dialogues occur between the reader and the past. Princess Elizabeth of Hungary, Saint Elizabeth, is remembered for the sacrificial care she provided for the sick in the thirteenth century. Thomas More, Lord Chancellor of England in the sixteenth century, has been immortalized as "the man for all seasons" and is remembered for his struggle to remain true to his conscience as his patriotism was being tested. Both saints were in the world and both possessed ample supplies of grace and good humor, Elizabeth entertaining her court, Thomas entertaining his friends in his lively household. Both wore hair shirts, shirts made of haircloth and worn by ascetics and penitents. The shirt worn next to the skin, irritated the flesh and was sometimes painful. Why did they wear such a thing? Were they masochists? Consider the fact seriously and you enter into another world, one far different from that which is familiar to most twentieth-century Americans. It is a world where the scourging of the body is not evidence of mental distress or illness but of health, sanity, and holiness. For unlike the majority of persons who worship before mirrors and live for the sake of the belly and of vanity, Elizabeth of Hungary and Thomas More sought to subdue the body that they might live for God and for those for whom the Lord Christ died on the cross. The hair shirt was an ally, beneficent and good. It did not put an end to their good humors. Instead, it supported them.

Here is something to consider, to wrestle with: persons become more real to us as we realize their otherness. Indeed we might find ourselves learning from them how to love, how to live in obedience to the Lord.

An Anglican Perspective

The historical sense of which I speak is very much a part of that Anglicanism of which the Episcopal Church is an important member. At the time of the Reformation in sixteenth-century Europe the English reformers—William Tyndale, Thomas Cranmer, John Jewel, and others—were actively engaged in studying history. They sought for evidence in their study of the earliest Christian church concerning the essential nature of the Christian witness. This they did in order that the Church of England might be restored to its proper vocation under God as the One, Holy, Catholic, and Apostolic Church in England. On doing so they were following the leadership of the Christian humanists, amongst whom they counted Erasmus of Rotterdam as preeminent. Thus they studied Scripture, the writings of the Fathers of the early church, the records of the first four general councils, and the evidence of history in general from the beginning down to their own time.

The process necessitated distinguishing between those things necessary to salvation which must at all costs be preserved and those matters of indifference which must never be absolutized, which can and often must be changed with the changing circumstances of history. As regards things necessary—Scripture, creeds, sacraments, and episcopal ministry—the church was firm. It stood its ground on what it deemed to be true and necessary and would not budge. As regards things indifferent, it steered a careful, often quite political and compromising course. For instance, the threefold ministry of bishops, priests, and deacons was necessary, but details concerning it, including specific job descriptions and the clothing ministers wore, were matters of indifference and might be left in a fairly fluid condition, as in the case of a job description, or be ordered by the civil government, as in the case of vestments.

It must not be thought that this was worked out by those involved sitting around a table making decisions calmly and with perfect unanimity. The stance or attitude indicated above was worked out over years of difficult struggle. John Jewel, bishop of Salisbury and chief spokesman for the church during the early years of Queen Elizabeth I, was one who grasped and made his own that which might be called the Anglican attitude. Deeply influenced by the continental Reformation, Jewel at first regarded the vestments prescribed by the medieval church as "ridiculous trifles" which should be eliminated from the reformed church as "vestiges of error" and "relics of the Amorites." The queen, as supreme governor of the church, would not allow this. In time Jewel came to accept her stubbornness. The vestments were, after all, matters of indifference, and scruples concerning cope and surplice must not be allowed to jeopardize all that had been gained in England. The things which he acknowledged to be necessary to salvation had been secured. Jewel lamented those who contended about the vestments "as if our religion were contained in this single point; so that they choose rather to lay down their functions and leave their churches empty, than to depart one tittle from their own views of the subject."[3]

This willingness to adapt, adjust, and compromise on lesser matters has been the subject of concern and consternation to some Anglicans in later years. The church often appears to be uncertain, infirm, changing its colors to suit the changing situations. In reality, that which appears to be chameleonlike must be viewed in relation to the church's adherence to the main things, those things necessary to salvation. That which appears to be a sign of weakness may very well be a sign of strength, a recognition that salvation does not rest with vestments, titles, opinions, or the like, but rather with the faith conveyed through Scripture, creeds, sacraments, and episcopal ministry.

This discernment of the historical sense bears much fruit:

1) Some Christians, during the upheavals of the sixteenth century, renounced the past as full of corruption and error.

They might do so on the basis of that history encompassed in the Old and New Testaments, and they might salvage a John Wycliffe and a John Hus out of the Middle Ages, but by and large the evidence for their commitment to reform consisted in large part of their destruction of all that tied them to the past. The Church of England, with its understanding of things essential and things indifferent maintained through the ages, displays a vivid sense of continuity with the past. Tradition is valued and the unending chain of witnesses— from Augustine of Canterbury and Hilda of Whitby, Anselm and Julian of Norwich, to Cranmer and Elizabeth I, Donne and Herbert, Wesley and Keble, Christina Rossetti and Dorothy Sayers, Stephen Bayne and Janani Luvum—is remembered with powerful effects. Not the least of these effects concerns the way in which consciousness of continuity with the past can be a safeguard against overconfidence in this age's wisdom.

2) With the passing of the sixteenth century and the broadening of knowledge and understanding among the leaders of the Church of England, the historical sense made persons such as Lancelot Andrewes, John Donne, and Francis Bacon deeply conscious of membership in the Church Universal. Richard Church, one of the original Tractarians and nineteenth-century Dean of St. Paul's Cathedral, London, wrote of how they

> refused to forget . . . what God's Spirit had done in other portions of Christendom, perhaps far removed, perhaps for the time bitterly hostile. They learned to pray as Andrewes did, "for the Catholic Church, its establishment and increase; for the Eastern, its deliverance and union; for the Western, its adjustment and peace; for the British, the supply of what is wanting in it, the strengthening of that which remains in it.[4]

This vision, bred in large part of the historical sense, was not always and everywhere maintained in the Anglican Communion. There have always been times when narrower spirits have seized control to the detriment of the church. But the vision persisted against all that sought to destroy it and helped make this communion preeminent in the ecumenical movement of the twentieth century.

3) The historical sense has inspired and supported high standards of learning and produced amongst its bishops remarkable scholars. In the seventeenth century there was James Ussher, Archbishop of Armagh, whose works filled seventeen volumes in a nineteenth-century edition and included a treatise on the succession of the church which sought to vindicate Anglican doctrine as standing in continuity with the church's teaching from the Apostles to his own time. In the eighteenth century there came Joseph Butler, bishop of Durham, whose *Analogy of Religion* is one of the finest theological expositions and is imbued with the historical sense. In the nineteenth century there was Joseph Barber Lightfoot, bishop of Durham, whose commentaries on Philippians and Colossians display his immense historical knowledge and wisdom.

In the United States during the nineteenth century two learned priests maintained the high standards of learning demanded by Anglican tradition. William Porcher Dubose at the University of the South in Sewanee, Tennessee, wrote volumes of creative theology such as *The Soteriology of the New Testament* (1892) which were influential in England as well as in America. Alexander Crummell, the founder of St. Luke's, Washington, D.C., educated at Andover Seminary in Boston and at Queens College, Cambridge, England, and a teacher at the College of Liberia, was a vigorous and learned spokesman for the black church and was known as "An Apostle of Negro Culture."

There have also been outstanding examples of scholarship amongst Anglican laity in the twentieth century: Evelyn Underhill, the author of two influential books, *Worship* and *Mysticism;* Marianne Micks, Professor of Theology at Virginia Theological Seminary, whose study of the Eucharist, *The Future Present,* has been appreciatively read by many; William Stringfellow, controversial lawyer-theologian who has used his considerable learning to interpret the Gospel in terms of contemporary crises; T. S. Eliot, poet, dramatist, social commentator, theologian, whose *Four Quartets* constitute one of the greatest expressions of the Christian faith in our time; Dorothy Sayers, author of the Peter Wimsey mysteries and of the *Mind of the Maker;* and C. S. Lewis, Oxford scholar, author of the *Screwtape Letters,* the Narnia chronicles, and science fiction type novels all of which present the Christian faith in language and in images of the twentieth century. The historical sense has informed all of these and has done much to direct their scholarship as well as to call it forth.

4) The exercise of the historical sense in Anglicanism involves the willingness to accept the findings of historical investigations. Thus there could be no doubt that Anglicans would in time accept the findings of modern, historical/ biblical criticism. However, this does not mean that every apparent finding of historical investigation must be accepted as final truth. The findings themselves are subject to the criticism of the historical sense in the church and in individual Christians. There is an area of Christian faith and practice which cannot be surrendered to the findings of historical investigators. The firm center, however difficult it may be to define and discuss in our day, establishes the limits. The findings concerning the historical Jesus portrayed in the first three Gospels (Matthew, Mark, and Luke) must always be informed by biblical, creedal, and liturgical affirmations concerning the Christ of faith. And yet in large areas of Christian understanding and practice the dictum propounded by William Sparrow of the Virginia Theological Seminary in the nineteenth century—"Seek the Truth, Come Whence it May, Cost What it Will"—is adhered to with the expectation that fresh perceptions of the truth will necessitate alterations in the mode of theological expression and in the nature of Christian action.

There are, as might be expected, notable examples of failure on this score. Churches are fundamentally conservative. Nevertheless, Anglicanism possesses something which is widely shared by other Christians. This is the conviction that in order to conserve the Gospel the church must constantly be engaged in the interpretation of it, taking seriously the contemporary world, ever ready to embrace that which is revealed in the present as good and true. The church will do this even though it may at times seem to contradict and even destroy that which has been revered as valuable and necessary. The Gospel is alive! It is dynamic! It will never contradict the honest, verifiable findings of historical investigation, nor can those findings negate the essential truth of the Gospel.

5) The historical sense dictates the necessity for Anglicans to exercise tolerance toward one another, and especially toward those who appear to be in error. This is in tune with the Anglican conviction concerning the largeness of truth, its varieties and complexities. Richard Hooker, writing against the Puritans at the end of the sixteenth century, put it this way:

> Whatsoever either men on earth or the Angels of heaven do know, it is as a drop of that unemptiable fountain of wisdom; which wisdom hath diversely imparted her treasures unto the world. As her ways are of sundry kinds, so her manner of teaching is not merely one and the same. Some things she openeth by the sacred books of Scripture; some things by the glorious works of Nature: with some things she inspireth them from above with spiritual influence; in some things she leadeth and traineth them only by worldly experience and practice. We may not so in any one special kind admire her, that we disgrace her in any other; but let her ways be according unto their place and degree adored.[5]

The historical sense opens the mind to the immensity of knowledge and wisdom, inspiring awe and humility.

6) This attitude of awe and humility is appropriate to a church which is so greatly influenced by its liturgy. The liturgy of the Book of Common Prayer, from 1549 to the present has, in keeping with the tradition rooted in the Scripture, emphasized worship as bowing before the Lord God with thanksgiving and humility. Worship thus understood is expressed vividly when we pray:

> Almighty God, unto whom all hearts are open, all desires known, and from whom no secrets are hid: Cleanse the thoughts of our hearts by the inspiration of thy Holy Spirit, that we may perfectly love thee, and worthily magnify thy holy Name; through Christ our Lord. *Amen.*

The Plan of This Book

There are many possible ways of writing a history book, but the most familiar way is exemplified by the school textbook which begins at a certain date, proceeds year by year, decade by decade, century by century, until it stops at another date. The author may declare in a preface, which will not be read, that her book is not complete, she has not included *every* significant event or named *every* important name, and that she has exercised certain rational criteria for selecting that which she has included. But the reader will assume that the author is the authority on her subject and that her books say all that is worth saying about the administration of Millard Fillmore, the history of the church in Sikkim, or the history of the world from prehistory to the present.

This book must not, and indeed cannot, be approached in such a manner. Its scope is very large, but no attempt is made to cover everything, even everything important. It deals with themes involving issues. The second chapter is "The Christian Community: The Body of Christ, an Evolving Institution," and the issue addressed might be put this way: *What is the church and what constitutes its essential nature?* The third chapter is "Renewal and Reform: 'Behold I make all things new,'" and the issue addressed might be put this way: *How is a church which is faltering and weak to be renewed, reformed?* The fourth is, "Church and Culture: Christ and Caesar in Tension," a title which suggests an answer to the question: *How are Christ and culture, church and state related in history and how ought they to be related now?* The fifth chapter is, "The Mission of the Community: 'To Every Kindred and Tongue,'" and the issue is: *What has been the church's self-understanding of its mission in history and what ought it to be now and for the future?*

Each of these issues is then investigated historically, with a certain procedure being followed: (1) The theme is established in a biographical sketch. Here the importance of the study of history by means of biography is affirmed. (2) There is then a brief discussion of the organizing principle being used, the basis on which the historical investigation is conducted and the course of events surveyed. Here we affirm that history is always considered by concrete persons endowed with experience, prejudices, and presuppositions. (3) There follows the historical survey running from the first century to the twentieth. Much too much is made of divisions or periods in the writing of history, but in this survey section I have found it convenient to explore each theme in terms of events which occurred in the early church, the Middle Ages, the Reformation (especially in England), and in more recent times (from the mid-seventeenth century on). Here we affirm the importance in historical study of detailed knowledge over a large segment of time. In exploring history in this manner the student is forced to come to grips with change.

Given this structure it should be possible for the reader to tackle the book in various ways. The biographies could be read alone, as could the brief sections on method or the more extensive sections of historical survey. Periods could be isolated, using the table of contents, so that all sections concerning the Middle Ages could be read together. There will always be those who prefer to read the conclusions before the rest. Let them be warned! The author is aware of this device, having indulged in it on occasion, and has on the whole eschewed the grand conclusion, having already, at the beginning of each of the following chapters, revealed his method and his convictions.

Having said this, it must now be admitted that the chapters were written to be read as a whole and consecutively. They presuppose one another in the order in which they are presented. Thus we begin with self-scrutiny (Who are we?) and gradually turn outward to consider the mission of the church to the world. We begin by considering the church, its founding and its evolution, as an institution in space and time. We then consider the renewal and reform of the institution. Renewal and reform are presented as constant factors in the history of the church, necessary if the church is to function meaningfully in the culture in which it exists and be an effective instrument for Christ's mission to the world. Thus the chapters depend on one another. And yet all of the themes are involved in the treatment of each particular theme, so that as a whole the fabric is a blend of interwoven threads. This being the case, some overlapping, some repetition is inevitable.

Let there be no misunderstanding, however. This is not *the* way, but only *a* way of viewing the history of the Christian community. There is no one right way to narrate the history of the church for all times and all places. The history of the church will differ according to the differing people who exercise the historical sense. Roman Catholics, Eastern Orthodox, Christians from third world nations—all will perceive things from somewhat differing angles, reflecting their particular heritages and concerns. This book is unabashedly Anglican, which is both its weakness and its strength. It is most definitely reflective of the modern West: reality is here perceived by a twentieth-century American, a priest of the Episcopal Church, a seminary teacher whose scholarly interests are focused on the sixteenth-century Church of England. This is most clearly not the definitive history of the Christian Church!

I would be less than honest, however, if I did not express my hope that certain main themes such as those represented in this book are not limited in the way in which the author is limited. They are themes which are relevant to all Christians, to all churches, for all times:

- The quest for an understanding of the people of God in history, who they are, and those elements which constitute their essential nature.
- The historical processes for the renewal and reform of the holy community.
- Some understanding of the various ways in which Christ and culture, church and state relate and should be related.
- The mission which is the community's vocation in the world in obedience to Christ, what it is and how it should be understood and carried out.

It is with this conviction in mind that you are invited to proceed.

· 2 ·

The Christian Community:
The Body of Christ,
an Evolving Institution

Ignatius of Antioch and the Beginning
of the Church in History

A man sits huddled at a crude table writing letters by the light of the rising sun. There is little time left. In a few moments the Roman soldiers will arrive to escort him on another leg of the journey which will end in his death in the arena at Rome.

The man is Ignatius, bishop of Antioch-on-the-Orontes, the great city of half a million people at the eastern end of the Mediterranean Sea. Roads from Edessa beyond the Euphrates, from Tyre and Sidon, from Asia Minor, from Greece and Rome converged upon it making it a major political and commercial center. The city was cosmopolitan, a melting pot in which Jews, Greeks, and Romans mingled. Exotic religions abounded, including those dedicated to the worship of Daphne, Apollo, Venus, and Isis. It was said to be a decadent place with licentious rites performed in the suburban grove of Daphne.

Ignatius was the bishop of the small but growing Christian community in this city. The community began when follow-

Ignatius of Antioch, d.c. 117

ers of Jesus fled from Jerusalem during the persecution which resulted in the death of Stephen, an event recorded in the New Testament Book of the Acts of the Apostles. These refugees began their witness to Jesus in the Jewish community of Antioch. Soon they experienced such success that a special apostolic envoy, Barnabas, was sent to them. He obtained the assistance of Saul of Tarsus, whom we know as the Apostle Paul. In time the community of Christians commissioned Paul and Barnabas to go further, and a series of missionary journeys began reaching into Asia Minor, Greece, and beyond. The missionaries returned to Antioch telling of their success, particularly of the response of the Gentiles to the Gospel they preached. When news of this reached Jerusalem special delegates were sent to caution Paul and Barnabas and a struggle ensued which resulted in the recognition that the Gospel was for all people and was not limited to the Jews.

It was in this important Christian community that Ignatius was made bishop. The prisoner writing by the light of the growing dawn was believed to have been born during the lifetime of Jesus of Nazareth. Indeed, a legend identified Ignatius with the child whom Jesus took into his arms and presented to the Apostles as an example of humility. He was, as he sat writing, an aging man. The year is uncertain, but it was somewhere between A.D. 110 and 117 when Ignatius committed the offense which resulted in his arrest and condemnation. Most likely he had refused to participate in the "ruler cult," unwilling to pledge allegiance to the Emperor Trajan as to a divine being. Whatever the cause, it was sufficient to send him on the way to Rome and to death.

The letters are finished. The soldiers arrive. The journey starts again, a journey which seems at times to be more of a triumphal procession than the passage of a prisoner on his way to death.

Seven letters from Ignatius's pen have survived, providing us with valuable evidence concerning the earliest history of the church. Through them we become acquainted with a remarkable man, one who helped form the institutional church with its charter (Scripture and creeds), organization (bishops, presbyters, and deacons), and work to do (liturgy). We turn now to these letters and to consideration of the founding of the Church Catholic.

Christ stands at the center of Ignatius's faith. He pictured Christ as struggling against that evil which disrupts the original, God-given unity of all things on earth and in the heavens. The struggle continues in the church, which is composed of people who seek, with God's help, to live in harmony with God's will for them. To his mind the church is both the world seeking unity and the agency by which the world is led toward unity with the Creator.

The unity of which he writes involves much. It has to do

with unity of faith, faith which precedes all human efforts and is God-given. In a particularly difficult passage, where in both the original Greek and in the English translation there are problems of interpretation, Ignatius testified:

> I then did my best as a man who was set on unity. But where there is division and anger God does not dwell. The Lord then forgives all who repent, if their repentance leads to the unity of God and the council of the bishop. I have faith in the grace of Jesus Christ, and he shall loose every bond from you. But I beseech you to do nothing in factiousness, but after the teaching of Christ. For I heard some men saying, "if I find it not in the archives [the Law and Prophets of the Old Testament, perhaps] I believe it not in the Gospel." And when I said to them it is in the Scripture [Christ being foretold by the prophets, for instance], they answered me, "that is exactly the question." But to me the archives are Jesus Christ, the inviolable archives are his cross and death and resurrection, and the faith which is through him. In these I desire to be justified by your prayers.[1]

Here Ignatius demonstrates his understanding of the Gospel. At the heart of all there is a Person. The Scriptures (for Ignatius they are the Old Testament) witness to Christ as do the writings of the evangelists and others who knew and followed the Lord. Ignatius is certain of the proper order: first the revelation of God in Christ, which alone brings faith and is the ground for all that Christians think and do in harmony with the will of God. Over and over again he states in creed-like form that which is for him most essential: "be convinced of the birth and passion and resurrection which took place at the time of the procuratorship of Pontius Pilate; for these things were truly and certainly done by Jesus Christ, our hope, from which God grant that none of you be turned aside";[2] "Be deaf therefore when anyone speaks to you apart from Jesus Christ, who was of the family of David, and of Mary, who was truly born, both ate and drank, was truly persecuted under Pontius Pilate, was truly crucified and died in the sight of those in heaven and on earth and under the earth; who also was truly raised from the dead, when his Father raised him up, as in the same manner his Father shall raise up in Christ Jesus us who believe in him, without whom we have no true life";[3] and in another passage he states that the Gospel has preeminence over the Old Testament in that it concerns "the coming of the Saviour, our Lord Jesus Christ, his passion and the resurrection."[4]

In such creedlike statements we observe the beginnings of church doctrine. It is doctrine based upon knowledge of Jesus Christ as witnessed to by his followers. It is based too upon Old Testament prophecy and is worked out in the midst of the battle with the Prince of this world, in the midst of persecution, heresy, and schism.

It is unity in this doctrine, centered upon faith in Jesus Christ, to which Ignatius refers, unity which produces community among the faithful, community which is itself a witness to Christ. That is to say that Christian faith issues in a style of life characterized by love. Ignatius put it this way:

> None of these things are unknown to you if you possess perfect faith towards Jesus Christ, and love, which are the beginning and end of life; for the beginning is faith and the end is love, and when the two are joined together in unity it is God, and all other noble things follow after them. No man who professes faith sins, nor does he hate who has obtained love.[5]

Heretics are noted for their lack of love: "For love they have no care, none for the widow, none for the orphan, none for the distressed, none for the afflicted, none for the prisoner, or for him released from prison, none for the hungry or thirsty."[6] And why? Because they do not have Christ. They deny Christ in various ways, the Judaizers denying that he is more than a great teacher, those known as docetists denying that he suffered, died, and was buried. "They abstain from Eucharist and prayer, because they do not confess that the Eucharist is the flesh of our Saviour Jesus Christ, who suffered for our sins, which the Father raised up by his goodness."[7]

To preserve and perfect the unity which is from God and divine there is the bishop who presides over the Eucharist, assisted by presbyters and deacons. The bishop is the symbol of Christian unity and the agency by which union with God occurs. He is the guardian of the faith, God's representative in the congregation, the one who preserves the people from heresy and schism when they follow his leadership. Ignatius is not concerned with matters of power and jurisdiction. He is concerned for the faith and in the face of persecution, heresy, and schism he acknowledges the strategic importance of the bishop as the living symbol of the community's faith and unity in God. He sees this symbolic power of the bishop most clearly in relationship to the Eucharist. In one of his most quoted statements Ignatius said:

> Be careful therefore to use one Eucharist (for there is one flesh of our Lord Jesus Christ, and one cup for union with his blood, one altar, as there is one bishop with the presbytery and the deacons my fellow servants), in order that whatever you do you may do it according unto God.[8]

Here Ignatius built upon Paul's first Epistle to the Corinthians (10:16–17) and pursued a train of thought which has been of the utmost importance for the Christian community throughout history. It has provided the basis, not only for an understanding of salvation and of the church but for the church's social teachings. The emphasis falls upon providing love where there is hate, community where there is disorder, care for those in need where there is callous mistreatment of the weak and the poor.

Over against the lust for power and domination, Ignatius, reflecting the influence of Paul in the epistles to the Thessalonians, Colossians, and Corinthians, exhorts:

> Now for other men "pray unceasingly," for there is in them a hope of repentance, that they may find God. Suffer them therefore to become your disciples, at least through your deeds. Be yourselves gentle in answer to their wrath; be humble minded in answer to their proud speaking; offer prayer for their blasphemy; be stedfast in the faith for their error; be gentle for their cruelty, and do not seek to retaliate. Let us be proved their brothers by our gentleness and let us be imitators of the Lord, and seek who may suffer the more wrong, be the more destitute, the more despised; that no plant of the devil be found in you but that you remain in all purity and sobriety in Jesus Christ, both in the flesh and in the Spirit.[9]

Such a point of view was as difficult for most ancients to accept as it is for most moderns. For Ignatius it was inescapable for he had in mind the passion of his Lord, which was the culmination of his serving ministry. As he went on his way to his own death, Ignatius sought to emulate the sacrificial life and death of his Lord.

Escorted by the armed guard, Ignatius understood all that was happening to him in relationship to the revelation of God in Christ Jesus. Here we have his most famous statement:

> I am writing to all the Churches, and I give injunctions to all men, that I am dying willingly for God's sake, if you do not hinder it. I beseech you, be not "an unseasonable kindness" to me. Suffer me to be eaten by the beasts that I may be found pure bread of Christ. Rather entice the wild beasts that they may become my tomb, and leave no trace of my body, that when I fall asleep I be not burdensome to any. Then shall I be truly a disciple of Jesus Christ, when the world shall not even see my body. Beseech Christ on my behalf, that I may be found a sacrifice through these instruments. I do not order you as did Peter and Paul [he is writing to Rome]; they were Apostles, I am a convict; they were free, I am even until now a slave. But if I suffer I shall be Jesus Christ's freedman, and in him I shall rise free. Now I am learning in my bonds to give up all desires.[10]

It is difficult now to feel the intensity of the Christian life lived in those days. Exposed to an hostile environment, suffering persecution for the sake of the Gospel, engaged in life and death struggles concerning the faith within the community of the faithful, the earliest Christians felt that they were living at the end of time. This conviction was waning by the time of Ignatius but it was still there. We read:

> These are the last times. Therefore let us be modest, let us fear the long-suffering of God, that it may not become our judgment. For let us either fear the wrath to come, or love the grace which is present,—one of the two,—only let us be found in Christ Jesus unto true life. Without him let nothing seem comely to you, for in him I carry about my chains, the spiritual pearls in which may it be granted to me to rise again through your prayers, which I beg that I may ever share . . .[11]

To go to one's death in the arena, following in the way of the Lord, was to participate fully in the last events of history, to be perfected for participation in the messianic banquet in heaven. Already, in the course of his progress toward Rome, Ignatius was experiencing that which is beyond history. He was already escaping from the corrupt world into perfect unity with God.

Ignatius is counted among the martyrs of the church. What little we know of him we gather from the seven letters he wrote on his way to Rome. These letters are also of value for that which they reveal to us about the development of the church as an institution. It is hazardous to claim that what we read in these few letters is applicable to the church in Jerusalem, Alexandria, Rome, and elsewhere. The churches located in the various parts of the Roman Empire shared a common faith in Christ but differed in many ways, particularly in terms of those things which were not of the essence of the faith. And yet it is reasonable to regard these letters as evidence concerning the earliest development of the church.

Exploring its meaning and mission in and through concrete historical events, beset by persecution, heresy, and schism, the church came to acknowledge a body of writings as authoritative Scripture, faithfully preserving the original Christian experience; the church drew up creeds and creedlike statements which expressed the heart of the faith contained in Scripture; devised a ministry and organization centered upon episcopacy, intending that it be the guardian of the faith and the maintainer of peace and unity in the church; and administered sacraments, in particular Baptism and the Eucharist, as means by which persons were incorporated into the holy community and nourished to follow in the way of the Lord.

The Chicago-Lambeth Quadrilateral and the Visible Church

We now leap forward eighteen hundred years to the Lambeth Conference of Anglican Bishops meeting in London in 1920. It was a time when world leaders were intent upon establishing peace and strengthening the unity of nations recently divided by war. Regarding the divided condition of the Christian community and the contrary surge of the times, as well as the Gospel, the bishops issued an appeal for reunion entitled "To All Christian People." They made clear the minimal, essential elements which constitute the church and form the basis of the church's unity. In doing this they relied upon four points set down by the Lambeth Conference of 1888. These points had been devised by the American, William Reed Huntington, and incorporated in a Declaration concerning Unity adopted by the House of Bishops at the General Convention meeting in Chicago in 1886.

Huntington was a prominent leader of the Episcopal Church toward the end of the nineteenth century. Rector of Grace Church, New York, he was instrumental in the revision of the Book of Common Prayer, resulting in the Prayer Book of 1892. In his book, *The Church Idea: An Essay Towards Unity* (1870), Huntington was concerned to isolate "the absolutely essential features of the Anglican position." He dismissed many of those things which immediately come to mind when the word "Anglican" is mentioned: "a flutter of surplices, a vision of village spires and cathedral towers, a somewhat stiff and stately company of deans, prebendaries, and choristers." The Anglican principle, as he called it, was far more substantial than that: it is nothing less than that which identifies the Church Catholic, the foursquare combination of Scripture, creeds, sacraments, and "the Episcopate as the key-stone of Governmental unity."[12]

By 1920, after years of discussion and revision, this Quadrilateral "of pure Anglicanism," as Huntington put it, was established in this form:

> We believe that the visible unity of the Church will be found to involve the whole-hearted acceptance of:-
>
> The Holy Scriptures as the record of God's revelation of Himself to man, and as being the rule and ultimate standard of faith; and the Creed commonly called Nicene, as the sufficient statement of the Christian faith, and either it or the Apostles' Creed as the Baptismal confession of belief.
>
> The divinely instituted sacraments of Baptism and the Holy Communion, as expressing for all the corporate life of the whole fellowship, in and with Christ.

A ministry acknowledged by every part of the Church as possessing not only the inward call of the Spirit but also the commission of Christ and the authority of the whole body.[13]

The last paragraph, concerning the ministry, was at the time, as it was before and has been since, a source of considerable controversy. The Chicago-Lambeth Quadrilateral (1888) put it in the form which has been most widely accepted in the Anglican Communion: "IV. The Historic Episcopate, locally adapted in the methods of its administration to the varying needs of the nations and peoples called of God into the unity of His Church."[14]

There is a fundamental agreement between the letters of Ignatius of Antioch and the appeal of the bishops at Lambeth in 1920. They both call for unity based upon personal experience of the Gospel as a dying and rising again in the one body, the holy community, the Church Catholic. Christ is known through participation in that body, the Church Catholic, which has as its outward marks and living instruments of grace, Scripture, creeds, sacraments, and the historic episcopate. It has these things not as absolute in and of themselves, but as gifts of God for participation in Christ.

Furthermore, we learn from Ignatius to view the Church Catholic with Scripture, creeds, sacraments, and episcopacy not as static but as dynamic and growing. Jesus did not leave his followers with any of these things in a finished, final form so that they simply took up a "manual" and made the machinery go. The institution as we know it evolved. The essential elements, all derived from and gaining authority from the Lord, gradually took shape and have continued to grow and change down through the years. The church in its external structures has been in a continual process of change, influenced by the changing historical situation, the dynamic struggle of human sin and error and the divine goodness and truth.

We turn now to consider the evolving of the church out of the encounter with Jesus as the Christ. That the evolution took place under the inspiration and with the guidance of the Holy Spirit is an affirmation of faith. That it was affected in the course of this evolution by human sin and error, so that from the beginning it was less than divine, is an affirmation of common sense, and of faith as well. The church, from Ignatius to the present, has existed not to draw people to itself but to its Lord, who indwells it as living Spirit, and judges it as well.

The Gospel, the Scripture, and the Rule of Faith

In the beginning the witness to God's acts in Christ was not contained in a written record, but was transmitted by word of mouth and by the actions of believers. The Bible for the earliest Christians was the Jewish Scriptures in Hebrew and in the Greek version from Egypt known as the Septuagint. That Bible was interpreted in relation to the unwritten Gospel: the prophets foretold Christ's coming.

In the Book of Acts and in the epistles of Paul we have the earliest presentation of the Gospel in the so-called apostolic preaching. Here we can discern the beginnings of the New Testament and of Christian doctrine. The preaching went something like this: "The age of fulfillment foretold by the prophets has dawned. This has occurred through the ministry, death, and resurrection of Jesus of Nazareth." A brief account of the facts is ordinarily given along with proof from the Scripture that everything took place through "the determinate counsel and foreknowledge of God." In relation to this, note is taken of Jesus' Davidic descent. The preaching continues with the observation that by virtue of his resurrection this Jesus has been exalted at the right hand of God as the Messiah, the head of the new Israel. The Holy Spirit in the church is the sign of Christ's continuing power and glory among us. The preaching insists that the present age will shortly come to an end with the return of Christ out of the heavens. The preacher, whether Peter or Paul, closes with an appeal for repentance and the offer of forgiveness and of the Holy Spirit, together with the promise of salvation, that is to say the promise of the life to come for those of the community of the elect.[15]

In time that which was transmitted by preaching was written down. Some of the letters which now are found in the New Testament were written to preach or transmit the Gospel by a preacher absent from those he sought to reach. Some were written much as business letters might be written today, in order to convey some necessary information and bring about some desired outcome. Other parts of the New Testament were written, as for instance the Gospels, in order to preserve a true witness to God's acts in Christ. As time passed and the letters and Gospels were read at meetings of the Christian community it became necessary to determine which letters and which Gospels among a great number should be read publicly and which excluded. In time there was a great mass of written material available for use in the congregations. Besides that which now constitutes the New Testament there were works of the Apostolic Fathers— Clement of Rome, the *Shepherd* of Hermas, the *Teaching of the Twelve Apostles* (or *Didache*), for instance—and works which were suspect from the *Acts of Paul and Thecla* and the *Apocalypse of Peter* to the gnostic *Gospel of Truth* and the impressive *Gospel of Thomas* containing secret sayings of Jesus. It became vitally important by the second century to determine which of the writings among all of the contenders were authoritative, could safely and usefully be read in public worship, and were derived from the Apostles and did not contradict the apostolic preaching.

The threat of heresy was not overcome by Ignatius and his letters to the churches. False teaching continued and grew, as one might expect given the volatile religious situation of the Roman Empire. Religious pluralism, the weakening of the Roman rule on which the Roman peace depended, the relative fluidity of the church in its beginning stages are all factors which must be taken into account. In particular one must note a great variety of gnostics, persons who claimed to possess a hidden knowledge which could effect salvation. Some gnostics were Jewish, some heathen, and some Christian, but all shared the conviction that the world is a bad place, under the control of evil forces or ignorance or nothing. As such it could not be redeemed. The divine spark within every person is the only thing that can be rescued out of this hell, and it is saved when by divine mercy and grace it is enabled to know itself, from whence it came, and to what it is destined. Basilides in Egypt and Valentinus in Rome, whose groups stood closest to the church, embraced gnostic dualism and in doing so regarded all flesh as corrupt. To them it was impossible that God should become flesh. It may have seemed that he did so in Jesus Christ but it could not have actually happened.

Standing to one side of the mainstream of gnoticism there was Marcion, whose origins were in Asia Minor, who came to Rome and was excommunicated there in A.D. 144. Sharing the gnostic attitude toward the world, Marcion rejected the Old Testament as being the record of the God of the Jews, the creator of this hopeless world. The God of the Jews he contrasted with the God of Jesus. However, Marcion rejected the Incarnation because he could not accept that the divine redeemer could have condescended to be born of a woman. Of the writings regarded as authoritative witnesses to God's acts in Christ, Marcion chose the letters of Paul and the Gospel of Luke, both of which having to be amended due to the corruptions perpetrated upon the original texts by the Jews or by Jewish sympathizers.

In the eighteenth century there was discovered a list of the Scriptures acknowledged by the Church of Rome about A.D. 190. Known as the Muratorian Fragment, it was named after its discoverer and begins in mid-sentence with the clear indication that among the authoritative writings the Gospels of Matthew and Mark have been mentioned. There follow Luke and John, Acts, the letters of Paul, Philemon, Titus, Timothy, Jude, and two letters of John. The writer mentions that there are other letters in circulation: "one to the Laodicenes, another to the Alexandrians, both forged in Paul's name to suit the heresy of Marcion, and several others, which cannot be received into the Catholic Church; for it is not fitting that gall be mixed with honey." Mention is made of the *Wisdom of Solomon* and of the *Revelation of John* and the *Apocalypse of Peter* "which some of our friends will not have read in the Church." As to the *Shepherd* of Hermas, the apocalypse written in Rome about A.D. 140, we read:

the Shepherd was written quite lately in our times in the city of
Rome by Hermas, while his brother Pius, the bishop, was sitting in the chair of the church of the city of Rome; and therefore
it ought indeed to be read, but it cannot to the end of time be
publicly read in the Church to the people, either among the
prophets, who are complete in number, or among the
Apostles.[16]

Works of Valentinus and Miltiades are refused: "those who
have also composed a new book of Psalms for Marcion,
together with Basileides and the Asian founder of the Cata-
phrygians are reject."[17] Other lists argue differently and contain variations, but by the end of the second century a consensus seems to have emerged, which does not mean that
there was from that point on a legal, closed, and authoritative
New Testament canon.

Once more we must attempt to see things in perspective.
We can best do this by reference to Irenaeus, Bishop of Lyons
in Gaul from about A.D. 178. He came from Asia Minor where
he had been a pupil of Polycarp of Smyrna, a contemporary
of Ignatius of Antioch. A theologian and ecclesiastical
statesman of considerable power, Irenaeus recognized the
gravity of the gnostic assault on the Gospel and did battle
against it and against Marcion. In opposition to the gnostic
claim to possess a secret knowledge or tradition, Irenaeus
referred to a public and apostolic tradition, preserved in the
Gospels and in the oral tradition of the faith as contained in
the rule of faith. This tradition is safeguarded by the succession of bishops in each locality, but preeminently in the city
of Rome. Thus he wrote:

> The true knowledge, the teaching of the apostles, and the primi-
> tive structure of the Church throughout all the world, and the
> nature [character] of the body of Christ according to the succes-
> sions of the bishops to whom they entrusted the Church which
> is in every place; this teaching has come down to us, having
> been preserved without any use of forged writings, by being
> handled in its complete fulness, neither receiving addition nor
> suffering curtailment; and reading without falsification, and
> honest and steady exposition of the Scriptures without either
> danger or blasphemy; and the special gift of love which is more
> precious than knowledge, and, further, more glorious than
> prophecy, and also superior to all the other sacred gifts.[18]

It is important to note here the place of the rule of faith to which Irenaeus referred. The rule of faith contains the key to that which the church believed to be essential in Scripture. Here in capsule form they described and proclaimed the apostolic tradition. It is not a creed because it is more fluid than creeds tend to be. It is the Gospel in miniature, as understood by the faithful student of the Scripture and expressed in his or her own words. There are numerous examples, but this one from Irenaeus is especially valuable given the importance of the man and of the heresies with which he did battle:

> For the church, although disseminated to all the world, even to the ends of the earth, has received from the Apostles and their disciples this faith, which is in one God, the Father Almighty, who made heaven and earth and sea and all that is in them: and in one Christ Jesus the son of God, incarnate for our salvation: and in the Holy Spirit who through the prophets proclaimed the dispensations and the advents and the birth from a virgin and the passion and the resurrection from the dead and the bodily ascension of our beloved Lord Jesus Christ and his coming from heaven in the glory of the Father "to sum up all things," [Eph. 1:10] and to raise up all flesh of the entire human race, in order that to Christ Jesus our Lord and God and Savior and King, according to the pleasure of the invisible Father, "every knee should bow, of things in heaven, and things in earth, and things under the earth, and that every tongue should confess" to him, [Phil. 2:10–11] and that he should execute just judgement toward all: that he may send "spiritual wickednesses" [Eph. 4:12] and the angels who transgress and become rebellious together with the ungodly and unjust and wicked and blasphemous among men into eternal fire: but the just and holy, and those who have kept his commandments and have persevered in his love, some from the beginning and others through their repentance, he will by grace give incorruption and surround them with eternal glory.[19]

The rule of faith, expressing the essence of the Scripture, points to the Person through whom faith is given to the humble and penitent. It provides a rule by which to measure all other witnesses to Christ, whether they be persons or books or letters. It constitutes a beginning for the development of doctrine and dogma, but is declaratory rather than definitive, ambiguous rather than philosophically exact. And it provides a link to the creeds which we shall consider next.

It remains to consider briefly that debate over the content of the New Testament continued into the Middle Ages and has continued down to our own day. By the seventh century there were three canons or collections of New Testament books in the world: the Athanasian (or Greek-Latin), containing twenty-seven books; the Syrian, containing twenty-two; and the Ethiopic, containing thirty-five, our twenty-seven being supplemented by such works as *I Clement* from the Apostolic Fathers and the *Revelation of Peter*. The *Revelation of John* continued to be disputed well into the Middle Ages, while some New Testaments continued to include the *Shepherd* of Hermas. But with the increasing acceptance of St. Jerome's Vulgate, (Latin) Bible in the West, adhering as it did to the Athanasian canon of twenty-seven books, the debates subsided. By the time the Council of Trent in 1546 closed the canon for the Roman Catholic Church, there was virtual unanimity among Christians concerning the contents of the New Testament.

Creeds and Councils

The Lambeth Quadrilateral, referring to that which is essential to the unity of the church, spoke of the Apostles' Creed "as the Baptismal confession of faith," and the Nicene "as the sufficient statement of the Christian faith." Thus the bishops chose, out of a great mass of creeds devised by Christians down through the ages, the two which had emerged in time as the most widely used and most authoritative. Both creeds are similar to the rule of faith and the apostolic preaching. Both witness to Christ and against those who distort the Christian understanding of God and of the Incarnate Son. But they also differ, one from another, as we shall see.

The Apostles' Creed is so called because of the legend which had each of the Twelve Apostles contributing a clause to its composition. It has also been understood that the title is appropriate because the creed dates from the earliest age of the church and to our knowledge is the creed which has been in continuous use for the greatest length of time. It first appeared in Rome, but had its origins in the simple confessions of faith required from the beginning of candidates for baptism. The statement "Jesus is Lord," of 1 Corinthians 12:3, is one of many examples of such a simple confession of faith found in the New Testament. It is reasonable to suppose that as time passed and the church grew there were baptismal creeds formulated for use in every local church. As was natural, the great churches, such as those of Jerusalem, Antioch, Alexandria, and Rome, commended their creeds for use in the provinces which they came to dominate. At Rome in the beginning of the third century one Hippolytus, forced into schism by those who resisted his attacks on the immorality and theological incompetence of the bishops of Rome, composed a manual called the *Apostolic Tradition* in which he reports that the convert to Christianity is to be given

over to the presbyter who baptises, and let the candidates stand in the water naked, a deacon going with them likewise. And when he who is being baptized goes down into the water, he who baptizes him, putting his hand on him, shall say thus:
Do you believe in God, the Father Almighty?
And he who is being baptized shall say:
I believe.
Then holding his hand placed on his head, he shall baptize him once. And then he shall say:
Do you believe in Christ Jesus, the Son of God, who was born of the Holy Spirit of the Virgin Mary, and was crucified under Pontius Pilate, and was dead and buried, and rose again the third day, alive from the dead, and ascended into heaven, and sat at the right hand of the Father, and will come to judge the living and the dead? And when he says:
I believe,
he is baptized again. And again he shall say:
Do you believe in the Holy Spirit, and the holy church, and the resurrection of the flesh? He who is being baptized shall say accordingly:
I believe,
and so he is baptized a third time.[20]

This was the creed in interrogatory form. In the fourth century we note its existence in declaratory form, much as we have it in common use today. With the passage of time other clauses were added and the creed gradually ousted all rival creeds in the West. It should be noted that it was not used in the East. It should also be noted that the clause "He descended into Hell . . . ," which first appeared in the fifth century, is still debated in some places, even though scriptural warrant can be adduced for it, for instance, Acts 2:31 and 1 Peter 3:19;4:6.

The Nicene Creed is of a different order. It is a conciliar creed, that is to say, a creed propounded and authorized by a council of the church. The Nicene Creed as we have it in liturgical use was the product of the first general council, held at Nicaea in Asia Minor in 325. We have it as revised for use at Baptisms in the East and as such adopted and promulgated by the second general council, held at Constantinople in 381. Both councils were largely gatherings of Eastern bishops seeking, at the behest of Emperors Constantine and Theodosius, to settle the vehement quarrels which were destroying the unity of the church and disturbing the peace of the empire. It is difficult for us today to imagine a theological debate so heated that it at times erupted into physical violence, and that the nature of the Trinity and the relation of the divine and human in Christ could be matters of such concern to the general populace that people could be heard chanting theological slogans in the streets of Alexandria, but such was the case. The theological controversies became matters of concern to emperors and common people, in part because they involved political and economic factors. The theological contentions were between great metropolitan centers of the Roman Empire, Rome and Alexandria, Alexandria and Antioch, Constantinople and Rome. The nontheological factors were very real and affected the course of theological debate. But the theological struggle itself was on center stage and involved nothing less than the survival of the Gospel: belief in salvation through Jesus Christ, the Son of God.

Eusebius of Caesarea, the great historian of the early

church, was present at Nicaea and, when writing to his church about the council, gave the creed which was drawn up on the basis of the creed in use at Caesarea. This is the original Nicene Creed:

> We believe in one God, the Father almighty, maker of all things visible and invisible;
> And in one Lord Jesus Christ, the Son of God, begotten from the Father, only-begotten, that is from the substance of the Father, God from God, light from light, true God from true God, begotten not made, of one substance with the Father, through Whom all things came into being, things in heaven and things on earth, Who because of us men and because of our salvation came down and became incarnate, becoming man, suffered and rose again on the third day, ascended to the heavens, and will come to judge the living and the dead;
> And in the Holy Spirit.[21]

The emphasis falls on the second section of the creed and in particular on "from the substance of the Father," and "of one substance with the Father." These were phrases aimed against one Arius, presbyter of the church in Alexandria, who was alarmed at the teachings of his bishop, Alexander, believing him to teach the divinity of Christ in such a way that one could only conclude that there were two gods. This was heresy to Arius's mind. In opposition to Alexander, Arius following the lead of Origen, the great teacher of Alexandria, taught:

> that the Son is not unbegotten, nor in any way unbegotten, even in part; and that he does not derive his subsistence from any matter; but that by his own will and counsel he has subsisted before time, and before ages, as perfect God, only begotten and unchangeable, and that he existed not before he was begotten, or created, or purposed, or established. For he was not unbegotten. We are persecuted, because we say that the Son had a beginning, but that God was without beginning. This is really the cause of our persecution, and likewise, because we say that he is from nothing.[22]

In order that it might be perfectly clear that the Nicene Creed was aimed against this teaching of Arius, this paragraph was appended:

But as for those who say, There was when He was not, and,
Before being born He was not, and that He came into existence
out of nothing, or who assert that the Son of God is of a different
hypostasis or substance, or is created, or is subject to alteration
or change—these the Catholic Church anathematizes.[23]

This rejection of Arius was not immediately successful. The
struggle went on through the Council of Constantinople in
381. Here the teaching of Nicaea was affirmed and the teaching of the Cappadocian fathers, Basil of Caesarea, Gregory of
Nyssa, and Gregory of Nazianzus was adopted: God is one,
one substance in three perfect persons, Father, Son, and Holy
Spirit. The Trinity was thus defined by the bishops of the
Eastern Church. Mindful of the Gospel as found in Scripture,
they used Greek philosophical terms to guard against tri-
theism (three gods) and also against such subordination of
the Son to the Father that Christ's divinity was denied and
the Incarnation rejected. This highly technical language was
not always helpful and indeed at times the fathers had to
twist and bend the words to suit their needs. In the end they
were forced to express their convictions in words and phrases
which seemed to those without faith to be irrational and
contradictory.

Two further general councils dealt with the problem of divinity and humanity in Christ. The Council of Ephesus (431)
condemned Nestorianism which taught, or seemed to teach,
that there are two persons in Christ, the one divine and the
other human. The Council of Chalcedon (451) condemned the
Eutychians who were accused of denying the two natures,
human and divine, of Christ. This last council decreed that
Jesus Christ was "of one substance with the Father as touching His Godhead, and of one substance with us as touching
His manhood," and that he must be acknowledged in two
natures "without confusion, without change, without division, without separation," the difference of the natures being
in no way destroyed on account of the union.[24]

In all of the complex and confused process it was the person
of Christ, the Christ of the Gospel, known to those who believed in him, who was most in contention. Through all the
sordid and violent conflict the apostolic tradition was pre-

served and passed on to the next generation. Something of value was achieved, for the conciliar decrees, including the Nicene Creed, affirm in the strongest terms that our salvation is from God himself, that Christ Jesus is the only mediator of this salvation, and that in Christ there is both perfect divinity and perfect humanity.

The struggles of the bishops warrant our close attention because, as Richard Hooker, one of the greatest of Anglican theologians, said in the sixteenth century: "all heresies which touch the person of Jesus Christ, whether they have risen in these later days, or in any age heretofore," have occurred and do occur in terms of those heresies and those affirmations with which the Councils of Nicaea, Constantinople, Ephesus, and Chalcedon dealt.

> In four words . . . truly, perfectly, indivisibly, distinctly: the first applied to his being God, and the second to his being Man, the third to his being of both One, and the fourth to his still continuing in that one Both: we may fully by the way of abridgement comprise whatsoever antiquity hath at large, handled either in declaration of Christian belief, or in refutation of the foresaid heresies.[25]

By a gradual process the Nicene Creed became the most important and best known creed in all of Christianity. Its first use in the Eucharist seems to have been at the instigation of Peter the Fuller at Antioch in 473, and for polemical reasons. By the sixth century it was in use at Constantinople and in Spain. It was not adopted officially at Rome until Pope Benedict VIII, under the influence of Emperor Henry II, accepted it in 1014. Since that time it has had a secure place in Christian usage as "the sufficient statement of Christian faith."

The Apostles' and Nicene Creeds differ, the first being associated primarily with the confession of faith made by newly converted Christians at the time of their Baptism, the second arising out of the necessity to defend the apostolic teaching against the distortions and idiosyncrasies of heretics, however well-meaning their intentions. And yet they are similar in their strong witness to the Gospel and to the Person whom the Gospel proclaims in Scripture and in creed.

Episcopacy and the Christian Community

There was the beginning of an organization for the Christian community in Jesus' selection of the Twelve Apostles. It was through them and their followers that the organized church developed. It is evident, however, that on Jesus' death there were only the rudiments of an organization and not the elaborately structured church we know today. An elaborate structure must not have seemed necessary to a people who regarded the end of history as near and the return of the risen Lord imminent. They were a people inspired, full of the Holy Spirit, the new Israel, another race. Aristides, the theologian of Athens who flourished around A.D. 140, explained simply that there are three kinds of people in the world: pagans, Jews, and Christians. Justin, a teacher at Rome, martyred about A.D. 165, argued in addressing Trypho, the Jew, that Christians are God's chosen people, indwelt by His Spirit. The center of attention was upon the holy community scattered around the Mediterranean Sea but united in its head, Christ Jesus, partaking of one bread, the body of Christ. It is this sense of being an organic community, and not a mere organization, which seemed to dominate the minds of the earliest Christians.

When considering Ignatius of Antioch we noted the emphasis upon Christ, the community, and unity. It was to continue as a major emphasis for years to come. Two of the most prominent of the North African bishops, Cyprian of Carthage and Augustine of Hippo, serve as important witnesses to this fact. Cyprian, martyred in A.D. 258, suffered the persecutions of the Emperors Decius and Valerian and fought to protect the church in the midst of controversies over those who had lapsed during the persecutions and sought reentry into the church, and over the re-Baptism of heretics. He believed that the church not only should be but is in fact one, its unity being "handed down by the Lord through the Apostles" and grounded in God himself. Like Ignatius he taught that this unity is expressed and guaranteed by the bishops, episcopacy constituting the God-given principle of unity.

Augustine, Bishop of Hippo Regius, justly famed as the author of the *Confessions* and the *City of God*, died in A.D. 430, mourning the death of the Roman Empire. He defended the Catholic Church against the schismatic Donatists. The roots of Donatism were in the Diocletian persecution of A.D. 303–305 and in the protest of moral rigorists in the city of Cirta in Numidia, North Africa, against those in the church who had yielded to the pressures of persecution. The Donatists separated themselves from what they saw to be a soiled and corrupt church. They were also Numidians, conscious of their national identity and separating themselves from a church they identified with an alien Roman culture. For them the true church consisted of the pure in heart and in outward discipleship.

In opposition to such Donatist teaching, Augustine taught that the church is truly catholic, teaching the entire truth, extended over the whole world and not confined to the visible society on earth called the church. The church includes all who have believed in Christ in the past and will believe in the future. It comprises the good and the bad. It is "a mixed community." He also believed that the Christian society is Christ's mystical body: Christ existing as the eternal Word, the Mediator God-man, and as the church, of which he is the head, and that the faithful are members. Its unity is in this:

> There are many Christians but only one Christ. The Christians themselves along with their Head, because He has ascended into heaven, form one Christ. It is not a case of His being one and our being many, but we who are many are a unity in Him. There is therefore one man, Christ, consisting of head and body.[26]

Augustine also believed that the church is a fellowship of love, its members being united with one another as one body. The society of Christ is then his focus, that is, as the mystical body of Christ.

This point has been labored here because any discussion of the development of the church's organization and ministry must be grounded in an understanding of the church as an organic entity, the body of Christ.

The church of the first two centuries was thus a community first of all. Within it two kinds of leadership were expressed:

(1) that which we designate charismatic because it exists as a result of the direct inspiration of the Holy Spirit, and (2) that which served functional needs of the community. The two sorts of leadership could be found together in a given individual or in different individuals working side by side. Amongst the charismatics were Christian prophets. *The Teaching of the Twelve Apostles* (the *Didache*), a document consisting of two sources edited as one work around A.D. 150, lays down rules for the congregation and their treatment of the prophets. In relation to the Eucharist it specifies that the congregation is to "suffer the prophets to give thanks as they will."[27]

There were also those whose tasks were more specifically functional, such as the elders or presbyters and the deacons who cared for the affairs of the local congregation, visited the sick and needy, presided at community meetings, and distributed the offerings of the people to those in need. There is some question as to how distinct presbyters and deacons were in the earliest period. Our literature demonstrates more concern for the moral qualities of such officers than for any exact definition of their tasks and authority. The letter of Clement of Rome (c. A.D. 90) concerns the church of Rome at an early time, where it would appear that the community was governed by a college of presbyters. It also seems that one of the presbyters would function as a chairperson to preside at meetings and to represent the congregation in external matters. Indeed, the development of this prebyterial government was most likely influenced by non-Christian organizations in the same city, as well as by the Jewish body of elders who were elected for life and served the community caring for civil, administrative, judicial, and financial concerns. Ignatius might very well have been the president of such a board of directors and might have been advocating a single or monepiscopacy because he realized the necessity for such if chaos was to be avoided and a sufficient center of unity provided in the midst of contention with heretics and schismatics.

The struggle against the gnostics and others whose teaching ran counter to the Gospel provided much of the impetus for a concept which quickly caught on. Irenaeus argued that if you want to know the teaching of the Apostles then you must go to the successors of the Apostles, the lawful bishops of the churches, and in particular the bishops of the Church of Rome. Thus he wrote that "the whole Church, that is, those who are everywhere believers, cannot fail to agree with that church, on account of its commanding position of leadership, in which the tradition which derives from the apostles is perpetually preserved by those who come from all quarters."[28] There is a living chain of persons providing a direct link with the Apostles. It is this succession of bishops which was to prove most effective against the unbridled exercise of spiritual gifts by ignorant or unscrupulous persons. What is true? Consult the teaching of Rome, protected by its bishops. These bishops have handed on the true doctrine from the Apostles who initially appointed them. Is it true that the first bishops were appointed by the Apostles? Of course it is. At least it is true to say that all of our evidence indicates that, in each community they visited, the Apostles appointed those officers who constitute the beginning of that which we call apostolic succession.

The Montanists provided another kind of pressure upon the church, accelerating its development of an hierarchical organization. We have this account of their beginnings around the middle of the second century:

> There is reported to be a certain village in that Mysia which borders on Phrygia [in Asia Minor], called by the name Ardabau. There it is said that a certain recent convert to the faith named Montanus (while Gratus was proconsul of Asia), in the immeasurable longing of his soul for pre-eminence, first gave the adversary a passage into his heart; and that moved by the spirit he suddenly fell into a state of possession, as it were, and abnormal ecstasy, insomuch that he became frenzied and began to babble and utter strange sounds, that is to say, prophesying contrary to the manner which the church had received from generation to generation by tradition from the beginning.[29]

This account, hardly objective, openly alarmist, points to the prophecies of Montanus, Priscilla, and Maximilla.

Maximilla spoke of the coming end of history, "After me

shall be no prophetesses any more, but the consummation," and referred to her special role, "The Lord sent me to be the party-leader, informer, interpreter of this task, profession and covenant, constrained, whether he will or nill, to learn the knowledge of God." Thus did she, like Montanus and others, claim to be a special channel of revelation alongside the Scriptures. Priscilla was reported to have said: "Christ came to me in the likeness of a woman, clad in a bright robe, and He planted wisdom in me and revealed that this place (Pepuza) is holy, and that here Jerusalem comes down from heaven." Maximilla said: "I am driven as a wolf from the sheep. I am not a wolf. I am word and spirit and power."[30] Such sayings, along with the moral rigor which accompanied them, deeply disturbed the church. Montanus and his followers won over many people, including Tertullian, the father of Latin theology who lived in Carthage at the end of the second century. But their activities also led to the waning of the prophetic element as a separate entity in the church and to the absorption of the prophetic into the ministry of bishops and presbyters.

There is a sense in which the crucial development was that of a growing conviction that bishops and presbyters were more than officers charged with caring for the church, governing its affairs, and defending it against internal and external threats. Cyprian, in the middle of the third century, viewed bishops as priests, giving them a special sacred character which, together with the presbyters, separated them from the community as a whole. They were no longer simply representatives of the people. Cyprian recognized the bishop as possessing power by virtue of the gift of the Holy Spirit in his consecration, power to act as the viceregent of Christ, transmitting this power to those presbyters and others who served under him. In time the one presiding at the Eucharist was no longer viewed as the offerer of the prayer of the community, but as "another Christ," standing in the place of Christ, making sacrifice for the sake of the community. Thus Cyprian wrote:

> If Christ Jesus our Lord and God is himself the high priest of
> God the Father and first offered himself as a sacrifice to the

Father, and commanded this to be done in remembrance of himself, then assuredly the priest acts truly in Christ's room, when he imitates what Christ did, and he offers then a true and complete sacrifice to God the Father, if he so begin to offer as he sees Christ himself has offered.[31]

We are here well on our way to the realization of a distinct hierarchy in the church, with bishops who are priests, from whom other priests derive their power and authority. In time bishops, priests, and deacons came to occupy a special order apart from the community, an order which was absolutely necessary to the welfare and continuance of the community.

Finally, we must take note of the bishops of special sees such as Jerusalem, Antioch, Alexandria, Rome, Carthage, and, after the arrival of the Constantinian peace in the beginning of the fourth century, Constantinople. Each of these sees exercised preeminence in the territories surrounding them, but Rome claimed primacy over all the churches, for it was with Rome that Peter and Paul were most firmly associated. It was also true that Rome was the center of the empire, as Constantinople was to be in the fourth century. In the beginning the primacy accorded the great sees was that of honor. The development of jurisdictional power was gradual and in part dependent upon rivalries which grew between the most important and powerful churches.

Cyprian acknowledged the supremacy of Rome, but after entering into a vehement struggle with the bishop of Rome qualified his earlier statements. While he accorded Rome the primacy of honor, the church's unity was located in the college of bishops of the church. Thus he wrote, first quoting from Ephesians 4:4–6:

There is one body, and one Spirit even as you are called in one hope of your calling: one Lord, one faith, one baptism, one God. This unity firmly should we hold and maintain, especially we bishops presiding in the Church, in order that we may approve the episcopate itself to be one and undivided. Let no one deceive the brotherhood by falsehood; no one corrupt our faith in the truth by a faithless treachery. The episcopate is one; it is a whole in which each bishop enjoys full possession. The Church is likewise one, though she be spread abroad, and multiplies with the increase of her progeny: even as the sun has rays many, yet one light; and the tree, boughs many, yet its strength is one, seated in the deep-lodged root; and as when many streams flow down from one source, though a multiplicity of waters seems to be diffused from the bountifulness of the over-flowing abundance, unity is preserved in the source itself.[32]

This is not, of course, the whole story. We shall probably never know enough about the development of the church as an institution, and in particular the emergence of its hierar-chical structure during the first two or three centuries of its history. Those who could have provided us with the evidence we need were more concerned for the Lord of the church, their unity with him and his mission, than for organizational planning and development. The organization developed in accordance with their needs. They would claim that it was the work of the Spirit of God alive in their midst inspiring and guiding the community, the body of Christ.

Liturgy and Sacraments: The Worshiping Community

The Lambeth Quadrilateral specified the sacraments of Bap-tism and the Lord's Supper as essential to the church's unity. These sacraments must be understood, however, in the con-text of the New Testament worship in general. Worship in the Gospels and Epistles is defined not in terms of particular rites or places but rather in relation to all of a person's life. To worship in spirit and in truth the faithful Christian must bow down, making obeisance before God as before the emperor, serving God with the service of a slave. The center of worship in the New Testament was not the Temple in Jerusalem. The Temple is at that place, wherever it may be, where God con-fronts the worshiper in Christ by the power of the Spirit. It may be on the road to Emmaus or it may be at the Temple in Jerusalem. It may be anywhere and everywhere in life. It involves not so much structured liturgies as the liturgy of a life lived in obedience to the Lord. Specific liturgies, times, and places for worship are of value and, given human nature, are necessary in order that life may be lived in communion with the Lord of life in the community of the faithful.

Thus, we find the early Christians worshiping around the clock, their lives permeated with prayer. We may be inclined to call it private prayer, but the distinction between private and corporate prayer for them might very well be regarded as artificial. There was a tradition, derived from Jewish practice and widely shared by Christians from the beginning, of prayer at certain hours, day and night. They came to associate these times with events in the passion of the Lord. We find reflections of this practice in the Book of Acts (3:2;10:3,9) and evidence of such worship, sanctifying all of life, in the *Didache* and in the writings of Clement of Alexandria, Origen, Tertullian, and Cyprian. In the manual called *The Apostolic Tradition*, dating from the beginning of the third century, Hippolytus of Rome reports:

> Let all the faithful, whether men or women, when early in the morning they rise from their sleep and before they undertake any tasks, wash their hands and pray to God; and so they may go to their duties.

He then speaks of instruction at the place where the community meets early in the morning.

> But if on any day there is no instruction, let everyone at home take the Bible and read sufficiently in passages that he finds profitable.
>
> If at the third hour you are at home, pray then and give thanks to God; but if you chance to be abroad at that hour, make your prayer to God in your heart. For at that hour Christ was nailed to the tree. . . .
>
> At the sixth hour likewise pray also, for, after Christ was nailed to the wood of the cross, the day was divided and there was a great darkness. . . .
>
> And at the ninth hour let a great prayer and great thanksgiving be made, such as made the souls of the righteous ones, blessing the Lord, the God who does not lie, who was mindful of his saints and sent forth his Word to enlighten them. At that hour therefore, Christ poured forth from his pierced side water and blood, and brought the rest of the time of that day with light to evening; so, when he fell asleep, by making the beginning of another day, he completed the pattern of his resurrection.

Pray again before your body rests on your bed.
At midnight arise, wash your hands with water and pray.
And if your wife is with you, pray together; but if she is not a
believer, go into another room and pray. . . .
And at cockcrow rise up and pray likewise, for at that hour of
cockcrow the children of Israel denied Christ, whom we have
known by faith. . . .[33]

The worship of the religious, monks and nuns living in
communities, was influenced by this development of regular
prayer. It also forms the basis for the practice of personal
devotions amongst many Christians, monastics and others,
living now.

Next we must take note of the existence of a liturgy of the
Word at an early stage of the church's development. Again,
the Christians seemed to be perpetuating, and at the same
time transforming, a custom familiar to them as Jews; in this
instance the worship of the synagogue. In the First Letter to
Timothy, dated some time in the second century, we read:

Till I come, attend to the public reading of scripture, to preaching, to teaching. Do not neglect the gift which you have,
which was given you by prophetic utterance when the elders
laid their hands upon you.[34]

It would seem that the Christian version of synagogue worship included an opening greeting, a reading from Scripture,
the recitation of psalms, and another reading. The readings
would be from the Old Testament and from the apostolic
writings, concluding with a lesson from one of the Gospels in
which Christ's own words would be recited. Then there
would be a sermon (the bishop's special liturgy), dismissal of
those not belonging to the congregation, the prayer of the
faithful, and another, final dismissal.

Baptism arose out of the Jewish rite of initiation for non-
Jewish converts. It was also influenced by John the Baptist
and the rite with which Jesus was baptized. Its use depends
most, however, upon Jesus' command and the interpretation
of its meaning by himself and his early followers. Evidence
concerning the development of Christian Baptism comes
from the New Testament, the *Didache*, Justin Martyr, and the
Hippolytan *Apostolic Tradition*. In general we find that Bap-

tism consisted of preparation, including fasting, the renunciation of the kingdom of evil and of the person's attachment to
it, which may have occurred as the candidates faced West and
shed their clothing in preparation for going into the water.
This divestiture was viewed as removing the clothes of this
world in order to put on the new clothes of Christ. There was
then a formal declaration of faith with the candidate, perhaps
facing East. How early this became a part of the sacrament we
do not know. It was certainly there in the beginning of the
third century as we have already noted in considering the
baptismal creed of *The Apostolic Tradition*. There was then the
descent into the water with the pronouncement of the baptismal formula: Baptism in the name of the Father, and of the
Son, and of the Holy Spirit. The exact nature of this formula is
not clear in the earliest evidence and it may have been incorporated as a part of the confession of faith. The person baptized was then brought up out of the water and clothed,
symbolic of "putting on" the risen Christ, being clothed in
the new humanity, becoming the body of Christ. There then
followed the breaking of the fast with, by Hippolytus's time,
participation in the Lord's Supper.

In many ways Christian Baptism was similar to other water
initiation rites. It differed in that it was Baptism into the
name of Jesus and involved reception of the Holy Spirit.

As Baptism was the sacrament of entry into the Christian
community, so the Lord's Supper was the sacrament of continuation and growth in that community. The Last Supper,
which the Lord commanded his disciples to continue in
memory of him, was basically a Jewish meal with the customary blessings in the form of thanksgivings over the bread
and wine. It was a Jewish meal transformed by Jesus so that
where the Jews remembered thankfully God's deliverance of
his chosen people from the bondage of Egypt, now the followers of Jesus would remember the acts of God in and
through their Lord releasing them from bondage to sin and
death, delivering them into the kingdom which would reach
its consummation in the heavenly, messianic banquet. The
Christians gave thanks for Christ and their deliverance
through him. The postresurrection appearances of Christ at

meals with the faithful were interpreted in the light of the
Lord's Supper and Eucharist, as thanksgiving. Christians
gave thanks for his presence with them as they remembered
him. Furthermore, it was at the Eucharist that the Christians
not only felt united to Christ but knew themselves to be
united with one another in love, love which overflowed the
community in deeds of service in their everyday lives. 1
Corinthians 10:16–17 spoke to their experience and they gave
thanks for the community of love. They broke bread, remembering the Lord: it was the sacrament of his body given for
them. They took the cup of wine, remembering the Lord: it
was the sacrament of his blood, shed for them. As they did it,
he was with them and they gave thanks, in words and
through their lives.

The earliest Eucharists, for instance, those mentioned in
Acts, must have been quite simple, attached to a meal, located at some convenient place. In all likelihood the sacrament was celebrated in the house of one of the faithful, a
house with an adequate upper (or dining) room. The houses
of the Roman nobility with their courtyards provided all that
was needed for the community meetings. In the fourth century the basilica with its apse would provide a more formal
and spacious alternative. At the meal the Lord would be remembered, bread and wine blessed with thanksgivings to
God, the bread broken and distributed, the cup passed
around, the people partaking mindful that the bread was the
body and the wine the blood of the Lord.

By the time of Justin Martyr, in the middle of the second
century in Rome, we have evidence that the meal itself was
separated from the sacrament, although it is clear that this
happened much earlier. The liturgy then began with the
ministry of the Word consisting of readings from the prophets
and from the letters and Gospels of the New Testament, instruction by the president of the Eucharist based on the readings, common prayers in litany form, and psalms to separate
the readings. In the sacrament proper there was a kiss of
peace, the presentation of bread and wine and water, and a
prayer of thanksgiving including thanksgiving for creation,
providence, and redemption, a memorial of the passion, and

the people's Amen. This was followed by the communion of all present.

We are uncertain as to whether by that time the eucharistic or thanksgiving prayer included a recitation of the events of the Last Supper with the Lord's words, an invocation or call-ing down upon the people, and/or the bread and wine of the Holy Spirit (or the Word). The dominant emphasis was still upon remembering with thanksgiving, in the course of which the Lord was known to be present. This continued to be the emphasis at the end of the second century when Irenaeus acknowledged that "the Eucharist is an offering of the firstfruits of the earth as an expression of gratitude to God and as sanctifying the creature."

The Hippolytan *Apostolic Tradition,* at the beginning of the third century, presents us with a Eucharist which, partially because of the scarcity of detailed information concerning any liturgy of that time or earlier, appears to be a connecting link between the simple rites of the first and second centuries and the elaborate, formal rites which developed into the classic liturgies of East and West: that of Rome in the West and in the East the Ethiopic Church Order, the Clementine liturgy or the Apostolic Constitutions, and the liturgies of Saints Basil and Chrysostom. The eucharistic or thanksgiving prayer of Hippolytus consists of (1) a thanksgiving for Jesus Christ, the Word of God through whom all things were made, our Savior and Redeemer, (2) a remembrance of him, his suffering and death, his resurrection and the events of the Last Supper, including the Lord's own words, which are the charter for making Eucharist. All of this is done for the re-membering of him. Then (3) there followed an invocation:

> And we pray you to send your holy Spirit upon the oblation of your holy Church, granting to all the saints who partake to be united to you that they may be fulfilled with the holy Spirit for confirmation of their faith in truth, that we may praise and glorify you through your child Jesus Christ through whom be glory and honor to the Father and the Son with the holy Spirit in the holy Church now and world without end.[35]

It has been argued that we see here a development of the Eucharist. The pronouncing of the Lord's words given at the

Last Supper and the invocation of the Spirit on the bread and wine shift attention from the remembering with thanksgiving to the transformation of bread and wine into body and blood. Furthermore, Cyprian's sacrificial view of the Eucharist, involving the celebrating priest's doing what Christ did, shifted attention from the remembering community toward the priest who was instrumental in the transformation of bread and wine. It would seem that during the first three centuries the emphasis moved from the temporal remembering of God in Christ to the spatial transformation of the elements of bread and wine affecting both ritual and meaning in important ways. And yet, through it all the Eucharist remained the sacrament of unity, unity with the Lord and with one another in the congregation, a foundation for the church's realization of its true nature in Christ, and a means for strengthening worship in all of life.

The Church and the Four Essentials in the Middle Ages

It is a long way from the fifth century to the thirteenth. Between those dates we witness the fall of the Roman Empire and the Mohammedan conquest bringing lands, from the Balkans in the East around through the Holy Land, across Africa, and up into Spain, into subjection to a non-Christian people. The church in the East was devastated, although it persisted. The church in the West gradually assumed more and more authority for government, became less and less urban and suburban, and found its greatest vitality in lands once controlled by heathen peoples. Between the fifth and thirteenth centuries there was a massive alteration affecting geography, economics, society, and religion. In time, feudalism provided the major social structure in Christian Europe. One indication of the importance of this is to be seen in the fact that alongside the major city and monastic ecclesiastical centers there arose private churches located in villages on manorial lands, controlled by the local landlord to whom the priest of the village church owed fealty. Furthermore, many of the members of the church hierarchy exercised authority as feudal lords, themselves owing allegiance to dukes or kings or emperors. This provided for much stress and strain, as we shall see in a subsequent chapter.

Then too, in this passage of time relations between the church of the West—centered in the papacy at Rome—and the church of the East—centered in the patriarchate of Constantinople, or the New Rome—deteriorated until in 1054 the Patriarch Michael Cerularius closed all churches of the Latin rite in Constantinople, an act sealing the schism. There were specific areas of disagreement between East and West, such as the use of unleavened bread in the Eucharist, the clause in the Nicene Creed which has the Spirit proceeding from both Father and Son, the date of Easter, and the use of icons or sacred images. But the differences ran more deeply, involving a fundamental difference in mind set and world view, and influenced by the difference in languages, Latin and Greek. The Latin West strove for precise definitions of doctrine and practice. The Greek East emphasized mystery and community. To the Eastern mind the worshiping community could encompass a diversity of opinions, especially concerning doctrines such as those related to the nature of our humanity, sin and grace, and the ways of salvation. The separation between East and West demonstrates the degree to which the church can be and is culturally influenced not only in outward matters but in the innermost ways.

At the height of the Middle Ages the fourth Lateran Council was convened by Pope Innocent III in 1215. Because of the schism between East and West it could not technically be called ecumenical, but it was a great council nevertheless, widely representative of Western Europe, and not only of the church in the West but of society at large, church and society at this time being virtually one entity. There were 412 bishops, 800 abbots and priors of religious houses, and lay delegates of various sorts. In spite of all that had transpired in the intervening centuries, the council first of all affirmed the faith as it was defined at Nicaea, Constantinople, Ephesus, and Chalcedon, beginning: "We firmly believe and openly confess that there is only one true God, eternal and immense, omnipotent, unchangeable, incomprehensible, and ineffable, Father, Son and Holy Spirit; three persons indeed, but one essence, substance, or nature. . . ."[36] In this paragraph and the following one, concerning the Incarnate Son, the faith was set forth in opposition to dualistic heresies, such as that of the Cathari in Southern France. Thus the struggle to maintain the faith of the Apostles continued and was to result in the establishment of the Inquisition in 1220.

Concerning the church, the creed of the Lateran Council declared:

> There is one Universal Church of the faithful, outside of which there is absolutely no salvation. In which there is the same priest and sacrifice, Jesus Christ, whose body and blood are truly contained in the sacrament of the altar under the forms of bread and wine; the bread being changed (transubstantiated) by divine power into the body, and the wine into the blood, so that to realize the mystery of unity we may receive of Him what He has received of us. And this sacrament no one can effect except the priest who has been duly ordained in accordance with the keys of the Church, which Jesus Christ Himself gave to his Apostles and their successors.[37]

There follows a paragraph on Baptism.

Here we have an affirmation of the sacrament of the Eucharist, now commonly called the Mass, and a reference to the sacerdotal hierarchy, or ministry of bishops and priests rooted in sacramental power and function.

Where is the Scripture? Without doubt during all of the time from the fifth to the thirteenth century Scripture was highly regarded. For those living at the time of the Lateran Council, the Bible was the expression of the Word of God, and its authority was to be accepted and obeyed. John Scotus Eriugena had at an earlier time, in the ninth century, cried out:

> O Lord Jesus, no other reward, no other blessedness, no other joy do I ask than a pure understanding, free of mistakes, of thy words which were inspired by the Holy Spirit. This is the acme of my felicity, the climax of perfect contemplation. For there is nothing beyond. Nowhere else art thou more openly discovered. Thou livest in them. Thy seekers and lovers thou inducest therein. There thou preparest for thine elect the spiritual banquet of true knowledge. There, passing, thou ministerest unto them.[38]

This prayer is not that of someone who understood Scripture in a literalistic or legalistic manner. Scripture has "two feet. One is the natural meaning of visible creatures. The other is the spiritual sense of divine Scripture." Furthermore, the quality of the various parts of Scripture was known to vary, not all writings being of equal value to the Christian.

In the twelfth century, Heloise, the companion of the theologian Abelard, led the nuns under her at the Oratory of the Paraclete in the serious study of Scripture. For this purpose she wrote out a series of questions known as the *Problems of Heloise*, which indicate not only her devotion to Scripture but her struggles to understand it, for she could not even accept the words of Christ as true and authoritative until her brilliant and critical mind was satisfied. The questioning was so intense, not because Heloise sought to reject the authority of Scripture but because she acknowledged that authority and must bring her mind under its sway. Scripture was primary. All doctrine must be rooted in it. The great *Summas*, or summations of all theology, composed by the medieval theologians offer ample proof of this, although modern scholars tend to disagree concerning the effectiveness of this rooting, claiming that medieval theologians chose from Scripture that which supported them and ignored the rest. Nevertheless, Scripture was held in high regard and there was seldom any conflict between the authority of Scripture and the authority of the church.

The agreement of Scripture and church began to crumble in the fourteenth century. On the one hand there was Henry of Ghent openly opposing Scripture to church, stating that the believer relies on the "words of Christ" in Scripture rather than on any preacher or on the "testimony of the Church, since he believes in the Church already on account of Scripture. And supposing that the Church herself taught contrary to Scripture, he would not believe her."[39] On the other hand there was Guido Terreni who, at the beginning of the fourteenth century looked upon Scripture as the books of the Bible quite distinct from the doctrinal tradition of the church, arguing the superiority of the church's authority to that of Scripture. He was laboring a distinction which would have made no sense to earlier generations. Guido thus fortified the distinction found in Henry of Ghent, but instead of glorifying Scripture, he glorified the church.

The belief in the superiority of the church's authority to that of Scripture was grounded in a developing understanding of the hierarchy of the church. By the time of the Lateran Council of 1215, the priest was no longer regarded as the minister or servant of the holy community, but rather as the intermediary between that community and God in heaven, dispensing the sacraments without which there could be no salvation. Higher than all priesthood there was the bishop of Rome, the successor of Peter to whom Christ had said: "You are Peter, and on this rock I will build my church, and the powers of death shall not prevail against it. I will give you the keys of the kingdom of heaven, and whatever you bind on earth shall be bound in heaven, and whatever you loose on earth shall be loosed in heaven." (Matt. 16:18) Alongside this understanding which had been growing at least since the time of Pope Leo I (440–461), there was the assertion that both swords, temporal and spiritual rule, were lodged in Christ's hands and in those of his vicars on earth, the popes of Rome. All of this led to the conviction that the Church of Rome was the head of the entire Christian universe.

The theory was buttressed by the remarkable organization of the Church of Rome. The pope, as the head of the church, possessed "fullness of power," wielding the authority of government—executive, legislative, judicial—with the assistance of his *curia* or court. The papal curia consisted of cardinals who were principal bishops, priests, and deacons of the Church of Rome, and who by 1059 were empowered to elect the pope. In 1179 they were formed into a legal corporation, the College of Cardinals, with specific duties and benefits. Their chief duty was that of government and in this they were assisted by secretaries, clerks, notaries, auditors, and others. Such organizational machinery assisted the process by which the papacy was to exert close control over the church of the West, down to the local bishop and his clergy.

This assertion of the church's authority did not go unchallenged. So-called heretics, such as the Lollards in England

and the Hussites in Bohemia, spoke out against the papal pretensions. Councils and conciliar theorists in the fourteenth and fifteenth centuries, confronted by papal schism with more than one pope claiming exclusive rule of the church, sought to return the power of the church to the entire community for which the councils should act as representative bodies. And there were bishops guarding their own prerogatives who argued that where the sacraments were concerned the pope did not differ from any other bishop. His power was related not to order (sacraments) but to jurisdiction (government).

At the other end of the hierarchical society ordinary people were deeply influenced by the sacramental system. All of life was touched by the sacraments for in addition to Baptism and the Eucharist, there were other sacraments, the number varying according to the theologian or council consulted. Usually the list of sacraments included Baptism, Confirmation, the Eucharist, Matrimony, Holy Orders, and Extreme Unction—the anointing of one near death with holy oil. At the fourth Lateran Council there was enacted a canon (or law) enforcing the Sacrament of Penance. This was considered a merciful provision for those who sin after Baptism. The sincerely contrite penitent would go to the parish priest or some other and there confess his or her sins, privately receiving absolution, which conveyed God's forgiveness. Both the guilt of sin and eternal punishment were remitted thereby, although God's justice required that some "satisfaction" be rendered. Such satisfaction must be made now or in the life to come. Thus the priest prescribed a "penance," some act of a spiritual nature such as the saying of certain prayers, fasting, or going on pilgrimage to a sacred shrine. Those whose satisfaction was incomplete at death went to an intermediate state called purgatory. The prayers of the faithful were efficacious on their behalf. But an indulgence whereby the ecclesiastical authority might draw upon the treasury of merits accumulated by Christ could remit all or part of their purgation. Finally, those who failed to confess and do penance, according to the Lateran Council, "shall be cut off from the Church (excommunicated) during life and deprived of Christian burial after death." This meant the denial of all sacraments to the impenitent sinner and ostracism within medieval society.

The penitential system was the most potent instrument for discipline in the medieval church and was directly related to the Eucharist. The Sacrament of Penance prepared the faithful for worthy participation in the Mass. The Mass for which such stringent preparation was provided was the drama of God's epiphany. It was the redeeming work which the faithful beheld and through which rich blessings came to them. It was the drama which involved the entire course of salvation from Eden to the end of time. The focus of attention was on the celebrating priest who continued the sacrifice of Christ as he offered the consecrated bread and wine at the altar. As he elevated the sacred Host (consecrated bread) the people gazed upon it and adored the body of Christ sacrificed for them. Berthold of Regensburg in one of his sermons admonished his listeners:

> At the elevation of the Sacrament the priest seems to be saying three things to you: See the Son of God who, for your sakes, shows His wounds to the Heavenly Father; see the Son of God who, for your sakes, was thus lifted on the Cross; see the Son of God who will come to judge the living and the dead.[40]

To grasp the full impact of the drama one must imagine it as taking place within the soaring structure of the perpendicular Gothic cathedral, accompanied by the rising sounds of Gregorian chant, resplendent with a rich and dignified ceremonial.

Viewed thus, the medieval Mass was quite different from the Eucharist of the early church, occurring in someone's house, with the focus on the people gathered there, with one out of their midst set aside to preside, with the emphasis on remembering with thanksgiving, ending with the communion in the body and blood of Christ whereby the community was reformed and empowered to do the deeds of Christ in the world. It was different, but in its own way it was true to the Gospel and effectual for the ordinary Christian.

Ailred, the Abbot of the great Cistercian monastery of Rievaulx in twelfth-century England, viewed the liturgy as

the representation in sacred action of the divine Word proclaimed in Scripture. "Jesus, our Lord and Savior . . . has, in
his care of us, given us not merely the record in the Scriptures
of his saving deeds, but re-presented them for us through
symbolic actions."[41] As the divine Word in Scripture makes
known to the faithful the meaning of history, so the Mass
speaks to them of their redemption, hope, and beatitude.
"We see what Christ suffered on our behalf; what, even at
present, he bestows on us; what he has waiting for us in the
life to come."[42] Furthermore, here, in action, truths are expressed through symbols, truths which words and concepts
can never express.

The emphasis upon redemption expressed through symbolic action was important for the medieval Christian who
might very well possess a limited intellectual ability and be
incapable of reading, but whose imagination and perception
might be quite lively. It was important during an age when
people were faced with either perpetual bliss or perpetual
torment, when mere existence was tenuous for most and all
were afflicted by plagues and wars. The church with its sacramental system reminded the faithful of the alternatives confronting them but also provided them, principally through
Baptism, Penance, and the Mass, with the means of grace
whereby they might be assured of eternal bliss.

The Sixteenth Century Church of England and the Quadrilateral

The Lambeth Quadrilateral, with its definition of the
church's unity in terms of Scripture, creeds, sacraments, and
ministry, expressed a conviction that was basic to the Reformation in sixteenth-century England. That is, the necessity to
define that which is essential to Christian faith and practice
and to emphasize it and insist upon conformity to it. All else
was to be regarded in the light of the essential—and neither
emphasized nor made the authoritative—basis of faith and
practice. For instance, the Sacrament of the Eucharist is essential, but the ceremonies surrounding it, such as the clothes

the priest wears, although important, are nonessentials, and thus the universal church need not agree on them. The state may legislate concerning them, hopefully all being done in accord with St. Paul's injunction that decency and order be the rule.

In part this distinction between essentials and nonessentials had always been present, in part its renewed emphasis came from the Christian humanist criticism of the medieval church. Humanists, such as John Colet, Dean of St. Paul's Cathedral, London, and Desiderius Erasmus, the wit and scholar of Rotterdam, were intent upon removing all that hid the Gospel, stripping away the accretions so that the pure light of Christ might shine forth. The development of this important attitude also involved a growing conviction that the recent centuries had been ones of decline from the purity of the early church. The years from A.D. 600 to 1500 were defined as a period of mediocrity. The more avid Protestants and those on the left wing of the Reformation went further, regarding those centuries, notably in terms of the growth of the power of Antichrist. The main task was that of restoring that which had been lost with the growth of papal power in the West. Leaders of the Church of England subscribed to this view of things and looked upon the years extending through the first four general councils, from Christ to the middle of the fifth century, as providing a model.

Upon the accession of Queen Elizabeth I to the throne of England, John Jewel went to Paul's Cross in London, the most prominent preaching station in the land, and challenged:

> If any learned man of all our adversaries, or if all the learned men that be alive be able to bring any one sufficient sentence, out of any old catholic doctor, or father: Or out of any old general council: Or out of the holy scriptures of God; Or any one example of the primitive Church whereby it may be clearly and plainly proved, that there was any private mass in the whole world at the time, for the space of six hundred years after Christ. . . . Or that the bishop of Rome was then called an universal bishop, or head of the universal Church. . . . Or that the people was then taught to believe that Christ's body is really, substantially, corporally, carnally, or naturally, in the sacrament. . . . [I will] give over and subscribe unto him.[13]

In all, Jewel specified twenty-seven items, most of them concerning the sacraments. Although the challenge had a negative impact, seeking to eradicate much which his opponents considered necessary, Jewel's underlying intent was positive. He was seeking to emphasize that which is essential to the church and to personal salvation, looking to the early church for guidance, working to ground the unity of the faithful and the prosperity of the people in general in Scripture, creeds, sacraments, and the threefold ministry of bishops, priests, and deacons.

We can observe the same intent in the work of the bishops and other clergy who gathered at the Convocation of Canterbury in 1563. Among other things, they established articles of religion which were given the force of law by Parliament in 1571. Articles of religion do not form a creed, but rather provide direction for the church in its struggles against those who disturb and challenge its unity, in this instance Roman Catholics and so-called radical reformers lumped together under the name of Anabaptists.

The articles which these representatives of the English church propounded were authoritative in their time and for centuries to come. They therefore provide an important source of evidence. First of all, they affirm the historic faith of the church: ". . . in the unity of this Godhead there be three persons, of one substance." Spelling out the contents of faith in terms of the Trinity, the convocation then asserted the authority of Scripture:

> Holy Scripture containeth all things necessary to salvation: so that whatsoever is not read therein, nor may be proved thereby, is not to be required of any man, that it should be believed as an article of the faith, or be thought requisite to salvation.[44]

The church was defined in relation to the Scripture as the Word of God, and the sacraments, widely called the visible words of God. Thus the convocation decreed:

> The visible Church of Christ is a congregation of faithful men [the word is used generically, as the Latin indicates], in the which the pure word of God is preached, and the Sacraments be

duly ministered, according to Christ's ordinance in all those things that of necessity be requisite to the same.

Furthermore:

> The Church hath power to decree Rites and Ceremonies, and authority in controversies of faith: And yet it is not lawful for the Church to ordain anything that is contrary to God's word written, neither may it so expound one place of scripture, that it be repugnant to another. Wherefore, although the Church be a witness and a keeper of holy writ: yet, as it ought not to decree any thing against the same, so besides the same, ought it not to enforce any thing to be believed for necessity of salvation.

Thus Scripture was considered to be supreme over all else, including the church. And yet, as Richard Hooker, the late sixteenth-century English theologian, put it: Scripture presupposes the operation of God-given reason in human beings. It is this reason, which is more than a human faculty and is called by some "right reason," spirit-filled reason, which receives the truths of Scripture and discerns truth amidst falsities. It is no good saying, "the Spirit says" this or that unless that which is said yields its reasons, convinces us of its essential merit.

Human reason, however, has need of the revelation which comes through Scripture, for reason has fallen. It is involved in the tragedy of universal sin. To redeem reason so that it may function as it was created to function, we have the grace of God, freely given, conveyed through God's Word in Scripture and attested to in the tradition of the church, which for theologians such as Jewel and Hooker was primarily the tradition of the early church. Three strands are woven together to compose the fabric of authority for Anglicanism: Scripture, reason, and tradition; but supreme among them is Scripture as the living Word of God.

The Thirty-Nine Articles of Religion had little to say about ministry and nothing about bishops. One article defined the ordained ministry as the "office of public preaching" and "ministering of the Sacraments in the congregation." Yet by statutory law enacted by parliament during the reign of King Henry VIII and through the provision of an official Ordinal, or manual for ordinations, under King Edward VI, the threefold ministry of bishops, priests, and deacons was preserved, and continuity with the church through history, including the Middle Ages, was maintained.

The papacy was repudiated under Henry VIII and the equality of bishops was widely affirmed. Archbishops over the two provinces of Canterbury and York were retained, but their authority was qualified by the power over the church asserted by king in parliament and to a lesser degree by the authority of the two convocations. John Jewel, who became Bishop of Salisbury in 1559, wrote:

> . . . the wealth of the bishops is now diminished and reduced to a reasonable amount, to the end that, being relieved from that royal pomp and courtly bustle, they may with greater ease and diligence employ their leisure in attending to the flock of Christ.[45]

John Hooper provided an example as bishop of Gloucester under King Edward VI. The bishops who preceded him were mostly nonresident, living abroad but drawing on the revenues of the see. Hooper resided among his people, visited the parishes, presided at court sessions, and sought to build up the clergy, most of them being underpaid and ignorant. A stern disciplinarian, insisting on high moral standards for clergy and laity alike, he was nevertheless sensitive to the hardships which his people suffered, protesting to the government against the high cost of things, particularly of food, and striving to correct the injustices which weighed heavily upon the poor. The bishop daily invited a number of poor to dinner where they "were served with hot and wholesome meats." Before they were served they were examined as to their knowledge of the Lord's Prayer, the Creed, and the Ten Commandments. When they were examined and sat down to eat, Hooper himself sat down. Thus he demonstrated the proper character of the ministry and of the episcopacy in particular.

Most prominently, the church in sixteenth-century England was characterized by its public worship. There might be some controversy concerning the ordained ministry, and some disagreement concerning the interpretation of Scripture, but most controversy seemed to revolve around the Book of Common Prayer. The Puritans, dissatisfied members of the Church of England and hoping and working for further reforms, objected to the Prayer Book and its ceremonies, which to them so closely resembled the worship of the medieval church. Their protests and efforts were thwarted during the sixteenth century. The Prayer Book, as authorized by the queen and parliament in 1559, was to provide the basis for the religious settlement of the Church of England.

The Book of Common Prayer which drew upon medieval structures, early church examples, and the liturgies of the Eastern Church and of German Lutheran churches, provided for the needs of the nation at prayer. The Sacrament of Holy Eucharist brought together the people of each geographical locale to hear the Word of God and to partake of the body and blood of Christ, mindful of their redemption in him through his sacrifice on the cross. Through Word and sacrament the people were reformed by grace to be the means by which the godly commonwealth was established and prospered.

The majestic words and phrases of the Book of Common Prayer worked on the minds and hearts of Christians so that by the end of the century it echoed and reechoed in the plays of Shakespeare and, during the early decades of the seventeenth century, provided much of the inspiration for the poetry of John Donne and George Herbert. Its effects upon the ordinary people were various, but at its best it inculcated a piety which was liturgical in one sense, but deeply biblical at the same time. Such doctrines as transubstantiation and consubstantiation were rejected as unbiblical and, it could be said, unnecessary.

Richard Hooker disdained all attempts to define the manner of Christ's presence in the Holy Communion:

> what these elements are in themselves it skilleth not, it is enough that to me which take them they are the body and blood of Christ, his promise in witness hereof sufficeth, his word he knoweth which way to accomplish; why should any cogitation possess the mind of the faithful communicant but this, O my God thou art true, O my Soul thou art happy![46]

Hooker, having studied the philosophy of ancient Greece and Rome, as well as the works of the medieval theologians, was most concerned for the ends to which things were intended. The end or purpose of the sacraments is our participation in Christ. The elements of bread and wine are not ends in themselves but causes instrumental toward our participation in Christ. The purpose of the Eucharist is not to be found in the transformation of the bread and wine into the body and blood of Christ but rather in the transformation, that is to say the salvation, of the worshiper from death to new life in Christ. This was a sacramental conviction widely shared in Hooker's day.

Lancelot Andrewes, who died in 1626, a translator of the Authorized Version of the Holy Bible and the Bishop of Winchester came onto the scene long enough after the Reformation had begun in England to internalize its chief accomplishments. His *Private Devotions* express something of the inner meaning of all that had happened and provide evidence as to where the emphasis fell:

> Shed abroad Thy love in my heart,
>   so that I may love Thee,
>   my friend in Thee, my enemy for Thee.
> O Thou who givest grace to the humble-minded,
>   also give me grace to be humble-minded.
> O Thou who never failest those who fear Thee,
>   my Fear and my Hope,
>   let me fear one thing only,
>   the fearing ought more than Thee. . . .[47]

The visible church, with Scripture, creeds, sacraments, and episcopal ministry, was meant to serve such an end, the love of God and the love of others in him.

The Holy Community Adapts to a New Place in a New Time

When the American colonies revolted against the British crown and parliament in 1776, the holy community in this place was confronted by a new set of circumstances. As the new nation was being born it became apparent that there would be no official, established, state-supported, national church. This was a practical impossibility. It was also against the principles of Founding Fathers such as Madison and Jefferson. Furthermore, there was a proliferation of churches in the colonies. Congregationalists, Baptists, Presbyterians, Roman Catholics, Quakers, Methodists, Anglicans, and others coexisted, sometimes unwillingly, with their chief strength in particular colonies. Now a new attitude to suit the new situation was emerging.

The Church of England in the colonies had been greatly weakened. Its clergy and people were split, some maintaining loyalty to the British crown, others fervently supporting the revolution. Many of the loyalists fled to England and to Canada. Furthermore, the colonists had never had a resident bishop. Now, cut off from England, with no bishops, a reduced church membership, fewer clergy, and growing opposition to having established churches, there was intense pressure on the remaining leaders of the church to adjust to the realities of the changed situation.

William White, who was to be the first Bishop of Pennsylvania, writing in his *The Case for the Episcopal Churches in the United States Considered,* noted: "all denominations of Christians are on a level, and no church is farther known to the public than as a voluntary association of individuals, for a lawful and useful purpose."[48] White himself was very much influenced by the statesmen working out the implications of their theories in the plan for a federal government. Like them, he had read John Locke on the contract theory of government and adopted the concept of voluntary association as practical application of that theory. Thus a group of people volunteer and contract to form a parish and parishes agree and contract to work together in larger units: dioceses, provinces, and a general convention.

The American descendant of the Church of England was to be a democratic church among other democratic churches cooperating with one another for the sake of the Gospel. The founding of the Protestant Episcopal Church in the United States, which we can date from the General Convention of 1789, involved something dramatically new in Anglicanism, appropriate to the realities and aspirations of the new nation. And yet, William White did not consider that he was suggesting anything radically new. The democratic episcopal government for the Protestant Episcopal Church was modeled upon governmental structures in the early church, where "it was customary to debate and determine in a general concourse of all Christians in the same city; among whom the bishop was no more than a president."[49] It was restoration not innovation which concerned him.

Furthermore, those first American Episcopalians did not desire a complete break with the Church of England. They were as concerned to preserve continuity with her as to adapt to the new circumstances. In the Preface to the first edition of the new Book of Common Prayer (1790), they said: "it will also appear that this Church is far from intending to depart from the Church of England in any essential point of doctrine, discipline, or worship; or further than local circumstances require." Here they relied on the distinction between that which is essential to salvation and that which is not, that which may change and, indeed, must change with the times. The changes which were occurring as the Episcopal Church adapted to new circumstances in a new nation affected only nonessentials and did not to their minds impinge on anything essential.

They accepted the teachings of the Thirty-Nine Articles of Religion concerning Scripture: it contains all things necessary to salvation. For many people in the early days of the new nation every part of the Bible was authoritative, directly inspired by God's Holy Spirit and intended as the only rule of faith. As such it was above the church and at times against the church. William Meade, third Bishop of Virginia, regarded the preaching of the Word as a mighty weapon for the conversion of souls, a weapon which in his time had to be defended within the Episcopal Church against those whose regard for the authority of the church and its traditions challenged the authority of the Bible. Meade wrote in this manner in 1841 when Tractarians, spearheading a Catholic revival in the Church of England under the leadership of John Henry Newman and others, were beginning to gain enthusiastic adherents in the United States. Old High Churchmen such as John Henry Hobart, Bishop of New York, by and large shared Meade's evangelical concern for the Scripture. Now, as America approached mid-nineteenth century and a devastating civil war, Benjamin T. Onderdonk, Bishop of New York and a professor in the General Theological Seminary, was teaching his students that while Scripture contained all that is necessary to salvation, one must regard "primitive catholic tradition as a rule for the right understanding of Scripture."[50] William I. Kip, first Bishop of California, went further in his book *The Double Witness of the Church* (1843), advocating the double witness of Scripture and catholic tradition.

This challenge to the authority of Scripture was mild compared to that which affected and aroused most Christians in nineteenth-century America. This greater challenge involved the appearance of a new kind of critical attitude toward the Bible. For a long time, and certainly since the time of the Renaissance beginning in fourteenth-century Europe, there had been textual criticism. This was the so-called "lower criticism," or study of ancient manuscripts of the Bible in order to determine, insofar as possible, the original text and thus to eliminate corruption and errors. Now out of nineteenth-century Germany there came another kind of criticism much influenced by the philosophical trends of the time, the rising importance of historical investigation and the growth of the natural sciences. This was dubbed "higher criticism." The Bible was to be analyzed in a scientific manner, much as the texts of Homer and Shakespeare were analyzed by literary critics and historians. The practitioner of higher criticism labored to penetrate behind the text to the essential meaning of the text, to the author or compilers of the text, and to the events and circumstances which influenced the text. New quests were pursued, such as the quest for the essence of Christianity and the quest for the historical Jesus. In the process much that was accepted as true was brought into doubt; much that was cherished was rejected.

The American Episcopal Church moved gradually from the outright condemnation of such biblical criticism to the acceptance of it. In 1865 the General Convention joined the Church of England in condemning John William Colenso, Bishop of Natal in South Africa. Colenso had cast doubt on the Mosaic authorship of all but a small portion of the books ascribed to Moses. He had even questioned the existence of Moses. In one place in the book, which contained his alarming views, he wrote that "the ordinary knowledge of Christ was nothing more than that of any educated Jew of his age,"[51] a statement which was condemned as blasphemous. But by 1897 the American bishops were largely in accord with the judgment of the Lambeth Conference of that year that: "The critical study of the Bible by competent scholars is essential to the maintenance of the Church in a healthy faith."[52]

The struggle was to continue between those who insisted upon the complete authority of the entire Bible and those who accepted the results of biblical criticism. The latter regarded the scientific study of the Bible not as destructive but as a defense against corruption and error and as an aid to the cultivation of faith. By the mid-twentieth century, a renewed understanding of the church as the holy community was influencing most of the churches in America so that the opposition of Scripture and church began to wane. Scripture and church and tradition were increasingly viewed as interdependent, the indivisible parts of the one body. St. Ambrose of Milan in the fourth century was remembered as commenting: "The traditions of the Scriptures are his [Christ's] body; the Church is his body."

The Apostolic and Nicene Creeds were accepted as described in the Thirty-Nine Articles of Religion and as found in the Book of Common Prayer. Evangelicals, such as Meade of Virginia, accepted them in that the doctrines they contain can be proved out of Scripture. They also accepted them as setting forth that doctrine necessary to salvation, as guarding against error, and as promoting true faith. The advent of liberal theology and biblical criticism brought the creeds, as well as the Scripture, into question. Like the Scripture the creeds must be treated as historical documents. In particular, the virgin birth was questioned on scientific grounds and the language of the councils of Nicaea, Constantinople, Ephesus, and Chalcedon was regarded as suitable for the fourth and fifth centuries but not for the nineteenth and twentieth.

Broad Churchmen, such as Phillips Brooks, bishop of Massachusetts (1891–1893), accepted the creeds, recited them in public, taught them in private, but having done so believed that they had discharged their duty and turned to the interpreting of the truths they contain in modern terms. They did not believe that the Holy Spirit had been silent or inactive since Chalcedon, and they were convinced that the Spirit was shedding new light on the eternal truths in their own time. And yet in spite of the questioning the creeds continued to occupy places of prominence in the worship of the holy community and to exert their influence as witnesses to the eternal Gospel in their own age and in all subsequent ages.

The two sacraments, Baptism and Holy Communion, were retained in the American Episcopal Church, basically as understood in the Thirty-Nine Articles of Religion and as historically contained in the Book of Common Prayer. The 1789 Convention of the Episcopal Church made the use of the Prayer Book compulsory for all state (or diocesan) churches belonging to the Convention. This Prayer Book was the English book, amended to take note of the changed circumstances. For instance, it was obviously no longer possible to pray for the English king as their sovereign. The Book was also influenced by the struggle between reformist and conservative leaders of the church. Bishop White favored the more revised and, according to some, radical "Proposed Book" of 1785. Samuel Seabury, as a result of pledges made to the Scottish bishops who consecrated him bishop of Connecticut, and as a result of his own preferences, objected to the 1785 Proposed Book and tenaciously insisted that the rather conservative Scottish Eucharist be included in the new American Prayer Book. Both views affected the outcome. The 1789 book reflected the adjustments necessitated by the changed circumstances and also preserved continuity with English and Scottish tradition. This book persisted, as revised in 1892 and 1928, until 1976, when General Convention adopted as a "Proposed Book" a Prayer Book which, while maintaining continuity with the past, goes far beyond any other revision and reflects the influence of the modern liturgical movement.

The liturgical movement has been one of the most dramatic events in the history of the Episcopal Church and other

churches in the twentieth century. The High Church movement and the Anglo-Catholic movement of the nineteenth
century enhanced the authority and appearance of sacraments in the church, largely under medieval and romantic
influences. Under the influence of those movements the
Eucharist was more frequently celebrated and with more
elaborate ritual, challenging the dominance of Morning
Prayer with Sermon in many places. The liturgical movement, beginning in nineteenth-century France and Germany
reached England and the United States effectually in the
twentieth century. Through this movement, which had its
origins in a theological and liturgical revival in the Roman
Catholic Church, increased emphasis was placed upon the
seriousness and wholeness of Baptism, and the Eucharist was
increasingly regarded as the chief and central corporate act of
celebration of the holy community. In both instances, Baptism and the Eucharist, the aim was to restore the understanding and practice of the early church in language and
actions amenable to the modern world. The emphasis was on
community and on the laity, whose active participation in the
giving of thanks was considered essential. Thus a central altar, the use of contemporary English, and the closest possible
relationship between priest and people were becoming
norms by the last quarter of the twentieth century.

Finally, episcopacy was retained in the Protestant Episcopal Church. This is more remarkable than is apparent on
first glance. The Church of England in the colonies had had
no resident bishops, as has been remarked. The bishop of
London maintained jurisdiction, exercising his authority
through resident ecclesiastical commissioners. Many Anglicans strove earnestly to have a bishop in the colonies. They
met strong opposition on the part of those who associated
bishops with monarchy and tyranny and who resented the
idea of being taxed to support Lord Bishops with their grand
retinues and pompous ways. The advocacy of bishops on the
part of the founders of the Episcopal Church in America was
therefore a matter of serious conviction. William White, writing in 1782, foresaw the difficulty in obtaining a native episcopacy and entertained the possibility that the American

church should have to begin without lawfully consecrated bishops. Bishops were important to him. Nevertheless, his Federal Plan was not centered on bishops but on presbyters and laity. Lay participation was emphasized, not only on the basis of the example of the early church but also in terms of precedents in the British Constitution. Convocation and the two houses of parliament governed the Church of England under the crown. In both houses of parliament laity participated in the control of ecclesiastical ideas and activities. Thus in parishes, in dioceses, in provincial synods, and in the continental or national representative assembly there were to be laity participating with bishops and presbyters in the government and discipline of the Episcopal Church.

The Federal Plan was opposed by the clergy of New England. There an Episcopal Plan was promoted by those who believed that the reorganization of the church should begin with the establishment of a valid episcopacy. Connecticut led the way, obtaining the consecration of Samuel Seabury in Scotland in 1784. The Connecticut clergy not only stressed episcopacy, they also objected to the participation of laity in the government of the church. The result of the contention between those supporting the opposing plans was a compromise. A House of Bishops, led by a presiding bishop, was established as a part of General Convention. At first the bishops could not initiate any legislation, but exercised the right of veto, which could be overruled by a three-fifth vote of the convention. By the end of the convention of 1789, the bishops had obtained the right to initiate legislation. Furthermore, their veto could only be overruled by a four-fifth vote of the lower house of General Convention.

The result of all the maneuvering in 1789 was a church government based upon local control by voluntary associations of persons in parishes. Dioceses and the national convention possessed power in relation to and for the sake of parishes. The larger organizations functioned as agencies preserving and strengthening the unity of the church. White agreed that "the great art of governing consists in not governing too much."

The subsequent history of the development of government

in the Episcopal Church is largely one of growing central or national power, beginning with the establishment by General Convention in 1820 of the Domestic and Foreign Missionary Society. It seemed obvious that the missionary work of the church must be a cooperative endeavor. In time a General Board of Religious Education and a Joint Commission on Social Service were established for similar reasons. In 1919 a central organization was created by General Convention and called "The Presiding Bishop and Council" to "administer and carry on the missionary, educational, and social work of the Church, of which work the Presiding Bishop shall be the executive head." All of the previously established organizations were absorbed by this National Council (now Executive Council), the creature of General Convention, with powers strictly limited, but with the advantage of meeting, deliberating, deciding, and executing all manner of ecclesiastical affairs on a day-to-day basis in the years between the triennial meetings of General Convention.

If the original polity of this church at first seemed patterned after the states-rights polity of the confederation of the colonies, the government after 1919 seemed more and more to emulate the federal government with its concentration of power, its great responsibilities, its growing bureaucracy, and its continuing dependence upon the will and whims of those responsible for its existence. The great power of General Convention was and remains its control of the budget of the Presiding Bishop and Council. Dioceses and parishes can indicate their approval or disapproval of its policies and activities by giving or withholding the money necessary for its work. At crucial moments ordinary people in parishes are able to exert their power in telling ways, indicating that they of the holy community provide the basis upon which all else exists.

The church as an institution which has developed through history is an instrument of the Gospel. It belongs to its Lord and is not its own possession. As the body of Christ it is most true to itself when it gathers to worship; to hear God's Word read and preached; to confess its faith in unity with all Christians, past, present, and future; to administer the sacraments, Baptism and the Eucharist, that it may deepen its communion with its Lord, with one another, and with those outside its community through loving service. It does this under the leadership of its bishop, the symbol and agent of its unity and its task. The holy community of living and breathing people is the church.

This community of the faithful is holy, but it is, of its very nature, human and fallible. Bishop Meade of Virginia put it this way in 1852:

> Let it not be supposed, that because we love the Church, we consider it perfect. Viewing it as made up of men—the redeemed of the Lord—of course it is a society of poor sinful beings, in whose hands every thing is liable to be perverted and corrupted. The history of the Church is the history of human frailty, though kept down by divine grace. She has often degenerated from her first love and fidelity. If she has been persecuted, she has also persecuted in turn, when it was deemed a duty so to do. But still, by means of her saints of all ages, and martyrs at various times, and holy bishops and other ministers, she has been the salt of the earth, and the light of the world.[53]

From our vantage point in the last quarter of the twentieth century we might add something concerning the growing weakness of the church in a world where less and less attention is paid to its theological pronouncements and its teaching in the practical areas of ethics and morals. This is widely acknowledged to be the post-Christian era, bearing considerable resemblance to the first years of the early church, with the society largely urban, opposition to Christianity widespread and often intelligent, and with Christians seeking more and more for the strengthening which comes when the faithful gather to worship their Lord.

The church of the post-Christian era does more than look back to a comparable era, however. As the early church faced the future with expectation of the end of history, so Christians living in the twentieth century increasingly look to the future with the realization that there is an end and that that end is not in the triumph of any institution as an institution. The triumph is that of the Lord and of those who gather with him around the heavenly banquet table giving thanks to God for his never failing love and goodness.

· 3 ·

Renewal and Reform: "Behold I make all things new."

Thomas Cranmer and Reform of Church and Society

In 1503 there arrived at the University of Cambridge in England a young man of fourteen known as "Thomas Cranmer, the sonne of Thomas Cranmer." He was born and raised in the rural town of Aslocton, in the County of Nottinghamshire, and was thus rooted in the rural countryside which was most characteristic of sixteenth-century England. To be sure there was London, with perhaps 60,000 people in 1503, a great trading and commercial center situated on the Thames River, which conveyed merchant ships from the European continent to the city's busy wharves. Upstream, at Westminster, there was the seat of government where the king lived at least a part of the time and the parliament met when summoned. Across the Thames at Lambeth there was the official home of the Archbishop of Canterbury, the chief ecclesiastic in the realm. One day Thomas would be the archbishop and live at Lambeth Palace. But that would have been unimaginable to the growing country boy who had never been to London and must have regarded Cambridge with awe.

Located in the fen country, Cambridge was a damp, chill

Thomas Cranmer, 1489–1556

place, a study in contrasts. Side by side were the medieval university of some 4,000 people and the town with roughly the same number of people. The university was one of the oldest and most famous in Christendom, a place which in 1503 was already beginning to feel the stimulating fresh air of humanistic studies. It housed its scholars and conducted its academic business by means of hostels (rather like inns or boarding houses), monastic houses, and the colleges which were coming to dominate the scene. While a student at Cambridge, Cranmer would have seen the final construction of King's College Chapel, the summation of all that is most impressive and beautiful in medieval Gothic and in Renaissance stained glass. It was a place to awe a youth from Aslocton. The town possessed the advantages and disadvantages of a medieval market and trading center. It was a busy place, with employment for willing workers, and with thriving business concerns such as the slaughterhouses behind the Augustinian friary which the scholarly Erasmus found so offensive. It had the smell of a busy town, emanating not only from the slaughterhouses but from the open sewers running down the streets pouring their stinking refuse into the King's Ditch. But there were also open fields, orchards, and gardens, sweet-smelling and gracious, in the town and in the colleges. The river which ran by the university was used for commerce, but there were swans gliding on it and paths alongside it for long and pleasant walks. By modern standards it was a small town, virtually overwhelmed by its rural setting. It was also a Christian town, for all of its inhabitants were nominally Christian. The town had its parish churches and the colleges had their chapels. The chief task of the university was to train men for the ordained ministry of the Church in England.

Cranmer was a member of Jesus College where he was engaged in the study of the Trivium and the Quadrivium: the former consisting of grammar, logic, and rhetoric; the latter consisting of arithmetic, geometry, astronomy, and music. To these were added the three philosophies, moral, natural, and metaphysical. Of all these subjects, logic and metaphysics (we might say theology) were given the greatest attention in the late Middle Ages. The regimen for the young student was harsh, with long hours of intense study. The Bible was read and interpreted, not according to the plain sense of the words but rather allegorically and mystically. Aristotle was studied, along with Peter Lombard's *Sentences,* and the works of the early church Fathers from Irenaeus to Chrysostom. Students gradually accumulated a great store of knowledge to use in the dialectical debates which provided a chief means of education and testing in the university. In 1511 Cranmer took his B.A. and in 1514 his M.A. after studying such "moderns" as Erasmus and Faber Stapulensis, as well as old Latin authors, and after learning Hebrew and Greek. It was around this time that Cranmer became a fellow of his college and began his teaching career. The way ahead seemed peaceful and assured. But then it all changed. Two events intervened, one of deep personal concern to Cranmer as a growing human being, the other also deeply personal but with important ramifications for the church and the nation, setting Cranmer on the road to Lambeth Palace and further on to a fiery death in Oxford.

The first event occurred when (in the words of an un-friendly witness) Cranmer became "clogged with a wife." The story is simply told by Ralph Morice, the archbishop's secretary:

> . . . it chaunced hym to marye a wif, by meanes wherof he was constrayned to leave his fellowshipp in the same colledge, and became the common reader at Buckingham colledge in Cam-bridge. And within one yere after that he was maried, his wif travailing with childe, both she and the childe died.[1]

We know very little more. She was, so we believe, the kins-woman of the owner of an inn at Cambridge. What she was like, what caused Cranmer to give up a secure position in order to marry her, how the death of his wife and his child affected him, we cannot know. But we do know that after his wife's death Cranmer regained his fellowship at Jesus Col-lege and began to study for Holy Orders, something he could not do if married.

The second event concerns Cranmer's conversion from al-legiance to the Church of Rome to espouse the Reformation associated with Martin Luther. Once more the necessary evi-dence is not forthcoming. But it does seem that the beginning of that conversion was in his growing concern while studying for Holy Orders to pursue the truth through the study of Scripture. The process whereby he proceeded was gradual and slow. An anonymous biographer records that for three years prior to his being made Doctor of Divinity at thirty-four years of age, in 1523, Cranmer "applyed his whole studye . . . unto the seyd scryptures."[2] Indeed, for the rest of his life he submitted all to the test of Scripture which he regarded as the living Word of God. To interpret it, discerning the Word in the words, he relied on the early church Fathers and his own God-given reason, rather than on the traditions of the theologians and the papal hierarchy.

It was as a biblical scholar that Cranmer first came to the attention of King Henry VIII and advised him concerning the annulment of his marriage to Queen Catherine of Aragon. Cranmer supported his king believing that by marrying his brother's widow, Henry had violated the Scriptural law contained in Leviticus 18:16, "You shall not uncover the nakedness of your brother's wife; she is your brother's nakedness." He defended the separation of England from allegiance to the Roman Church on the basis of Scriptural proofs, especially the teachings found in Paul's Epistle to the Romans and in the first Epistle of Peter which made clear the Christian's primary duty to obey the civil ruler and not the bishop of Rome. He argued for clerical marriage and against clerical celibacy, believing that the marriage of priests and bishops was legal according to the Scripture and that the church's law to the contrary should not be heeded, for it was in conflict with a higher authority. He labored to obtain an English Bible, so that the ordinary people of the realm might grow up reading, or at least hearing, the Scriptures in their own language. The Great Bible (1539), the work of William Tyndale, Miles Coverdale, and others was the result.

Throughout King Henry's reign the goals of reformers such as Cranmer were not to be sustained. For whatever reasons, personal and political, the king sought for independence from the Roman Church while retaining the outward appearance, and the basic doctrine, of the medieval church. With his death, the floodgates opened and Cranmer saw to the devising and promulgation of many things, including a book of homilies, or sermons, a doctrinal standard, the Forty-Two Articles of Religion, and a common order of worship, all grounded upon Scripture and all making Scriptural teaching more accessible. The crowning achievement came with the publication in 1549 of his Book of Common Prayer. He had been working quietly and steadily toward this, as he had been working toward a book of homilies and a set of articles during Henry's reign. When the Prayer Book was finally published it came forth as a model of liturgical creativity and reform, preserving continuity with the liturgical tradition of the West, but refreshing and innovative where Scripture was concerned. Its content was mostly biblical. To worship by the Prayer Book was to engage in the very heart of the Scripture. Its lectionary provided that the entire Bible was to be read through once a year, the New Testament three times a year, and the Psalms once every month. This meant that Scripture was read in large segments, entire chapters, and together with the preaching upon it, was to be dominant in the lives of English Christians.

The Scripture was the basis upon which not only freedom from the Church of Rome was to be achieved, but also a corrupt and dying church reformed and a people restored to godliness in their daily lives. As he explained in the Preface to the 1549 Prayer Book "the common prayers of the Churche" were established for the "advauncement of godliness." Therefore the whole Bible was to be read over every year in order that the clergy should "(by often readyng and meditacion of Gods worde) be stirred up to godlines themselfes, and be more able also to exhorte other by wholsome doctrine, and to confute them that were adversaries to the trueth. And further, that the people (by daily hearyng of holy scripture read in the Churche) should continuallye profite more and more in the knowledge of God, and bee the more inflamed with the love of his true religion."[3]

Cranmer's ultimate aim was to reform the church in order that the pure Word of God might effect the reform of individuals after the image of God and thus of the society in which they lived, extending from the king at Westminster to the lowliest plough-hand at Aslocton. All stood in need of salvation. No one knew this better than Cranmer himself whose liturgy, with its strong note of repentance, expresses the conviction that all have fallen away from God and that as a consequence there are plagues, wars, famine, rebellion, and the like as the just rewards of sinners. There was about England in the late Middle Ages an "odor of despair" preventing the "scent of optimism" accompanying the dawning new age of science and progress.

The way out was to be found in Scripture. If there was a

strong note of repentence in Cranmer's liturgy, it was there as the springboard to the new life in Christ. Amongst the homilies or sermons which were prepared for use in all the pulpits of the land, but especially for those which had no licensed preacher, there are the three homilies by Cranmer on salvation, faith, and good works. These homilies provide a powerful explanation of what Cranmer and others had learned from their study of the Scripture concerning reform. The message is basically the same as that delivered by Luther in Germany and Calvin in Geneva:

All are sinners, having broken God's laws, and none therefore can do anything to earn God's mercy and favor. Indeed, all deserve eternal punishment. But God is the God of mercy. God justifies the sinner who receives righteousness from God. "And this justification or righteousness, which we so receive by God's mercy and Christ's merits, embraced by faith, is taken, accepted, and allowed of God for our perfect and full justification."[4] Thus three things are involved in salvation through justification: (1) God's mercy, freely given, (2) on "Christ's part, justice, that is, the satisfaction of God's justice, or price of our redemption, by the offering of his body and shedding of his blood, with fulfilling of the law perfectly and throughly." That is to say, justice would be effected if we paid for our sin through eternal punishment, but God in his mercy sent his Son who paid the price for us. (3) And there is our part, which is faith, faith which is not passive but lively, a dynamic response to the love of God shown in the sacrifice of Christ for us.[5]

Cranmer makes it clear that because good works are not required of anyone in order to be justified or accepted and made righteous, this does not mean that the saved sinner is free to do anything at all. He carefully explains that true Christian faith is

. . . not only to believe that holy scripture and all the foresaid articles of our faith are true, but also to have a sure trust and confidence in God's merciful promises, to be saved from everlasting damnation by Christ: whereof doth follow a loving heart to obey his commandments. And this true christian faith neither any devil hath, nor yet any man, which in the outward profession of his mouth, and in his outward receiving of the sacraments, in coming to the church, and in all other outward appearances seemeth to be a christian man, and yet in his living and deeds sheweth the contrary.[6]

Reform thus involves the condemnation of hypocrites: of all those who profess the faith, attend church, and receive the sacraments but behave selfishly, denying authority or cheating the poor. Cranmer attacked the Christian community of his day, revealing glaring abuses and demanding that love and justice be actualized.

In his homily on good works, Cranmer refers to the vows of obedience, chastity, and poverty, and to the monks and nuns who take them.

First, under pretence of obedience to their father in religion, (which obedience they made themselves,) they were exempted, by their rules and canons, from obedience of their natural father and mother, and from the obedience of emperor and king, and all temporal power, whom of very duty by God's laws they were bound to obey. And so the profession of their obedience not due was a renunciation of their due obedience. And how their profession of chastity was observed, it is more honesty to pass over in silence, and let the world judge of that which is well known, than with unchaste words, by expressing of their unchaste life, to offend chaste and godly ears. And as for their wilful poverty, it was such, that when in possessions, jewels, plate, and riches, they were equal or above merchants, gentlemen, barons, earls, and dukes; yet by this subtle sophistical term . . . "proper in common," they deluded the world, persuading that, notwithstanding all their possessions and riches, they might neither help father nor mother, nor other that were indeed very needy and poor, without the licence of their father abbot, prior, or warden. And yet they might take of every man, but they might not give aught to any man, no not to them whom the laws of God bound them to help.[7]

The accusations were extreme, but as Cranmer viewed the church of his day he had to speak out, decrying the corrupt state of the holy community.

Cranmer did not, however, consider that he was speaking out on his own authority as a Christian or as archbishop of Canterbury. He spoke as informed by the Word of God. It was the Word which he uttered against hypocrites. The same Word provided a defense for King Henry's actions: the rejection of the papacy, the establishment of a national church, and the dissolution of the monastaries. In obedience to the Word of God a reformed church emerged in England, much in need of further reform, but a church which nevertheless recalled the people of God to the essentials of the faith and put all else in proper perspective as nonessential, however beneficial.

To represent God's Word in the world called for humility and courage. Cranmer was ideal for the task possessing both qualities. Power did not seem to preoccupy him, although much power was available to him. Nor did he claim to have full possession of the truth. He was always ready to listen to others. But when he was certain of the right in any matter, the mild scholar could be fearless and strong. At times when it was not politic to do so he interceded for those marked for destruction by the powers of the state. Sir Thomas More, Anne Boleyn, Thomas Cromwell, and Princess Mary were all recipients of this courage as he pled for their lives. Furthermore, he could and did oppose King Henry in such matters as the Six Articles Act with which he was in strong theological disagreement. And during the reign of King Edward VI he opposed the government's avaricious policies which deprived the church and the people of lawful possessions. Such acts of courage were always the result of careful consideration and thus when engaged in had to be taken seriously even if rejected. That he survived as long as he did, given his actions and the strength of his enemies, is remarkable.

When King Edward died and the Roman Catholic Queen Mary, daughter of Henry VIII and Catherine of Aragon, came to the throne in 1553, Thomas Cranmer was dismayed and troubled. He had done his part, however reluctantly, to prevent her accession and when this failed he, along with other bishops, was seized, imprisoned, and tried. For long he stood firm in his convictions, resisting pressures to recant his reformation principles and achievements and return to Roman allegiance. But he eventually weakened. We do not know what went through his mind in those last months of his life.

But he should not be faulted for experiencing fear and revulsion in the face of violent death as a heretic and a traitor. We should certainly understand the dilemma he experienced between a conscience which commanded that he renounce all papal authority and a conscience which ordered that he obey his sovereign. He confronted a queen who demanded that he submit to the papacy and for a moment in time he obeyed her, admitted the evil of his reforming activities and recanted his faith.

That recantation was not, however, his last word. The day of his execution began with heavy rain and with the gathering of crowds in St. Mary's Church, Oxford, and on High Street outside, to witness the final events in the life of the once great and now shameful archbishop. In the church he was commanded to speak and expected to confirm his recantation. Instead, he ended by recanting his recantations and affirming his faith:

> And now I come to the great thing that so troubleth my conscience . . . and that is my setting abroad of writings contrary to the truth, which here now I renounce and refuse as things written with my hand contrary to the truth which I thought in my heart, and written for fear of death, and to save my life, if it might be; and that is all such bills which I have written or signed with mine own hand. . . . And forasmuch as my hand offended in writing contrary to my heart, it shall be first burned. And as for the Pope, I refuse him as Christ's enemy and Antichrist, with all his false doctrine. And as for the Sacrament. . .[8]

At that he was cut off, stopped in mid-sentence, and amidst cries of indignation dragged off to his death by fire, the death of a heretic. His death was not an end, however, but a beginning, for with this final act of courage the continuance of the English Reformation was assured.

Renewal and Reform: A Persistent Theme

Reform may be personal or institutional, or both. In the early church it was understood almost solely in personal terms.

Reform meant to be reformed according to or in the image of God. Romans 12:2, a text which John Colet as Dean of St. Paul's, London, used to urge reform on the clergy, put it this way: "Do not be conformed to this world but be transformed [or reformed] by the renewal of your mind, that you may prove what is the will of God, what is good and acceptable and perfect." Reform involved conversion, turning away from the world—that which denies God—and turning to the Lord, to worship him in spirit and in truth. The argument goes this way: People have fallen away from that original integrity and innocence which was theirs before the fall of Adam and Eve in the Garden of Eden. Now by virtue of God's sending his Son to die for us it is possible to turn, to be reformed in accordance with the image of God in Christ. It is possible to return to the Garden, to Paradise, and to regain integrity and innocence, according to the Greek Fathers. Gregory of Nyssa expressed himself in these words:

> It is indeed possible for us to return to the original beatitude, if we now will run backward on the same road which we had followed when we were rejected from Paradise together with our forefather [Adam].

And so we must behave

> as those who have become strangers from their homes: after they have turned back in the direction whence they started, they leave that place first which they had reached last when setting forth.[9]

Such returning, or reform, involves renunciation. Gregory speaks of leaving behind marriage, things of the flesh, and the illusion of taste and sight. Reform thus involves asceticism or discipline, which is highly personal but not devoid of communal aspects. The holy community itself was the embodiment on earth of the heavenly city, the Communion of Saints. So St. Augustine of Hippo understood. Insofar as the church is truly the church it does not need to be reformed. The people who compose it, however, are pilgrims on the way to the full realization of the heavenly city and must constantly be reformed.

The idea of reform was probably first used with application to the church during the rule of Pope Gregory VII in the eleventh century. But this does not prevent us from considering church reform in relation to events preceding the Middle Ages. Sociologists of religion have identified reform as a major element in the development of religions. For instance, it can be argued that the world religions which have particular founders, such as Buddhism, Mohammedanism, Jainism, Manichaeism, and Christianity, all follow a certain pattern. The first stage in their development consists of the founder with a band of disciples. The second stage occurs when the founder dies and the disciples become apostles forming a close fellowship which worships or professes allegiance to the founder. In time there is a third stage with organizational development becoming a necessary preoccupation for a fellowship which cared little or nothing for organization in the beginning. During this third stage doctrine is elaborated, the oral tradition is written out, worship becomes increasingly formal, and governmental organization with an hierarchy and law occurs.

There then arise protests against the compromises and modifications of the original meaning and message as the organization becomes more and more enmeshed in the surrounding society and the leadership becomes corrupt. The forms which these protests take vary. Some reject the parent organization altogether and found new groups. Others remain within the parent organization and either seek to live out a basically internal protest and reform, or seek to alter the structures and forms of the organization. However the protest is expressed, those involved have in mind the original experience of revelation in and through the founder. But they can also have in view some sort of ideal future which judges the present. Monasticism, which is not restricted to Christianity, is viewed as a protest movement in this context and shall shortly be considered as such.

Reform, whether personal or institutional or both, can be either backward-looking or forward-looking. If it is backward-looking it is carried out in terms of a perfect form or state which has been changed or corrupted but may hopefully be restored. This involves an incarnational view of the church. An example here in the modern church is found in the liturgical movement and in particular in the work of Dom Gregory Dix, monk of Nashdom Abbey, an Anglican Benedictine house. In his book, *The Shape of the Liturgy* (1948), he searched for and found the essential nature of Christian worship in the Eucharist, not in the words used but in a four-action shape: "taking" bread and wine at the offertory; "giving thanks," or blessing in the Eucharistic prayer; "breaking" bread at the fraction; and "sharing," or communion as the body and blood of Christ is presented to the faithful. All of this was based on New Testament evidence but also on early evidence such as the Hippolytan liturgy of the third century. Liturgical reform was thus to involve a return to the "original" shape and this has in fact been the aim of much liturgical revision.

If reform is forward-looking it will involve change from one form to a new and different form. It will involve reshaping and innovating. It is to be found in Christian millenarianism, which is the expectation of a thousand years of happiness at the end of history, yet still within history. Such millenarianism has its roots in the Jewish messianic hope and in Hellenistic cosmology, and it is to be found prominently in persons from Irenaeus in the second century down to the present among certain Christian sects and charismatics. St. Augustine stands out here, reinterpreting millenarianism, identifying the millennium of Revelation 20 with Christian history in the sixth age, the present Christian age preceding the end. Joachim, the monk of Calabria (d. 1202), modified Augustine's teaching to speak of three ages, those of the Father (up to Christ), the Son (from Christ to Joachim), and the Holy Spirit. Joachim's followers engaged upon reform activities, including attacks on the clerical hierarchy, on the basis of their expectations of the dawning ultimate age. Their views in Christian and secular forms, rooted in a past Golden Age and culminating with the dawning age of perfection, have been influential in the history of the West. Some historians speak of utopianism in various forms, from Thomas More to Karl Marx and the American dream. However we describe it, whether in Christian or secular terms, we are speaking of that which is rooted in the past but directed forward, with present activities determined by some vision of the future. A modern Christian example is provided by the theology of hope.

Jürgen Moltmann, the German Protestant theologian is a prominent expositor of the theology of hope, which is basically reformist, critical of the church's entrapment in the past, and committed to revolutionary action. Moltmann speaks a language of promise, the central figure of which is Jesus Christ. He speaks of hope, which is hope in the God "who gives life to the dead and calls into existence things that do not exist" (Rom. 4:17). He acknowledges that the promise was spoken in the past and that Jesus is an historical figure, but he does not view revelation as that which happened and happens no more. Revelation belongs to the future. God is the future. Christ will be revealed in the future. And while the Christian does not pretend to know what is coming, the faithful look to the future with expectation and hope. Over against the narrowness, irrelevance, and dogmatism of the church as it has come to be, the theology of hope inculcates an attitude of openness and expectation: God is in the future bringing about new things. Christians who understand this will free themselves from the traditional shackles of cult, creed, and hierarchy; and, living with ambiguity and contradiction, they will rejoice in change.

We must beware, however, of making distinctions too rigidly. Thomas Cranmer was backward-looking, but insofar as he was in tune with the historical and theological perspectives of sixteenth-century England he believed that a new age was dawning when Christian people would be free from the dominion of Antichrist and enter into the promised land. Furthermore, theologians such as Richard Hooker, who subscribed to reform that looked back to an ideal past, were also concerned for ends, and for change in relation to ends. The end or purpose of Christian experience is participation in Christ, now and in the future. All should be directed toward that end and not toward the preservation of outmoded traditions and ceremonies which bind people to a dead past. Indeed, the modern ecumenical movement, which is reformist, has sought through the World Council Faith and Order Commission to prove that the most genuine turning back to the past provides the basis upon which to move into the future, the future which itself beckons us.

Whether we look backward or forward, if we are to engage in reform we shall seek to distinguish between essentials and nonessentials in the inward and outward manifestations of the faith. In this there is the conviction that whatever it is we wish to reform is deficient in terms of that which is necessary. The location of that which is essential to the faith is fraught with difficulties. People differ in their opinions; they tend to absolutize their own views; and conflict merely seems to strengthen their personal convictions. Humility is thus required, which we might define here as openness or availability. Reform, whether on the personal level of conversion or on the corporate level of institutional restructuring, requires openness, availability, whereby we are able to participate in that which is either deeply within or outside ourselves. Such humility is required if there is to be meaningful and far-reaching reform. For it must be understood that reform is not only a requirement but a gift which must be received, not as we would have it but in obedience as God commands. Matthew 18:3–4 has been recalled many times in relation to this consideration: "Truly, I say to you, unless you turn and become like children, you will never enter the kingdom of heaven. Whoever humbles himself like this child, he is the greatest in the kingdom of heaven."

Once the gift has been given and received another attitude is called for in the Christian. Call it courage, or call it arrogance, it does not negate humility but testifies to the gift received without apology and without flinching in the face of opposition. Martin Luther, on trial at the Diet (or assembly) of Worms, standing before the Holy Roman Emperor, having been confronted by the demand that he recant, is reported to have replied "in Latin and in German, humbly, quietly, and modestly, yet with Christian courage and firmness." After speaking and hearing the Emperor respond, Luther is reported to have said:

Since then your serene Majesty and your lordships request a simple reply, I will give it without horns and hoofs, and say: Unless I am convinced by the testimony of Scripture or by plain reason (for I believe in neither the pope nor in councils alone, for it is well-known, not only that they have erred, but also have contradicted themselves), I am mastered by the passages of Scripture which I have quoted, and my conscience is captive to the word of God. I cannot and will not recant, for it is neither safe nor honest to violate one's conscience. I can do no other. Here I take my stand, God being my helper. Amen.[10]

We now turn to consider some of the highlights of the history of the reform of the church through the centuries.

Monasticism and Reform from the Early Church to the Middle Ages

In the first three centuries Christianity constituted a persecuted minority. To be a Christian required commitment and discipline. It necessitated training such as that which athletes underwent. Emphasis was placed on moral discipline involving renunciation of worldly pleasures and even worldly necessities. Christ was the exemplar for such discipline and the martyrs provided examples of discipleship, attaining the highest possible life on earth, life in process of being freed from earthly existence. In turn all church leaders were to live exemplary lives of moral rectitude. Thus the second-century *Shepherd of Hermas* looked for the leaders of the church to "reform their ways in righteousness, to receive in full the promises with great glory."[11]

The necessary training could entail fasting, praying, chastity, and renunciation of worldly possessions. Women were in the forefront of such training. Virgins were consecrated and given the veil as early as the second century, living a basically contemplative life. Widows, who were called deaconesses, engaged in an active life of almsgiving and caring for the homeless and for travelers. In Rome during the fourth century a community of virgins and widows was founded on the Aventine hill where they lived lives of austerity and prayer.

This training for the holy life could be rigorous to the point of fanaticism. There were times when moral rigorists had to be cautioned against excess. But with the cessation of persecution and the official recognition of the church by the emperor in 313, the growth of moral laxity in the church became the urgent concern of many.

This decline from the examples of Christ, the martyrs, the virgins, and the widows, was partly a result of compromise with the surrounding society as members of that society began to seek entrance into the church. Some have seen the problem in terms of the sudden expansion of the church in numbers and geographically. In 301 King Tidrates III proclaimed Christianity the religion of Armenia and an entire nation entered the holy community. Such an occurrence placed a great strain on the community and its rigorous standards. But there was also present then, as there is now, that element of human existence which constantly seeks for self-gratification. St. Jerome (347?–420), perhaps best remembered for his Latin translation of the Old and New Testaments (the so-called Vulgate Bible of the West), and himself an ascetic, was mercilessly critical of the clergy of Rome. He wrote of one of them:

> He arises in haste with the sun. The order of his calls is arranged for him. He seeks short cuts. The old gentleman arrives unseasonably and practically forces his way into the bedchambers of his sleeping parishioners. If he catches sight of a cushion, an attractive piece of cloth, or some piece of household bric-a-brac, he praises it, marvels at it, strokes it, and laments that he is without things like that. He doesn't so much succeed in having it presented to him: he extorts it from the owner. All the ladies fear to offend the town gossip. Chastity doesn't appeal to him, nor does fasting. What he likes is a meal hot from the kitchen—a fattened bird, the kind usually called a chirper. His speech is barbarous and impudent, as he is always provided with abusive epithets. Wherever you turn, he is the first person you meet. Whatever news is noised abroad, he is either the author or the exaggerator of the tale. He changes horses every hour; and they are so sleek and so spirited that you would suppose him to be a brother of the King of Thrace.[12]

Monasticism began as a part of the ascetic movement of the church which preserved the ideal, so vividly presented by the martyrs and other ascetics, which was rooted in the hope, not for anything in this world, but rather for union with the Lord in his passion. Those who followed in this way were concerned for their own reformation, but they were also to provide combat troops for the faith and for the church. Monks and nuns seeking for the vision of God for themselves and for others were a means by which the church was brought under judgment. By their witness they recalled the church to its origin in the sacrifice of the Son of God and away from those things which were either nonessential or evil.

The development of Christian monasticism as it was to be known in the Middle Ages was gradual. It began in the Egyptian desert with ascetics who fled from the corrupt cities to do battle with the forces of evil on the edges of the world. In Christian tradition St. Antony is recognized as among the first to practice the asceticism of the hermit life, this in the latter half of the third century. Having heard the Gospel, "be not anxious for the morrow," Antony went out of the church where he was worshiping and gave all that he had to the poor, after providing for the safe keeping of his sister. Athanasius (295–373) writes:

> . . . he henceforth devoted himself outside his house to discipline, taking heed to himself and training himself with patience. For there were not yet so many monasteries in Egypt, and no monk at all knew of the distant desert; but all who wished to give heed to themselves practised the discipline in solitude near their own village.[13]

In time Egypt was teeming with hermits and Antony, recognizing the problems involved in the hermit life, acquiesced to the pleas of his admirers and organized a semicommunity. In the transitional period the hermits lived out of earshot of one another but came together for worship. They prayed, disciplined the body—sometimes by scourging, usually by renunciation—and wrestled with demonic spirits. Sometimes they went to extremes, such as Simeon Stylites who lived on a pillar, the Dendrites who lived in trees to be closer to heaven, and the Munchers who were vegetarians and ate grass. They were accused of avoiding the assemblies of the holy community and of casting aspersions upon the leaders of the church.

Pachomius formed a community of ascetics by the Nile at Tabennisi which provided a way of overcoming the hazards of the hermit life. His sister founded a community of women. In fact women were very much involved in this development, although the historical record seems to place emphasis upon men as founders. Pachomius organized those who committed themselves to his direction in military fashion, requiring their obedience and setting them to work. Aberrations harmful to monks and nuns were kept in check by the exercise of the most rigorous discipline. Something of the character of this community, which in time numbered some thirteen hundred at Tabennisi and extended in various places to several thousand more, is given by St. Jerome:

> The sick are attended to with wonderful devotion, food being made ready for them in plenty; those in good health practise a stricter abstinence. Twice a week, on the fourth and sixth day of the week, they fast entirely: except at Easter and Pentecost. On other days, those who wish to do so take their meal after midday: so too at supper the table is laid, for the sake of the sick, the old, the young, and those in high fever. . . . All take their meals together. If any one does not wish to come to table, he has an allowance in his cell of bread and water only, with salt, for one day or two, according as he desires.[14]

The full flowering of cenobitic (life together) monasticism came with Basil of Caesarea (330–379), one of the Cappadocian fathers encountered in the last chapter. Converted to the ascetic life by his sister, Macrina, who had evidently formed a religious community, Basil composed a rule for the discipline and government of monasteries. This rule provided for the authority of bishops, exercised restraint on ascetic practices, and instituted a formal and regular means of admitting new members. Obedience, chastity, and poverty were to be followed in the community, not only for the sake of the members themselves but for the benefit of others. Thus they not only provided an example of holiness but led the church in the practice of love and service toward one's neighbors. This was the intent of communal life. As Basil put it,

> . . . the love of Christ does not allow us to look each at his own good. For *love* we read *seeketh not its own* (1 Cor 13:5). Now the solitary life has one aim, the service of the needs of the individual. But this is plainly in conflict with the law of love, which the apostle fulfilled when he sought not his own advantage but that of the many, that they might be saved.[15]

Basil's rule established communal life as it was to develop in the East.

In the West the great name is that of Benedict of Nursia (c. 480–c. 543). In Benedict's time there were monasteries in Gaul, among the Celts, and in Italy, but they were Antonian in advocating the hermit life. The Benedictine ideal was to establish a school for God's service, characterized by moderation and clemency. The rule he provided was called a "little rule" for beginners. Chastity and poverty were emphasized but above all there was obedience and a commitment to stability, which involved staying in the community where one began rather than roaming about seeking for the most satisfying monastic house. Divine service was threefold: worship, self-discipline, and manual labor. Worship was central, seven times during each twenty-four-hour period: 2 A.M. Nocturns; dawn Matins or Lauds; 6 A.M. Prime; 9 A.M. Terce; 12 noon Sext; 3 P.M. Nones; dusk Vespers; and bedtime Compline. The end in view was the vision of God, perfection, and conformity to the image of God for the sake of both the church and the world. Benedict's rule, with its humanistic spirit and its care for firm but reasonable organization, was to spread throughout the West. By the eighth century it was the model rule, adapted to particular circumstances.

It is at this point that we become aware of another important aspect of monastic history: its changing nature which, along with the continuing weakness of the humans involved, requires reform. Then, too, there are the changing circumstances which make former goals and practices obsolete and require reformation of monastic institutions. In time the sins of a corrupt church were the sins of supposedly reformist monasticism. Furthermore, monasteries became economic and social centers. In them education was pursued and the heritage of the past preserved and transmitted to vast regions conquered by Vandals, Goths, Huns, and others. They grew in wealth and became increasingly more involved in the society around them. Benedict of Aniane established a house in Aquitaine which by 782 contained over a thousand monks seeking to live out the Benedictine rule with the greatest strictness. To help with this reform of Western monasticism he composed two works, the *Codex Regularum,* which was a compilation of the various rules of East and West, and the *Concordia Regularum,* in which Benedict took the chapters of the rule of Benedict of Nursia one by one and set out passages explaining them from the other rules of the *Codex.* At the Council of Aachen in 817, Benedict of Aniane succeeded in having the Benedictine rule, with both *Codex* and *Concordia,* accepted as binding on all religious, monks and nuns, as the one "Holy Rule, Teacher Rule," with which every monk and nun was to have a personal relationship binding them to a life covered in every detail.

The reform of Benedict of Aniane was not lasting, however. Furthermore, the historical circumstances were always changing. Every monastic establishment henceforth is in some sense a reform, whether in terms of a decline from the ideal or in terms of altered circumstances, or both. Cluniacs in 910, the Carthusians in 1084, and the Cistercians in 1098 were all provoked, at least in part, by a worsening situation in the religious life. By the time of Cluny a further difficult problem was recognized, reviving the old problem of control over the individual monastery. Basil succeeded in obtaining control for the bishop. In the Middle Ages, since monasteries were important economic and social institutions, kings and nobles sought to control them. Under lay control they were often exploited and their attempts at maintaining the rule frustrated. William the Pious, Duke of Aquitaine, placed the monastic house established at Cluny under the protection of the papacy and provided for a revival of the Benedictine rule interpreted in the strictest sense in accordance with the dictates of Benedict of Aniane. The emphasis at Cluny fell on worship and on the praise of God with beauty. By the time of the founding of the Cistercian order in 1098, the Cluniacs were criticized for their ostentatious luxury and another, different, effort was made to live by the Benedictine rule in the strictest sense.

The reform of the monastics was carried out for the sake of the underlying quest for reform of individuals in accordance with the precepts of the Gospel and the example of Christ, and for the reform of the church and the world. The fundamental aim was expressed in the twelve stages of humility in Benedict's rule. The way of salvation was by means of perfection, an ascent up the ladder of perfection and through the spheres to the empyrean heaven and the communion of saints everlasting.

Reform, the Pelagian Controversy, and St. Augustine

There was danger in the reformist emphasis on moral rigor. This is demonstrated by many incidents in the history of the church and certainly by the Pelagian controversy. Pelagius, whose views were condemned at the Council of Ephesus (431), was a lay monk from Great Britain or Ireland. He was in Rome for some time, leaving in 409 or 410 for Sicily and Africa. From 411 on he lived in Palestine. Initially, Pelagius reacted, as did St. Augustine of Hippo, against the superficiality of many conversions to Christianity, the abuse of wealth in the society, and the general moral decline of the times. He was convinced that some of the teachings of the church contributed to the decline by arousing such pessimism that moral responsibility was undermined.

In his *Confessions,* Augustine had written: "You [God] command continence; grant what you command and command what you will." It seemed as though there was nothing for the sinner to do. Grace was either given or not given and thus the person was altogether passive and might act in any manner. What was needed was an understanding which held people responsible for their moral behavior. Pelagius put his view in terms something like this:

Human beings possess quite naturally reason and an understanding of God's will for them. This is not, however, sufficient. What is needed is, objectively, revelation, and subjectively, clear, compelling knowledge in order that the human beings may come to know their true nature and claim it. There is a cloud of ignorance which covers the essential nature of human beings as rational and as in tune with the divine will. Knowledge given in Scripture, and in particular through law, teaching, and example (especially the example of Christ) dispels the cloud of ignorance making possible the effective recovery of true human nature, true human nature which has never been harmed by sin.

To put it another way: people behave in a dissolute way, not because they have inherited sin from Adam, but because they simply do not know their true nature. When they do, aided by the knowledge transmitted by Scripture, and especially knowledge of Christ as their example, they are freed from their former ignorance and can will and do that which is acceptable to God. Thus human beings must take responsibility for their actions. Everyone must be on guard, and particularly those Christians who, having been given the necessary knowledge, have no excuse for sin.

The basic teaching of Pelagius, which is so difficult to summarize because of the misunderstandings which have persisted concerning him and the paucity of materials from his own pen, was taken up by many. Some of those who accepted his teaching went far beyond him, such as the unknown Britain living in Sicily who took Pelagius's basic contention that when God commands (for instance, "Sell what you have . . .") the human must obey and advocated a kind of socialism which aroused the ire of many against Pelagius.

The formidable Augustine went on the offensive. He taught that the entire human family fell with Adam, that sinfulness is transmitted through the reproductive process, that babies are born corrupted by sin and unless baptized are damned, and that, such being the case, humans are incapable of any act of the will which is altogether good. The virtues of the pagans are but "splendid vices," as one of Augustine's followers said. For the acts of the will to be altogether good they must be aided by grace, which is not a teaching or an example but the love of God poured into the heart of the sinner by the Holy Spirit. It follows from this that God chooses those to whom he gives the gift of grace, a gift which cannot be resisted. Thus we speak of a part of humanity, elected, predestined to salvation, while the rest are consigned to that hell which all persons, the saved and the unsaved, justly deserve.

For Augustine this teaching against Pelagius was no mere intellectual exercise. He had known what it meant to be morally impotent. His *Confessions* speak to this eloquently and to his pervasive feeling of utter dependence upon God, his sense of awe and reverence before God whom he thus worshiped. He begins his telling of his conversion, his personal renewal and reform:

> I flung myself down I know not how, under a fig tree, giving full vent to my tears; and the floods of my eyes gushed out, an *acceptable sacrifice to thee*. And, not indeed in these words, yet to this purpose, spoke I much unto thee: *And thou, O Lord, how long? how long, Lord, wilt thou be angry for ever? Remember not our former iniquities,* for I felt that I was held by them. I sent up these sorrowful words; How long? how long is it to be? "Tomorrow, and tomorrow?" Why not now? why is there not this hour an end to my uncleanness?[16]

His deliverance was the act of God's love, unmerited grace, enabling him to be that which he could not otherwise be.

It must not be thought, however, that Pelagius was the only one against whom Augustine fought in his teachings on grace. He was also conscious of the danger inherent in those who believe that to trust in God means to relax one's own efforts. In particular he warned against the idea that a person who is baptized is by necessity altogether a child of God forever. Against such presumption, which is at the opposite extreme from the teachings of Pelagius, Augustine cited 2 Corinthians 4:16: "Though our outer nature is wasting away, our inner nature is being renewed every day." Baptism is followed by daily reform in the context of the holy community with its sacraments and pastoral care.

Augustine occupied a middle ground, establishing a balance between divine grace and human will. The initiative for human liberation from sin and movement toward salvation is always God's, but this does not obliterate human will. To be accepted, justified, made righteous before God involves consent on the part of human beings. Thus human responsibility is taken into account, but the grace of God is paramount. Augustine, in striking this balance, attempts to preserve what he understands to be the New Testament doctrine concerning salvation, as well as defending what he understands through his own and others' experiences. We might say that he maintains human responsibility, but that this sense of responsibility is not cruel: it does not lay an impossible burden on us. The God of this teaching is not always commanding: he is caring and gracious. But one must admit that the teaching on grace and human free will in Augustine is difficult to pin down with certainty. There is development in his thought and at times ambiguity. In part at least the difficulty rests with the subject and not the teacher.

Augustine was a Christian who viewed reform in terms of the willingness of the believer to regard one's life as a sacrifice. Sacrifice was at the heart of the matter for Augustine, sacrifice which is personal but also involves the entire holy community. In the *City of God* Augustine put it this way:

A true sacrifice then is every work which is done in such a way that we may adhere to God in a holy society. . . . Thus man himself, consecrated in the name of God and devoted to God, is a sacrifice, in as much as he dies to the world so that he may live to God. . . . This very same thing the Apostle says when he continues and adds: "And be not conformed to this world; but be reformed in the newness of your mind. . . ." (Rom 12:2). Since, therefore, true sacrifices are works of mercy toward ourselves or toward our neighbors, which are referred to God . . . it is actually brought about that this whole redeemed city, that is to say, the congregation and society of the saints, is offered to God as a universal sacrifice by the High Priest [Christ], who also offered Himself in His passion for us according to the form of a

servant, so that we may be the body of such a head. . . . Thus,
after the Apostle has exhorted us that we present our bodies a
living sacrifice . . . (see Rom 12:1) and that we be not conformed to this world, but reformed in the newness of our mind
. . . he says: "we being many are one body in Christ and every
one members of one another" (Rom 12:5). . . . This is the sacrifice of Christians: many are one body in Christ. And this the
Church observes in the sacrament of the altar, known to the
faithful, where it is made clear to her that she herself is offered
in that which she offers.[17]

In such a way Augustine keeps personal reform and that reform which involves the holy community—personal religion
and the corporate experience as members of the body—
together. For it is in the context of the church that salvation
comes for the Christian.

Two Ways of Reform in the Middle Ages: Pope Gregory VII and St. Francis

The eleventh century was known as the great century of reform in medieval Europe. That reform was needed was
widely understood. The church suffered from a lack of understanding itself as a "peculiar people," from a lack of
much needed instruction, and from a lack of spiritual
depth. The symptoms of this deep distress were various. The
papacy was at a low ebb in terms of both politics and morals.
In the middle of the tenth century Pope John XII was deposed
by the German king, Emperor Otto I, for living in adulterous
relations with prominent women of Rome. In the middle of
the eleventh century Pope Benedict IX aroused the anger of
the Romans. This thoroughly immoral man had obtained the
papal throne through the influence of his family at age six-
teen. The Romans having deposed him, Benedict sold his
right to the papacy to a third party who became Pope Gregory
VI. But Benedict soon regretted this action and reclaimed the
papacy. There were then three men claiming to be pope. The
muddle brought Emperor Henry III to Italy with his army to
straighten things out.

The church beyond the Roman see was deeply entangled in

the feudal system. Overlords sought to maintain control of all people and the lands under them, forbidding outside interference. In the diocese of Liège, the bishop owed ecclesiastical allegiance to the archbishop of Cologne and political allegiance to the duke of Lower Lorraine and to the German king. Furthermore, since his see involved very considerable feudal properties, he was a prince-bishop, regarded by his secular overlords as an important royal administrator. It thus behooved duke and king to obtain the "right" person for the diocese, a person loyal to them and able to assist them in times of trouble. The bishop, at first chosen by acclamation of clergy and laity, then by vote of the Cathedral Chapter, was more often than not now appointed by the German king. The result was that in the conflict between spiritual and secular responsibilities, the balance tipped in the direction of the latter. Simony, the buying and selling of ecclesiastical offices, was especially rife, one bishop buying the diocese from the German king for 300 marks and then selling lesser offices to the highest bidders. It was no wonder that there was more concern for what one could get out of the church than for serving the church.

On the local level—the town, village, and countryside— things were no better. Sacraments were sold. Clergy were often illiterate. People complained of the way clergy mistreated women. Clergy were often involved in drunken brawls, and they seized upon the offerings of the people as their own to do with as they pleased. Odo of Rigaud tells of a certain priest who sexually violated

> one of his parishioners whose husband on this account went beyond the sea, and he kept her for eight years, and she is pregnant; also he plays at dice and drinks too much, he frequents taverns, he does not stay in his church, he goes hawking in the country as he wishes . . .[18]

In reaction to this corruption reform movements arose. There was that of Cluny, begun in 910, which has already been mentioned. There were among the laity stirrings of dissent; lay people were preaching, without being ordained and without license, against corruption. But there is a sense in which the most important surge for reform, in terms of that which evolved, was the renewed assertion of the ascetic ideal, renunciation of the world through the discipline of the Christian. At Camaldoli, on a mountainside near Arezzo in Italy, the Egyptian "desert" was recreated. The most advanced monks lived austerely in hermitages within a wide enclosure high on the mountain. Lower down a monastery was built where monks were in training to ascend to the "desert." Such places as Camaldoli led the way. In 1084 the famed Carthusian order was founded on the desolate uplands of the Grand Chartreuse. In 1098 the Cistercian order began in dreary solitude among the reeds of the river Saône.

These ascetics, dedicated to withdrawal from the world so that they might focus on God alone, inspired many people of influence. The prime example is that of Peter Damian who, on the way to becoming a wealthy teacher at Parma in northern Italy, renounced all and began the practice of the ascetic life at a community over which he became prior in 1043. Throughout the rest of his life he fasted, eating vegetables three days a week and bread and water on the other four, scourged his body with cold water and a whip, and prayed fervently. But he also became a cardinal, a renowned preacher, and a man of great influence in the papal curia. He was critical of the ecclesiastical hierarchy, including the popes, but he, as a masterful politician, employed his skills in canon law and rhetoric to achieve reform through the papacy.

The papal reform movement of the eleventh century centered upon the imposing Hildebrand. He, as Pope Gregory VII, ruled the Roman Church from 1074 to 1085, although he exercised influence in papal affairs beginning in mid-century. The reform under Gregory was intended to result in the transformation of all society into a Christian society imbued with love toward Christ and the renunciation of bondage to the world. This was to be achieved by means of the reform and thus the centralization of ecclesiastical authority in the Bishop of Rome. It was to be realized, too, by means of the eradication of all interference by the laity in the control of the church. And it was to involve the reform of the clergy on every level. Simony was to be eradicated and clerical celibacy enforced. In brief, the aim was to ensure that the ecclesiastical hierarchy from the pope down to the lowest cleric should be motivated by spiritual and not worldly interests.

Under Pope Nicholas II (1059–1061) the election of the pope was made to rest with the College of Cardinals and the papal curia, dominated by pope and cardinals, was established for the administration of the church. As a result the papacy became in time a powerful instrument for the centralized operation of the Western church. Furthermore, the administrative reform was buttressed by an intensification of the theory without which it could not be effected. The body of Christ headed by the successor of Peter was now known to be the one true way of salvation. It was incumbent upon all to love the Roman Church and to obey its bishops, especially the pope. The institution thus in process of reforming itself moved to implement its policies. By means of legates, or ambassadors, the pope reached out to every nation and increasingly intervened in the election of bishops. Laity were forbidden to interfere. In 1075 Pope Gregory issued a decree forbidding prelates to receive their churches from lay rulers. This consolidation of power in the papacy was viewed as a holy thing, inspired by the Holy Spirit, and necessary if the church was to be reformed.

The clergy far and wide were to feel the cutting edge of this reform. The papacy viewed with horror the buying and selling of ecclesiastical offices, clerical concubinage, and clerical marriage. Simony and marriage were dealt with by a Roman Council in 1074 which decreed:

> Those who have been advanced to any grade of holy orders, or to any office, through simony, that is, by the payment of money, shall hereafter have no right to officiate in the holy church.
>
> Nor shall clergymen who are married say mass or serve the altar in any way. We decree also that if they refuse to obey our orders, or rather those of the holy fathers, the people shall refuse to receive their ministrations, in order that those who disregard the love of God and the dignity of their office may be brought to their senses through feeling the shame of the world and the reproof of the people.[19]

Through the forbidding of clerical marriage, as well as simony, reform reached into the village churches. It would seem that the clergy were to be reformed after the model of the ascetic monk. Many resisted, but in time it would seem that all were brought into line, or disciplined, or perhaps drifted into dissent.

Another way of reform, not controlled by those at the apex of the hierarchy and espousing ideals which could bring judgment on those wielding power for the church, is exemplified by Francis of Assisi (1182–1226). Without explicitly attacking those in power, Francis inspired spiritual reform and renewal at a time when society was undergoing great changes. He was not to be identified with such others of his time as the Waldensians, who vehemently criticized the church's hierarchy. He was simply concerned to imitate the life of Christ and the lives of the Apostles with wholehearted dedication, pursuing the ideals of poverty and simplicity.

In his testament, written shortly before his death, Francis spoke of his love for the church and its priests, who administer the only form in which the Son of God is corporeally known: "His most holy Body and Blood." He told of the beginning of his order, the Grey Friars, whom we know as Franciscans:

> When the Lord gave me some brothers, no one showed me what I ought to do, but the Most High Himself revealed to me that I should live according to the form of the holy Gospel. And I caused it to be written in few words and simply, and the Lord Pope confirmed it for me. And those who came to take this life upon themselves gave to the poor all that they might have and they were content with one tunic, patched within and without, by those who wished, with a cord and breeches, and we wished for no more.[20]

Thus was instituted a company of friars, called Friars Minor, dedicated at the beginning to lives of holy poverty. A second order of the Friars Minor was established with Clare, a disciple of Francis, as its head. Clare of Assisi (1194–1253) set forth a rule for her sisters, sometimes called "Poor Ladies" and sometimes "Poor Clares," in which the ideal of poverty was paramount:

> Let not the sisters appropriate anything to themselves, but as strangers and wayfarers on the face of the earth let them gather alms with confidence, and be content to serve the Lord in pov-

erty and humility. Nor ought they to be ashamed of living thus, for Jesus Christ for our sake made Himself poor in the world. This is the height, beloved sisters, of that Sublime Poverty which hath purchased for you a royal heritage, even the Kingdom of Heaven, and which rendering you poor in material things hath enriched you with spiritual treasures.[21]

It must be kept in mind that this emphasis on poverty was rooted in the Gospel and pointed to a life of penitence encompassing poverty, humility, and simplicity. It was as an act of penitence that Francis went amongst lepers and served. It was as a penance for his sins that Francis gave away to the poor all that he had and went naked into the religious life. In the 1221 rule there is a chapter (21) which provides a sample sermon which may be used by all brothers. Penance is the keynote: "Do penance," "bring forth fruit worthy of penance. Blessed those who die in penance because they will be in the Kingdom of God." His adherents were known at times as the "Brothers and Sisters of Penitence."

In an age when Western Europe was experiencing a major growth of trade and commerce, when towns and cities were become once more prominent, and when there was a seriousness concerning religion, Francis and the Friars Minor, along with a similar order of friars begun by St. Dominic (1170–1221), seemed well suited to proclaim the Gospel in a changing world. Dedicated to simplicity and poverty, unencumbered by great wealth, they traveled preaching the Gospel, ministering to the poor and suffering, going from town to town, pursuing the apostolic way. It is one of the ironies of history that this order which espoused Lady Poverty attracted wealthy merchants and great kings who in gratitude gave them money and property which soon encumbered them. Furthermore, Francis warned against books and learning, but in time the Friars Minor were to inhabit universities and produce some of the most learned scholars. Whether intended or not, the Franciscans were being assimilated into the society and the time would come when the Friars Minor would be virtually indistinguishable from others of the church.

That this assimilation should happen is not surprising. The

very existence of the Friars Minor was a judgment upon an overly wealthy and ambitious hierarchy. In England the monks feared the friars whose austerity contrasted so sharply with their opulence. John, abbot of Peterborough, writing of the year 1224, cried out: "In that year, O misery! O more than misery! O cruel scourge! The Friars Minor came to England!"

To be confronted by Francis was to be met by an overwhelming demand for a radical change of heart and mind. There were many who found the demand intolerable and rejected it. But the demand, encompassed in the medieval understanding of penitence, would be asserted again and again, not to be stifled for long. Catherine of Siena (1347–1380), witnessed to the necessity of reform and renewal in the next century after Francis, fearlessly confronting popes and bishops. To Pope Gregory XI she wrote:

> The world is in such a state of upheaval, how shall peace be restored to it? . . . First you must pluck out of the garden of Holy Church those flowers that spread the infection of impurity, avarice and pride: that is to say, the bad pastors and superiors who poison and corrupt this garden.

And to Pope Urban VI she wrote:

> Sweetest Father, the world cannot bear any more of this—so much do vices abound, especially in those who should be like sweet-smelling flowers in the garden of the Church . . . We see them give themselves over to vices so shameful and so blameworthy that they infect the whole world! Renew completely the garden of your Spouse; put in it good and vigorous plants; surround yourself with a brigade of saints . . . who do not fear death.[22]

Renewal and reform was not incidental to St. Catherine's life. She who was a mystic felt the inspiration for reform come through her innermost experience of the divine. Thus in a letter to Raymond of Capua she wrote:

> What tongue can relate the marvels of God? Not mine, poor miserable creature that I am. Therefore, I wish to keep silence and concern myself solely with God's glory, the salvation of souls, the renewal and exaltation of Holy Church, and, with the

grace and strength of the Holy Spirit, to persevere unto death. This desire drives and will drive me to cry with great love and compassion to our "Christ on earth" and to you, Father, and to all my dear sons. I asked and obtained your petition. Therefore rejoice, rejoice and be glad![23]

Whether with Francis or with Catherine renewal and reform began with the experience of the presence of God, a keen sense of personal responsibility for the sins of the world, and an awareness of the fire of divine love cleansing and restoring the image of God in them, bringing in the end perfect union with the Blessed Trinity. It was toward the end of her letter to Robert of Capua, after telling of how Christ explained the persecution of the church to her as a means of cleansing it, that Catherine wrote:

The fire of love increased in me and I was amazed because I saw Christians and unbelievers entering the side of Christ crucified. The desire and ardor of love made me go with them and enter Christ, sweet Jesus. . . .[24]

Renewal and Reform in the 16th Century: Luther and Erasmus

The late medieval church was neither as corrupt as its enemies thought or as exemplary as its defenders claimed. This is the judgment of most modern historians who scrutinize the evidence. The papacy was no more corrupt than it had been and was better in some ways. The monasteries, by and large, were not dens of iniquity as some sixteenth-century reformers said. There were orders, such as the Augustinians to whom Luther belonged, which were reformed and vigorous. Why then the revolutionary events which characterize this century?

There are numerous factors to be taken into account. Here we shall list a few. The institutional church was in trouble. It was gradually losing power as the new nation states, with their rising middle class and their increasingly secularized legal systems, were gaining strength and regarding their national needs as taking precedence over the needs of the common society of Christian Europe. In France and in the Germanies it was necessary for the papacy to negotiate agreements whereby the rights of temporal sovereigns over the church were recognized, however limited those rights might be. It is important to realize that inherent in the reform movements of Germany, England, Spain, various Swiss cantons, and the Scandinavian states there was a rising patriotism which resisted the international claims of the papacy and the Roman Church.

Alongside the growth of patriotism there was the increasing strength of late medieval lay piety and mysticism, issuing in such things as the veneration of St. Anne, mass pilgrimages, and Bible study. This was also an age of religious dissent. Dissent was not new except insofar as the dissenting bodies—such as the Lollards, the followers of John Wyclif, the fourteenth-century Oxford don; and the Hussites, led by John Hus of Bohemia, excommunicated by a general council in 1415—were strong and their influence widespread. The late Middle Ages was a time of intellectual and spiritual ferment. Basic things were being questioned. Dissidents attacked the wealth of the church once more in the name of holy poverty. The disaffected sought a direct, personal experience of God and the propagation of that experience through preaching, providing thereby a threat to the sacramental system and the sacerdotal hierarchy.

The late Middle Ages witnessed the rise of humanism through the Italian renaissance. This too has been acknowledged as a potential threat, although the popes of the time became patrons of the arts closely associated with the renaissance. In Italy new ways of viewing self and history were emerging, leading to a growth of individualism and the painful searching of the conscience, as well as an appreciation of the past and of its power to affect the present. As a result, the medieval understanding of reality was brought into question, as we shall observe when considering Erasmus.

In brief, there was a shaking of the foundations. It has been said that the twin pillars of the medieval church were the papacy and the monasteries. Now both were more seriously questioned as their power and credibility waned in a changing world. The papacy had been in turmoil, with various popes when, according to belief, there could be but one. Reality challenged belief. According to one Benedictine historian the monastics were suffering a loss of spirit, involving a loss of meaning concerning the vows taken and the life lived. There seemed to be an erosion of that uniformity of obedience which characterized the church at the height of the Middle Ages.

Our examination of the late medieval church, therefore, indicates that the Reformation occurred not so much because the church was immoral, but rather because the times were revolutionary and the church was having serious difficulty adjusting to the change. The result was not so much the purifying of the church as it was the fragmentation of it, at first into national segments and then into a pluralism of denominations within the nation states. Nevertheless, on the basis of those convictions shared by reformers, from the reforming cardinals of the papal curia to the left wing groups which range from the Mennonites to the Family of Love, the crisis was not so much political and social as it was moral and theological. We shall now consider Desiderius Erasmus (1466?–1536) and Martin Luther (1483–1546), their views and their conflict.

Erasmus was influenced greatly by the fact that he was the bastard son of a priest. He was educated by the reformist Brethren of the Common Life at Deventer in the Lowlands. Becoming a monk, because for him there was little alternative, he gradually made his way into academia, studied at the University of Paris, and began to write. His writings were entertaining. They were also disturbing, satirical, and provocative. His *Adages* and *Colloquies,* his *Praise of Folly,* and his *Enchiridion* were read all over Europe, and through these writings, as well as through his edition of the Greek New Testament and his editions of the works of the fathers of the early church, he gained an international reputation.

Erasmus was critical of the papacy. In commenting on Christ's arrival in Jerusalem on an ass, he contrasted the elaborate and splendid procession of the pope through the streets of Rome. In his *Praise of Folly* he exposed monks to ridicule: they will not touch money but they are not averse to women and wine. At the last judgment a monk will boast that he has never handled money—unless wearing gloves. Elsewhere he compared contemporary monastic practices with the ideals and rules of the founders and harshly judged his fellow monks and nuns. He railed at the theologians for their endless debates concerning the Eucharist and Christ's presence in it, and their pseudosophisticated quibbling over quiddities and entities. None escaped his sharp barbs. But he wielded his pen not just to criticize and entertain. He was concerned for the recovery of what he called "the philosophy of Christ." One of his best statements concerning this "philosophy" is to be found in this commentary on Matthew 11:30.

> Truly the yoke of Christ would be sweet and his burden light, if petty human institutions added nothing to what he himself imposed. He commanded us nothing save love for one another, and there is nothing so bitter that charity does not soften and sweeten it. Everything according to nature is easily borne, and nothing accords better with the nature of man than the philosophy of Christ, of which almost the sole end is to give back to fallen nature its innocence and integrity. How pure, how simple is the faith that Christ delivered to us! How close to it is the creed transmitted to us by the apostles, and apostolic men. The church, divided and tormented by discussions and by heresy, added to it many things, of which some can be omitted without prejudice to the faith. . . . There are many opinions from which impiety may be begotten, as for example, all those philosophic doctrines on the reason and the distinction of the persons of the Godhead. . . . The sacraments themselves were instituted for the salvation of man, but we abuse them for lucre, for vain glory or for the oppression of the humble. . . . What rules, what superstitions we have about vestments! How many are judged as to their Christianity by such trifles, which are indifferent in themselves, which change with the fashion and of which Christ never spoke! . . . Would that men were content to let Christ rule by the laws of the Gospel and that they would no longer seek to strengthen their obscurant tyranny by human decrees![25]

The Christian life involves living by the laws of the Gospel. For such living all that obstructs the Gospel must be removed. This was the radical side of his teaching. On the other side he advised that the reform be centered on knowledge and prayer. The humanist way was the way of peace and of education. It was reasonable and humanistic, concerned for the dignity of human beings as responsible participants in God's creation, whose wills have been crippled but not destroyed. Erasmus never claimed to be a theologian, but he did have a theology which has had its influence upon many and contributed something to the formation of the modern western mind.

Martin Luther was cut from different cloth. Born of a highly respectable and prosperous copper miner in Saxony, he studied at the University of Erfurt where he came under the influence of a philosophical school which was optimistic and stressed the common-sense attitude that before God one should do what one can. It was a philosophy which strove for a careful balance between the grace of God and human merit, but placed practical emphasis on the human will: doing what one can. According to Thomas Aquinas, the thirteenth-century theological giant, faith without love cannot save. To say that it can is as much as to say that a corrupt bride can contract a spiritual marriage with Christ. Love, human love, is involved in the process of salvation.

Luther, having become a monk of the Reformed Congregation of the Eremetical Order of St. Augustine, tried to live according to that which he had learned at Erfurt. He disciplined himself, fasted, confessed, but he was left uncertain.

> After vigils, fasts, prayers and other exercises of the toughest kind, with which as a monk I afflicted myself almost to death, yet the doubt was left in my mind, and I thought, "Who knows whether these things are pleasing to God?"[26]

Here he expressed the anxiety of the pilgrim on the way to the city of God.

In 1513 he began teaching at Wittenberg and lecturing first on the psalms and subsequently on the Epistle to the Romans. It was during this time that a new insight came to him. Luther, justly deserving divine wrath, stood trembling before God. This was not wrong; but it was not the place to stop. For thus abasing oneself before the righteous God, with no pretence of earning salvation, the sinner is justified, made righteous. In grasping this point and speaking and writing of it, Luther was doing something revolutionary. Jacob Hochstraten, the Dominican inquisitor of Cologne, exclaimed in horror:

> That rash advocate lists no preconditions for the spiritual marriage of the soul with Christ except only that we believe Christ, who promises all good things, and trust that He will bestow all the good things [which He has promised]. Not a single word is said about the mutual love by which the soul loves Christ, who is love, above all things. Nor do we hear anything about the other divine commandments, to the keeper of which eternal life is both promised and owed.[27]

On the basis of such accusations, Luther was declared a heretic, excommunicated, and excoriated as one who preached that Christians need not obey the law and could do anything they wished.

The ramifications of Luther's teaching of justification by faith alone without the necessity of any works or merits only gradually emerged and became in time confused with other issues, such as the growing national sentiment in the Germanies and elsewhere. In time Luther came to realize that Hus had been burned for similar teachings, that the Roman Church in opposing scriptural doctrine was the Antichrist, and that the religious orders and other aspects of the ecclesiastical organization must be changed or abolished. He was not, however, radically committed to change. In the spectrum of religious reform Luther is considered conservative. He changed much but he retained much which others abolished. In some ways the Lutheran church still had the appearance of the medieval church.

To a person such as Erasmus, Luther was anything but conservative. At first he had thought that they were brothers in a common cause, but they soon clashed. In a sense two such persons, with such different personalities, were bound to clash. Erasmus: erudite, sophisticated, witty; Luther: somewhat a German peasant, highly educated, constantly

tormented within, fiercely dedicated to his convictions.
Luther suspected Erasmus of holding Pelagian views:

> Though with your lips you pretend to confess Christ, you really
> deny Him in your heart. For if the power of "free-will" is not
> wholly and damnably astray, but sees and wills what is good
> and upright and pertains to salvation, then it is in sound health,
> it does not need Christ the physician, nor did Christ redeem
> that part of man; for what need is there of light and life, where
> light and life exist already?[28]

Erasmus was stung. He did not regard himself as holding an
untrue doctrine of free will and openly confessed that
Pelagius attributed too much to it. "But Luther mutilates it at
first by amputating its right arm. And not content with this,
he has killed the freedom of the will and has removed it
altogether."[29] Erasmus attempted to follow a middle course,
which he believed to be the right way:

> I like the sentiments of those who attribute a little to the free-
> dom of the will, the most, however, to grace. One must not
> avoid the Scylla of arrogance by going into the Charybdis of
> desperation and indolence.[30]

At one point Erasmus concluded:

> Luther behaves like a wild man; his adversaries goad him on.
> But if they prevail, we shall be left to write only the epitaph of
> Christ, dead without hope of resurrection.[31]

It was quickly apparent that Erasmus and Luther were
separated by a great gulf and that there was little possibility
of their being brought to agreement. Luther went on to recover the true church as he understood it and to arm it with
correct doctrine based on the Bible, in particular on the Epistles of Paul and the writings of Augustine of Hippo. His
reform movement, which was at first so personal, changed in
the course of time to become a political matter, a basis for
wars and treaties. Erasmus died a disappointed man, disturbed about both the Roman Church and its opponents, but
doggedly remaining within the obedience of that church.

There were Protestants as well as Roman Catholics who taught the doctrine which he set forth in his "philosophy of Christ."

The two men shared much, however. They sought for the reform and renewal of individuals. And because both believed that the institution of the church was designed to assist in the reform and renewal of individuals, and yet seemed to obstruct and not assist, Erasmus and Luther alike called for the reform of the institution from its head through all its members.

We know that there was more to the Reformation than that. We began this section by referring to the external and internal factors which necessitated change in the church. The world was changing. The church on mission to the world could not stand still. Thus Christendom was broken into segments, a freer spirit of inquiry began, and at the same time new challenges for future reform began to rise.

Renewal, Reform, and the English Reformation

The English Reformation began in a ferment of political events. While there were other important facets to the historical drama of the 1530s, the beginnings of the Reformation in England were dominated not by a Calvin or a Luther, but by King Henry VIII. A renaissance prince who coveted his individuality and independence, Henry sought to divorce his Spanish wife, Catherine of Aragon, in part because she did not bear him a son and heir and was past her prime, and in part because she represented a foreign power, Spain, which had misused him on the battlefield and engaged in trickery against him in diplomacy. He and his agent, Cardinal Wolsey, pressed the king's case at home and abroad, but at Rome where success counted most they were unsuccessful. The pope was influenced by Catherine's nephew, the Emperor Charles V, and could not acquiesce to Henry's wish. The result was that the English king first threatened to sever England's ancient ties with the Roman see. The threats taking no effect, the king with his faithful commons represented by parliament declared royal supremacy over the Church in England and rejected the authority of all foreign powers including the Church of Rome. The decisive action was taken in 1534 but its further development came slowly, with the dissolution of the monasteries by 1539, and the internal reform of the church only after Henry's death, during the reign of Edward VI. Indeed, it can be said that the English Reformation actually came to fruition during the reign of Queen Elizabeth I (1558–1603).

King Henry, needing all the support he could muster, called upon an emerging faction of reformist intellectuals. By and large they were at first humanists critical of the status quo and avid students of the Scriptures and the early church Fathers. Some of them also read Sallust and Livy and found their understanding of politics and society shifting. Some read the pamphlets of Luther when they first became available during the 1520s and became Lutherans. A person of great talent, William Tyndale, began a translation of the New Testament in English and visited Luther in Germany. The doctrine of justification by faith alone, without the aid of any works, shone through the first edition of Tyndale's New Testament. Subsequently, he came under the influence of Rhineland theologians with their emphasis not on justification but on the covenant-contract relationship between God and Christians. The Lutheran doctrine was still there, but it was supplemented (some would say diluted) by the necessity of maintaining the contract with God through the performance of good works. In 1528 Tyndale's *The Obedience of a Christian Man, and How Christian Rulers Ought to Govern* was published at Antwerp. Anne Boleyn persuaded King Henry to read it and he was reported to have exclaimed, "This is a book for me and for all kings to read." It is certain that Henry was not impressed by Tyndale's theology. What he liked in the book was the strong assertion of the rights and duties of rulers and their just claim to the total obedience of their subjects. Furthermore, Henry would note with interest Tyndale's arguments and evidence to prove that the Roman see provoked sedition in violation of divine law. The king, with his predilections and ambitions, found ready and useful allies in the Protestant humanists who rose to his defense.

It is important to realize that the English Reformation developed in an atmosphere of growing national sentiment and was guided by a strong ideal, that of the Christian commonwealth. It aimed at nothing less than the establishment of divine love and justice in the land. This involved the unity of all the people, clergy and laity, under the sovereign power of the king who operates with the representatives of the people in parliament. This is a large and complex subject. Take, for example, the literature aimed at overcoming the division between the spirituality (clergy) and temporality (all the rest). In 1532 Christopher Saint German wrote *A treatise concerning the division between spirituality and temporality* which placed the blame for the alienation on the clergy with their avarice and pride, and urged reform. Saint German was reflecting the sentiments of the laity whose discontents were enumerated by Simon Fish in *A Supplication for the Beggars* (1528). Fish referred to the clergy as an "idle, ravenous sort" who have seized hold upon a third of the realm, extort every available penny from the common people, and usurp the king's "rule, power, lordship, authority, obedience and dignity." In 1538 there appeared an anonymous *Treatise proving by the king's laws that the bishops of Rome had never right to any supremacy within this realm*, which argued:

> And where the clergy of this realm have made a difference or a distinction between spiritual men and temporal men, and spiritual causes and temporal causes: yet such difference is not as they have most commonly taken it. For by these terms, they of the clergy have taken and called themselves spiritual men only, and have not of long time admitted, that lay men were spiritual, wherein they did not well. For a lay man may be spiritual and he may also be carnal and temporal. In like manner a bishop, or a priest, may be carnal and temporal, and he may also be spiritual.[32]

Involved in this statement there is the realization of actual events involving ecclesiastical courts, wherein the clergy have asserted their separation from the laity and, by abusing the laity, have aroused their ire. Royal supremacy is justified in terms of the necessity to overcome such division and to realize the conviction that England is a commonwealth, a unity of people of all estates.

Stephen Gardiner, Bishop of Winchester, who was a strong supporter of King Henry VIII, and no Protestant, put the case this way in *Of True Obedience* (1535):

> The king (they [the papists] say) is the head of the realm but not of the church: whereas, notwithstanding, the church of England, is nothing else but the congregation of men and women, of the clergy and laity, united in Christ's profession: that is to say, it is justly to be called the church, because it is a communion of Christian people, and of the place, it is to be named the church of England, as is the church of France, the church of Spain, and the church of Rome.[33]

Inherent in this there was national sentiment, a social doctrine which was related to medieval ideals and yet attached to those aspirations which were to eventuate in a new age, and there was the theological perspective of the Protestant humanists. This theology insisted upon the unity of the people and sought to overcome the separation of the sacred and the secular. The Protestant Reformation emphasized the priesthood of all believers, promoted the reading of Scripture by the laity, sought to turn the monastic ideal into a style of life for all people in their daily occupations, and promoted the participation of all in the Holy Communion. The distinction between clergy and laity was retained in the Church of England, too much of a distinction for those who urged a further reformation and were called Puritans, but the distinction was not as great as it had been if only in terms of the assertion of power over the church by the king and parliament.

The distinction between sacred and secular was resisted in part because it seemed foreign to the experience of the people. The Church of England was not a denomination. It was a part of the fabric of the nation. All people were nominally members of the church and were ministered to through the Word and the sacraments, through the exercise of godly discipline, and through care for the poor and needy. The poor laws were administered through the parish structure on the local level. Furthermore, bishops served as justices of the peace and parish clergy were involved in occupations which took them out of the sanctuary to work with their hands. Hugh Latimer (1485–1555), bishop of Worcester, preached on the social trials of the people and instructed the court as to its social and economic responsibilities during the reign of Edward VI. In doing so he was exercising the church's responsibility on behalf of the oppressed. Dr. John Favour, vicar of Halifax during Queen Elizabeth's reign, not only did the ordinary things expected of the clergy in any age, but helped start a grammar school, took a lively interest in the industries of his parish, and served his people as both lawyer and physician. He tells of being kept busy

> preaching every Sabbath, lecturing every day of the week, exercising justice in the commonwealth, practising physic and surgery in the great penury and necessity thereof in the country where I live.[34]

Many clergy were farmers, tilling their glebes (farm lands belonging to the Church), tending cattle, caring for ploughs, carts, and other farm implements. In addition, the parish church was the social center of the community (along with the tavern), providing the largest, most hospitable space for the gathering of the people. This is not to suggest that other influences were not at work. The Elizabethan age was one in which dissent was growing, challenging the unity of the people. In the next century the nation would be torn apart by civil war. But for the time being the nation was, by and large, united under the crown and parliament, one people who were all members at one and the same time of the state and of the Church of England.

Encompassing all the people, this church developed certain emphases which have outlived the historical situation. First of all there was the concept of things indifferent. If all people are to be comprehended in one church, then it must be granted that differences can be allowed. But there are also areas, concerning things necessary to salvation, in which differences cannot be allowed. To distinguish between essentials and nonessentials was difficult but necessary in creating a spirit and an atmosphere which was both authoritative and charitable. Humility was another fruit of the time, as well as of the Gospel. Such humility was characterized by awe and reverence. It is expressed in lines concerning the Holy Communion attributed to Queen Elizabeth I:

> Christ's was the word that spake it,
> He took the bread and brake it,
> and what His word did make it,
> That I believe and take it.[35]

In this spirit an attempt was made to achieve a balance between "lawfull authority" and "just liberty." An example here is to be found in other words attributed to Queen Elizabeth and written in 1570 between two threatening rebellions: "In the word of a Prince and the presence of God," so long as her subjects demonstrated themselves to be quiet and comfortable to her laws through attendance at church, they would enjoy her accustomed favor, mildness, and grace, "without molestation . . . by way of . . . inquisition of their opinions for their consciences in matters of faith, remitting that to the supreme and singular authority of Almighty God, who is the only searcher of hearts."[36]

In a sense the English Reformation was epitomized by the Queen, a Protestant humanist by education and conviction, ruling under God, whose covenant with her required that she rule her commonwealth to bring about its perpetual prosperity and peace. As a child she studied the New Testament in Greek, the writings of Cicero, Sophocles, Cyprian, and the theology of the moderate Lutheran, Philip Melanchthon. Such was a Christian humanist's fare, inculcating a devout life, a simple faith, studious habits, and moderation in all things.

There were dangers in all this. The goals of the reformers were not always on target and those that were ran up against the intransigence of human material and the changes involved with the passage of time. There was a sense in which the reform was too closely identified with an intellectual elite out of touch with the lowest classes of the society. The quest for essentials could and did lead in the next century to a denial of the Christian faith as defined by the New Testament and the creeds. Burgeoning rationalism would reduce belief to a very simple affirmation such as the existence of God and the promise of immortality. The Christian cause as represented by the Church of England could be too closely identified with a waning and challenged royal power. It could become a department of state and seemingly lose its ability to prophesy and judge the powers that be. With the emphasis on justification and personal salvation, the Christian faith could become a private, individual matter to the neglect of its broader implications and the social responsibilities of the church. All of these things occurred and, as a result, new reform movements arose. We now turn to consider some of these new movements.

Reform in the 18th and 19th Century Church of England

It is possible to discern a pattern in the reform movements of the eighteenth and nineteenth centuries. While the eighteenth-century Church of England was not as badly off as some would claim, it was nevertheless beset by a number of problems. Chiefly, it would seem that Christian faith and witness was waning. Indeed, many prelates warned against enthusiasm and advocated both an emphasis on reasonable arguments to confound the irreligious and moral exhortation in preaching. The preaching of the age was often concerned to advocate philanthropic enterprises such as the charity schools. It could also be pastoral but, on the whole, it took little note of personal and corporate sin and was not likely to urge conversion. The church contained many outstanding persons, but it appeared to be weak and occasionally corrupt, providing the laity with little inspiration.

The Church of England was more and more apparently a department of the state. Whereas in the sixteenth century there was one church, now there were many churches, although only one established by law. The Church of England, as distinguished from the chapels of nonconformist Presbyterians, Congregationalists, and the like, was seemingly compromised by its official status. The fact that convocation did not meet between 1717 and 1852 was a symbol of sorts. The church had little independence, little understanding of itself as an organic entity, and little conviction concerning its sacramental life. Finally, the church seemed to be losing its hold on the nation. The population was growing, the Industrial Revolution got under way, changing the face of the land, and "new" cities developed around the factories, with masses of workers largely ignored by a church which in its parochial system was still largely rural and dominated by the higher classes.

The movements for reform during these two centuries all addressed the problem of the church and its mission in England. They did so in different ways, to some extent interacting with one another. Historians during the past decade have done much to illuminate the relationships between these movements, relationships characterized by mutual influence as well as antagonism. The evangelical movement, beginning in the eighteenth century, aimed at the cultivation of real as opposed to nominal Christianity. It was concerned to revive a sense of personal reform and renewal grounded in biblical doctrine, emphasizing sin and redemption. As Henry Venn (1725–1797) put it, the preachers of the church, largely moralistic in their preaching while neglecting sin and salvation,

> press the necessity of moral practice without first giving plain and full directions how to master the great impediment to well-doing, which is no better than reading our sentence of condemnation. What we all want is power to surmount . . . difficulties and . . . assurance of its vouchsafement.[37]

That power and assurance is to be found in God's Word, in heartfelt repentance and a lively faith. As William Wilberforce (1759–1833), a lay leader of the movement and member of Parliament, wrote:

> We must be deeply conscious of our guilt and misery, heartily repenting of our sins, and firmly resolving to foresake them: and thus penitently "fleeing for refuge to the hope set before

us," we must found altogether on the merit of the crucified Redeemer our hopes of escape from deserved punishment, and of deliverance from their enslaving power. This must be our first, our last, our only plea. We are to surrender ourselves up to him to "be washed in his blood," to be sanctified by his Spirit, resolving to receive him for our Lord and Master, to learn in his School, to obey all his commandments.[38]

It is difficult to determine the beginnings of this movement. We now believe that it began in relative obscurity during the first decades of the eighteenth century with religious revivals such as that of Griffith Jones of Llandowror in Wales during 1714. By the 1730s others were abroad in Wales, preaching in churchyards and on hillsides, leading a revival which was gradually spreading. George Whitefield (1714–1770) was widely acknowledged as the first of the great revivalist preachers. His outdoor, itinerant preaching began among the English miners in 1739 just a short time after he began correspondence with Howell Harris, one of the Welsh revivalists. John Wesley (1703–1791), who had undergone a conversion experience in the previous year—in which he felt his heart strangely warmed and knew the assurance of a real faith—heard Whitefield preach among the miners a little more than a month after he began. They were in the open air and Wesley, a priest of the Church of England, wrote:

I could scarce reconcile myself at first to his strange way of preaching in the fields. . . . Having been all my life (till very lately) so tenacious of every point relating to decency and order, that I should have thought the saving of souls almost a sin if it had not been done in a church.[39]

That same day Wesley began preaching, first to a little society of earnest Christians and then to the poor in a brickyard, and subsequently to growing numbers of people with powerful affects. His preaching brought on conversions accompanied by raving and screaming, the outbursts of souls struggling through the death of sin to the life of salvation.

Wesley remained in the Church of England throughout his life. The organization which he helped form eventually broke away and became the Methodist Church, but in the begin-

ning it existed as an adjunct to the parish church, not interfer-
ing with the regular church services. This organization consisted of societies which in turn were composed of bands or
classes. Normally there were twelve persons to a class, one of
whom would be the leader. They were intended to extend the
results of the revival through examination, edification, and
discipline. Wesley derived this structure in part from the
Moravians and in part from the societies of all sorts already
existent. Above the society there was the circuit, a grouping
of societies served by a group ministry, supervised by a
senior minister. Above the societies there was the conference
which met annually and provided leadership for discipline,
education, and the "stationing" of preachers. The hierarchy
of the Church of England objected to all of this, particularly as
the success of the movement became apparent and as, in
1744, the conference began to deal with doctrine. It is not
surprising that four years after Wesley's death Methodism
broke away from the Church of England forming a new
denomination.

The Methodists themselves were not entirely united.
George Whitefield and John Wesley differed in their estimate
of humanity and of God. The difference was basically that
some followed John Calvin in depicting God as the absolute
sovereign of inscrutable wisdom who chooses some persons
for salvation; while others, such as Wesley, followed the
teaching of Jacob Arminius (1560–1609), believing that God
wills all people to be saved, and allowing greater scope to
human will in relation to divine will. Whitefield objected that
Wesley's Arminianism dulled the awareness of sin, making
people complacent. He found his staunchest support in
Selina, countess of Huntingdon (1701–1791), a loyal member
of the Church of England, who employed Anglican clergy
such as Whitefield as her chaplains and preachers. Lady Huntingdon drifted away from the church when the hierarchy
rejected her plans to promote the faith, founding what came
to be known as the Countess of Huntingdon's Connexion.

Many Evangelicals remained in the Church of England,
largely Calvinist in their teachings, devoted to the preaching
of the Gospel, and loyal to the church so far as it was in
agreement with the Gospel. During the eighteenth century

there were evangelists such as William Grimshaw of Haworth (1708–1763), scholars such as William Romaine of London (1714–1795), and parish priests such as Samuel Walker of Truro (1714–1761). In the next generation, extending into the 1830s, there were organizers and pastors who kept the movement in the church. They included laity and clergy—the parliamentarian, William Wilberforce; the educator and moralist, Hannah More (1745–1833); the Thorntons and the Venns, backbones of the so-called Clapham Sect; John Newton (1725–1807), the ex-slaver; and Charles Simeon (1759–1836). In a way Simeon was the most impressive of them all, espousing the tenets of biblical evangelicalism, while loving the church, its polity, worship, usages, and doctrine as set forth in the Book of Common Prayer and the Articles of Religion. His emphasis on the church was so strong that it was heard said: "Mr. Simeon is not a Gospel-man, but a Church-man."

By founding societies such as the Church Missionary Society, by supporting the Bible Society, the Prayer Book Society, the Sunday Schools, by doing philanthropic work among the poor, and by struggling for reform of the factory laws and the abolition of slavery, these Anglican evangelicals contributed much toward the formation of Victorian England.

The second movement has been variously called the Tractarian Movement and the Oxford Movement. It evolved into Anglo-Catholicism, incorporated the ritual movement, and was the successor to the old High Churchmanship of the eighteenth century. The movement aimed at restoring the integrity of the Church of England in the face of political and theological liberalism. Its founders were alarmed that parliament, which had recently admitted to its membership persons not belonging to the Church of England, should make decisions concerning the internal affairs of the church, treating it as though it were merely a department of the state. In reaction to the suppression of ten bishoprics in Ireland, John Keble (1792–1866) preached in a sermon at Oxford, later entitled "National Apostasy," on July 4, 1833:

> Should it ever happen (which God avert, but we cannot shut our eyes to the danger) that the Apostolical Church should be

forsaken, degraded, nay trampled on and despoiled by the State and people of England, I cannot conceive a kinder wish for her, on the part of her most affectionate and dutiful children, than that she may, consistently, act in the spirit of this noble sentence [1 Sam. 12:23, in which Samuel vows to continue praying and teaching his people in spite of their opposition.] nor a course of conduct more likely to be blessed by a restoration to more than her former efficiency. In speaking of the Church, I mean, of course, the laity, as well as the clergy in their three orders,—the whole body of Christians united, according to the will of Jesus Christ, under the Successors of the Apostles.[40]

John Henry Newman (1801–1890) claimed that this sermon marked the beginning of the movement. We now regard this claim with some scepticism, aware of the many thoughts and feelings stirring in the early Tractarians. There were already existent High Churchmen such as William Palmer (1811–1879), who formed the Association of Friends in 1833 to sound the alarm against present dangers and to project a vision of the Church Catholic in accord with which the Church of England should be reformed. There was the group of Oxford scholars, including Newman, who in the 1820s sat at the feet of Charles Lloyd (1784–1829), subsequently bishop of Oxford, studying the ancient liturgies. There were Newman's conversations with Richard Whately (1787–1863), a liberal scholar attached to Oriel College, Oxford, who gave Newman a vision of the church as an independent, organic reality. There was romanticism which had been influencing some of the best minds of Europe, inspiring Newman and his close friend, Hurrell Froude (1803–1836), to look back to the medieval church with longing while despising the reformers of the sixteenth century as destroyers. And there was the influence of the evangelical movement on persons such as Newman who had had a conversion experience and sought for perfection as a "real" Christian.

From the Association of Friends there came in 1834 two petitions addressed to the archbishop of Canterbury, one signed by seven thousand clergy, another by two hundred thirty thousand laity. They requested, in polite but strong terms, that the church be reformed and that this reform be based on apostolic succession, the church, its doctrine and polity. This was a call for the bishops to assume leadership in the church. From Newman and Oxford came the tracts, essentially aiming at the same results. In the Second Tract, Newman set forth the One, Catholic, and Apostolic Church as a fact. After asking what the fact means and scoffing at the common opinion that it means all Christians, Newman wrote:

> Doubtless the only true and satisfactory meaning is that which our Divines have ever taken, that there is on earth an existing Society, Apostolic as founded by the Apostles, Catholic because it spread its branches in every place; i.e. the Church Visible with its Bishops, Priests, and Deacons. And this surely *is* a most important doctrine; for what can be better news to the bulk of mankind than to be told that Christ, when He ascended, did not leave us orphans, but appointed representatives of Himself to the end of time.[41]

This was the chief message at the beginning. This vision of the church involved much, both external and internal. It involved Newman's mysticism, his vision of the invisible penetrating the visible to transform it. It involved the recovery of the sacramental life, the enrichment of personal devotions and public worship. And it involved the incarnational views of theologians such as Robert Isaac Wilberforce (1802–1857), which were to have far-reaching implications for society. That is to say, in time something which began as a response to a specific challenge developed into a wide-ranging movement reviving the catholic emphasis of the Church of England, enriching its liturgy and inspiring reformist activities in the society.

The Oxford Movement, like the Evangelical Movement, found the going rough in the beginning. Newman and others despaired of the Church of England, having been attacked by members of its hierarchy, and fled into the Church of Rome. Such departures seemingly confirmed the opinions of those who believed that the Tractarians were "papists" in disguise. Furthermore, many who protested their loyalty were harassed by their bishops and the church courts for their ritual "innovations." The first court case was begun in 1855. The vicar of Knightsbridge was cited in the consistory court of

London for installing high altars, crosses, candlesticks, colored altar cloths, and credence tables. The case went all the way to the Privy Council which largely decided in favor of the ritualists. Case succeeded case until the cause was won, the ritualist movement inspiring even Evangelicals and Low Churchmen in the twentieth century to adopt such things as altars, altar cloths, crosses, candlesticks, and credence tables.

The Tractarians staying within the Church of England had no lack of leadership. Edward Bouverie Pusey (1800–1882) had been there from the beginning and provided a steadying hand through the troubles of the 1840s and '50s. The religious life was revived in England under the influence of Pusey and others. The missionary work of the church received fresh impetus. Anglo-Catholics led the way in ministering to the slums of London's East End. In short, the life of the Church of England was both troubled and reinvigorated by the Oxford Movement.

The third movement is that of the Christian Socialists, which shall be mentioned briefly here, for the next chapter begins with a consideration of its most prominent leader, Frederick Denison Maurice. Suffice it to say that Christian Socialism aimed, as Maurice said, at making Christians social and Socialists Christian. Its chief concern was to minister to society, to guard against the excesses of the continental revolutions of 1830 and 1848, and to promote the principles of cooperation and sacrifice. The Evangelicals were concerned for social action, but were often patronizing in their actions and intent on alleviating the sufferings of the poor rather than eradicating the ills of society at their source. The Tractarians were not without their social views and programs, but (until the Anglo-Catholic slum work in the latter part of the nineteenth century) they seemed to be inner-oriented, concerned chiefly for the church, its authority and self-respect. The Christian Socialist movement, which in its organized form was most active from 1848 to 1854, saw God working in the society at large and thus sought to direct Christians away from a church narrowly conceived to a church defined in terms of the activity of Christ in the world.

The three movements provided three approaches to the

reform and renewal of individuals and of the church. That they happened at all indicates the vigor of the Christian community and its ability to raise up prophets and leaders from its midst. It should also be noted that the three movements influenced each other, even though at times they regarded one another with disdain. Principally, the liberal spirit of the time, which the first two movements sought to combat, gradually transformed the movements themselves, so that we can speak of "liberal Evangelicalism" and "liberal Catholicism." Prominent Evangelicals and Anglo-Catholics came in time to accept the findings of modern science, modern biblical criticism, and to develop a lively concern for the mission of the church to the society in which God is at work. One might also speak of "liberal Mauricians," for the leader of the Christian Socialists was reluctant to accept the findings of modern science and biblical criticism. So-called Broad Churchmanship represents the further evolution of at least some of those who followed Maurice. Their principal dictum was to seek the truth, come whence it may, cost what it will. Firm in what they believed to be essentials, they maintained an openness toward the future. Their excesses caused some Evangelicals and Anglo-Catholics to reassess their positions, but they proved themselves to be well adapted to existence in the late nineteenth and early twentieth centuries.

Reform in America and in the Protestant Episcopal Church

American history has been punctuated by evangelical revivals. By evangelical we mean to indicate an emphasis on conversion. Revivalism concerns a technique for inducing conversion. It is the long debated thesis that such revivalism is inherent in the American ethos and in particular in Protestantism. If this is so then it helps to explain that while the same three movements which we have just discussed were effective in this country, chiefly amongst Episcopalians, yet they differ in important ways. In part they differ because the background of evangelical revivals impinges not only on the

Evangelical Movement, but on the Oxford and Broad Church Movements as well.

It is perhaps unwise to attempt to list all of the revivals. Doing such the historian is bound to miss some and include others which are questionable. But with that caution in mind, it is possible to list the high points, beginning with the first Great Awakening in the eighteenth century. The second Great Awakening, which is dated around 1801, followed and extends into that which some may consider separately, the revivals associated with the long conquest of the American frontier, between 1800 and 1840. Then comes the so-called "businessman's revival" of 1857–1859, which resulted in the creation of the Y.M.C.A. Billy Sunday comes next, leading a revival movement which lasted a decade, between 1909 and 1919. We could list subsequent revivals, perhaps mentioning Billy Graham's Crusades of the 1940s and '50s and the more recent resurgence of revivalism in the 1970s.

The beginnings in the eighteenth century were not found in any one place or related to any one person but concerned the reaction of many serious people to the spiritual decline and growing immorality of American society. Then too, most people in colonial America stood outside the churches and could only be brought in by extraordinary means. The revival began in various places but especially in the Middle Colonies with the arrival of the Dutch Reformed minister, Theodore J. Freylinghuysen in 1720. His fervent preaching stirred up the people, and by 1726 the revival he began was spreading among other Dutch Reformed congregations. In the same year the influence of Freylinghuysen reached a Presbyterian pastor, Gilbert Tennant, an emotional man who poured out divine wrath on the heads of those who stood in the way of the Gospel and portrayed in terrifying images the fires of hell awaiting those who resisted conversion. His activities provoked a split between the New Side Presbyterians, who flourished with the Awakening, and the Old Side Presbyterians, who experienced a serious decline.

George Whitefield roamed up and down the Eastern coast stirring up the fires of rebellion, impressing Ben Franklin with his power, and arousing the ire of many others. In New

England the central figure was Jonathan Edwards. Building on the revivals conducted by his grandfather, Edwards witnessed a dramatic increase in the effectiveness of his preaching about 1734. There was great fear that God was about to leave the land, and there were dramatic signs that religion was the greatest concern of the people who viewed the world around them as a passing thing. Edwards described the beginnings thus:

> This work of God, as it was carried on, and the number of true saints multiplied, soon made a glorious alteration in the town; so that in the spring and summer following, anno 1735, the town seemed to be full of the presence of God: it never was so full of love, nor so full of joy; and yet so full of distress as it was then. There were remarkable tokens of God's presence in almost every house. It was a time of joy in families on account of salvation's being brought . . . unto them. . . . Our public assemblies were then beautiful; the congregation was alive in God's service, every one earnestly intent on the public worship, every hearer eager to drink in the words of the minister as they came from his mouth; the assembly in general were, from time to time, in tears while the word was preached; some weeping with sorrow and distress, others with joy and love, others with pity and concern for the souls of their neighbors.[42]

Edwards based his preaching on his understanding of the true nature of religion and of human psychology. Alongside the human understanding, capable of perception and speculation, he placed the affections, vigorous and sensible exercises of will or inclination. The purpose of preaching is to stimulate the primary affection of love toward God. Edwards was a learned man with a clear understanding of what he was about and what the church should be about. He separated himself from both arid rationalists and hysterical fanatics. True religion involves both mind and heart.

The fruits of the awakening were manifold. Historians have referred to a new seriousness in religion, growth of denominations such as the Presbyterians and Methodists, an increase in religious controversy, a split between individual and corporate concerns, an aroused social consciousness, a deepening appreciation for the nation as a whole and of democracy in particular. In addition there was a greater interest in missions, particularly to those not already reached.

Also influenced by the recurrent evangelical revivals, and yet never prominently involved in them were members of the Protestant Episcopal Church. Evangelicalism was, however, prominent in this church during the late eighteenth and early nineteenth centuries, and has persisted since. Some have referred to it as a party, but there are dangers in doing this, for such a High Churchmen as John Henry Hobart (1775–1830), bishop of New York, wrote:

> Pardon, justification, eternal life, as the free gifts of God the Father, through the merits and intercession of his eternal Son, and through the renovating and sanctifying agency of the Holy Ghost—these are the great Evangelical truths which alone render of value or of efficacy the ministration and ordinances for which the High Churchman contends. . . . *Evangelical the High Churchman must be. . . .*[43]

And yet there was a party feeling in those who gathered to do battle at first against the irreligious and immoral spirits of the age and then against the popish Tractarians who seemed bent on destroying the Episcopal Church.

The situation in Virginia is a case in point. At the General Convention of 1811 the member dioceses reported on the "State of the Church" in each place. There was no report from Virginia, but there was entered into the Convention Journal this somber note:

> They fear that the Church in Virginia is, from various causes, so depressed, that there is danger of her total extinction, unless great exertions, favored by the blessing of God, are employed to raise her.[44]

The first disturber of the peace in Virginia was Devereux Jarrat (1732–1801), whose Calvinist doctrine and revivalist preaching aroused Bath Parish, Dinwiddie County, where he was rector for thirty-eight years. But William Meade, third bishop of Virginia, testified that in spite of the happenings in Dinwiddie County, vital religion was nurtured not in the churches but in the homes of committed parents. His father read the Prayer Book service, in lieu of a service at church. His mother had her children learn hymns, especially those of Bishop Ken, and had them pray with her at her bedside. At about the same time books of the English Evangelicals, such as Hannah More and William Wilberforce, began arriving. But the great change came with the consecration of Richard Channing Moore (1762–1841) as bishop of Virginia in 1814. He began with the intention "to preach the glorious doctrines of grace instead of mere morality." For the rest of his life he worked, preaching throughout Virginia, reviving old parishes, establishing new ones, rigidly enforcing discipline on clergy and laity alike. Strongly attached to the Book of Common Prayer, he required its full use in the parishes of his diocese. He also encouraged informal gatherings for fellowship and prayer. He began with seven clergy; at his death there were one hundred.

Such a story is not uncommon. There were many evangelical bishops at work: building their dioceses; inspiring their people; founding seminaries to provide more evangelical clergy (in Virginia in 1823, and in Ohio in 1824); and active in the formation of educational, missionary, promotional, and benevolent societies. They were influenced by the evangelical revivals at large, but also by English Evangelicals such as Simeon and Wilberforce, and were devoted to the church. Devereux Jarrat was a revivalist preacher, but he proclaimed:

> I dearly love the Church. I love her on many accounts—particularly the three following. I love her because her mode of worship is so beautiful and decent, so well calculated to inspire devotion, and so complete in all parts of public worship. I love her because of the soundness of her doctrines, creeds, articles, etc. I love her because all her officers and the mode of ordaining them, are, if I mistake not, truly primitive and apostolic. . . . These three particulars, a regular clergy, sound doctrine and a decent, comprehensive worship, contain the essentials, I think, of the Christian Church. As these are still the possession of the old Church, I have been, and still am, inclined to give her the preference.[45]

Such an evangelical protest of love for the church could not be altogether convincing to the American followers of the English Tractarians. The Catholic revival in this country, which began with troubles at the General Seminary in New York, was a matter of controversy at General Conventions and elsewhere through the latter half of the nineteenth century. Its chief aim was the restoration of the ancient constitution of the church and thereby the cultivation of sacramental piety. Ferdinand C. Ewer (1826–1883), founder and first rector of St. Ignatius's Church, New York, attacked Protestantism as "a failure, and worse, it is a delusion, a snare to souls, a heresy." He also turned his eloquence against the Roman Catholic Church, saying that Protestantism "is diversity without unity; Romanism unity without diversity; Catholicity [Anglo-Catholicism, etc.] diversity in unity. . . . Rome regards unity as that of a single person; the Catholic conceives unity as that of a family." He then added: "He who perverts from Catholicity to Romanism commits the sin of suicide."[46] This latter statement was warranted because many who left the Episcopal Church for the Roman did so via Anglo-Catholicism. And yet there were many who remained within the Episcopal Church to influence it. Parish churches were founded on Catholic principles: the Church of the Advent, Boston; St. Clement's, Philadelphia; and St. Paul's, Baltimore, being prominent examples. Such churches were liturgically rich, dedicated to the exercise of holy discipline, and self-consciously Catholic. Religious orders were founded, beginning with the Community of St. Mary in 1865. In 1881 the first order for men in this country began work, a house of the Anglican Cowley Fathers. The Catholic Club was organized in New York in 1886, the predecessor of the American Church Union.

What in a positive sense did this movement stand for? When Ferdinand Ewer was attacked by F. D. Huntington, bishop of Central New York, demanding to know how far the Anglo-Catholics proposed to go, he responded by listing his firm convictions, shared, so he believed, by all true Catholics. These included prayers for the dead; acceptance of a real and objective presence of Christ in the Eucharist; the centrality of the Eucharist in the lives of Christians; its superiority over Morning Prayer; and the necessity of adjuncts fitting to its celebration, such as vestments, lights, incense, song, and adoration. He spoke for the use of outward acts of devotion in the celebrating of the presence of Christ in the Eucharist. He regarded the Eucharist as a commemorative sacrifice as well as a sacrament and a communion and proclaimed loyalty to the Prayer Book while yearning for a better book. He insisted on the right to found religious orders, to make and hear confessions, to administer unction with episcopally blessed oil, and to regard Confirmation, Orders, Absolution, Marriage, and Unction as sacramental in character. Other persons might respond to such a challenge differently, but most would include the items listed by Ewer. Where such an understanding of the faith was practiced, there was devotion, awe, and respect for authority.

In the last decades of the nineteenth century a liberal spirit imbued with a strong sense of optimism permeated the American scene. It was there in the revivalism of Dwight L. Moody (1837–1899) and in the preaching of Henry Ward Beecher (1813–1887), Lyman Abbott (1835–1922), and Phillips Brooks (1835–1893). Liberalism was a strong element in the "New Theology" of Theodore Munger (1830–1910). Munger stressed reason believing revelation only insofar as reason was not contradicted, accepting evolution as the method of creation, and emphasizing the social solidarity of all mankind. In the Episcopal Church those called Broad Churchmen were not always prepared to go as far as Munger, and yet they believed that God had given human beings reason for the verification of revelation. Fundamentally, over against what they saw as the dogmatic rigidity of the Evangelicals and Anglo-Catholics, and Broad Churchmen sought for a larger freedom, more room in which to move about while influencing events in their society. Edward Washburn, at a meeting of the Church Congress in 1876, spoke for a "regulated liberty." Preparing for a meeting which was to eventuate in the founding of the national Church Congress in 1874, Phillips Brooks, Rector of Trinity Church, Copley Square, Boston, wrote in his diary:

> Next week we go to New Haven, all of us broad churchmen, to see what can be done to make the Church liberal and free. There is a curious sort of sensitiveness and expectancy everywhere in the Church. A sort of fear and feeling that things cannot remain

for ever just as they are now. One wonders what is coming out
of it all. Certainly some sort of broad church. A meeting such as
this I speak of could not have been possible ten years ago. Then,
the men could not have been found to go; now, men are asking
to be invited.[47]

We shall subsequently have cause to consider this movement again, in relation to the Social Gospel in America and
reactions to it in the Episcopal Church and elsewhere. For the
moment let us note that it influenced both Evangelicalism
and Anglo-Catholicism, which became more socially active,
open to the findings of science, facing toward the future as
well as holding fast to that which is of value in the past.

There is a sense in which all subsequent reform movements
in the Episcopal Church have been related to the three
movements discussed here. Among more recent movements
one should mention the Ecumenical Movement, perhaps
most deeply influenced by Broad Churchmen such as William
Reed Huntington, but also by Evangelicals engaged in world
mission and by High Churchmen yearning for the unity of
the Body of Christ. There is also the Liturgical Movement,
perhaps most deeply influenced by High Churchmen with
their emphasis on sacraments, but also by Broad Churchmen
concerned for a more socially relevant liturgy and by Evangelicals concerned for a stronger ministry of the Word. And there
are charismatic movements, healing movements, movements
concerned to eradicate racism and sexism in the church, and
many others all seeking to reform the church in relation to
those essential things which have been neglected or negated.
In all such movements, Evangelicals, Anglo-Catholics, and
liberal or Broad Churchmen have been and are involved,
which perhaps points to the merging and transforming of
them all. What will happen we cannot now know. But whatever the future holds we may be sure that there will be
movements for the renewal and reform of the church, its
people, and the institution.

· 4 ·

Church and Culture:
Christ and Caesar in Tension

F. D. Maurice
and Christ Transforming the World

In 1848 the forty-three-year-old chaplain of Lincoln's Inn, London, was preaching a series of sermons on the Lord's Prayer. His congregation was composed in large part of young lawyers employed in the Inns of Court, troubled by the signs of the times, drawn to the little upstairs chapel by the prophetic preaching of the chaplain. The preacher, Frederick Denison Maurice, was respected, not for his eloquence or fervor but for the exciting new insights and vision of the church and contemporary society which he conveyed to his hearers. Thirsting for more, some of his followers formed a "band of brothers" and met with Maurice for weekly Bible evenings at which their anxieties and perplexities would be discussed in relation to the Scriptures.

Maurice and his congregation had ample reason to be anxious and perplexed. Revolution was in the air. The government of Louis Philippe in France fell, signaling the start of a wave of revolutions sweeping across Europe. There was fear that this time England would experience that which she had hitherto been able to escape. This fear sprang in large part from the economic and social conditions of English society.

Frederick Denison Maurice, 1805–1872

The Industrial Revolution, which began in the 1760s, was transforming the nation into the major industrial and commercial power of the world. In the process the society was severely tested, peoples' lives were disrupted, and the greedy and ambitious prospered. Charles Dickens, in his novel *Dombey and Son*, transmits something of the feeling of the times in relation to the building of the railways:

The first shock of a great earthquake had, just at that period, rent the whole neighbourhood at its centre. Traces of its course were visible on every side. Houses were knocked down; streets broken through and stopped; deep pits and trenches dug in the ground; enormous heaps of earth and clay thrown up. . . .[1]

Masses of laborers, many of them immigrants escaping from famine in Ireland, were crammed into urban ghettos without sufficient sanitation, with wildly fluctuating wages and prices, and with working conditions which were often brutal. The working hours were long; women and children constituted a large portion of the work force and labored twelve to fourteen hours a day. Many children did not survive to maturity. Many women fell victims to the exploitation, dying young as a result, some drowning in the readily available cheap gin. Leaders of society were concerned about all of this. Reform legislation did in fact alleviate the situation. But the march of progress and the rapidity of change were such that in 1848 some doubted that legislation would right the wrongs in time to avert disaster.

The situation in England was ripe for revolution. The Chartist movement appeared to be the agency for its eruption. This was a vast organization of persons from trade and industry, embracing almost all of the urban working classes. Its charter, called "the People's Charter," called for annual parliaments, universal male suffrage, equal electoral districts, the removal of property qualifications for members of parliament, the secret ballot, and payment of M.P.s. Chartist hopes thus rested with a reformed parliament and legislation. There were those among its members, however, who agitated for the nationalization or redistribution of land, and others who labored for trade union organization as the means for securing justice.

On April 10, 1848, a great crowd of Chartists assembled on Kennington Common. Some expected that an uprising would result. Maurice volunteered to be a special constable, or policeman. It began to rain and the crowd quietly dispersed. The anxiety and perplexity remained, however, for the issues had not been resolved, indeed many of them had not been addressed. The Church of England, in particular, seemed to share the anxiety, but its official agents seemed incapable of addressing the issues except by means of denunciation, despair, or avoidance.

There were exceptions among Evangelicals and Tractarians. We should not ignore the contributions of the former toward the achievement of reform legislation or of the latter in raising the moral standards of many of the nation's leaders. But basically the Evangelicals seemed preoccupied with sin, echoing John Newton's sentiment that the vast cloud of smoke which habitually hung over London was an emblem "of that cloud of sin which is continually ascending with a mighty cry in the ears of the Lord of hosts." And the Tractarians regarded the church as supernatural, standing over against the world. There is, Newman wrote, "another world around us, though we see it not, and more wonderful than the world we see, for this reason if for no other, that we do not see it." Evangelicals and Tractarians exercised the insights and vocations given to them; these did not seem to include effective reform of the troubled English industrial society.

Maurice's appeal for those concerned to tackle society's ills came in large part from his conviction that it is not sin which lies at the root of human existence, but rather sacrifice. Sin is the denial of our true being. The deepest truth about anyone and everyone is that the fundamental law of humankind is sacrifice, not sin. In his book on *The Doctrine of Sacrifice* (1854), Maurice wrote that Abraham

> found sacrifice to be no solitary act, no sudden expression of joy, no violent effort to make a return for blessings which we can only return by accepting; but that it lies at the very root of our being; that our lives stand upon it; that society is held together by it; that all power to be right, and to do right, begins with the offering up of ourselves, because it is thus that the righteous Lord makes us like Himself.[2]

The law of sacrifice is not the exclusive possession of any group, not even the church. It is the law of all society, mankind's "spiritual constitution," proceeding from that society

which is the Holy Trinity. At the center there is Christ.
Maurice put it this way in 1833:

> God tells us, "In him," that is in Christ, "I have created all
> things, whether they be in heaven or on earth. Christ is the
> Head of *every* man." Some men believe this; some men disbe-
> lieve it. Those who disbelieve it walk "after the flesh." They do
> not believe that they are joined to an Almighty Lord of Life—
> One who is mightier than the world, the flesh, the devil—One
> who is nearer to them than their own flesh.[3]

Those who acknowledge the headship of Christ and live by
the law of sacrifice are the church, for the church is "human
society in its normal state; the World, that same society irregular and abnormal. The world is the Church without God;
the Church is the world restored to its relation with God,
taken back by Him into the state for which He created it."
There is, then, no absolute separation between the church
and the world. Both are composed of the same elements. "In
the Church, these elements are penetrated by a uniting, reconciling power."[4] On this basis, Maurice rejected the distinction between secular and sacred. He also objected to any
understanding of the church or the Christian life which based
the human relation to Christ on some form of "religion," on
external rites or narrow doctrines. Christianity is not a
religion. Christianity is Christ, "the head of *every* man,"
woman, and child.

Furthermore, Maurice attacked all rationalism and unbelief
which results in dehumanizing individuals by cutting them
off from their source, leaving them isolated. The restoration
of society to its true nature involved the restoration of belief
in the Triune God, the fellowship of Father, Son, and Holy
Spirit. In his *Lincoln's Inn Sermons* he explained:

> The Universal Church, constituted in its Universal Head, exists
> to protest against a world which supposes itself to be a collec-
> tion of incoherent fragments without a centre, which, where it
> reduces its practice to a maxim, treats every man as his own
> centre. The Church exists to tell the world of its true Centre, of

the law of mutual sacrifice by which its parts are bound together. The Church exists to maintain the order of the nation
and the order of the family, which this selfish practice and
selfish maxim are continually threatening.[5]

Church and state, thus, are not opposed. Both aim at the
same end, which is to promote the full realization of society
through the application of the law of sacrifice. Maurice
likened the state to the Law and the church to the Gospel. The
Law operates to put down all selfish, individualistic im-
pulses. The Gospel operates to obliterate all selfishness in the
minds and hearts of people. To put it another way, not altogether consistent with what has just been said, church and
state need one another. They aim at different ends. The state
is "by nature and law Conservative of individual rights, individual possessions. To uphold them it may be compelled (it
must be) to recognise another principle than that of individual rights and property."[6] That other principle is that which
constitutes the aim of the church. He calls that principle
communism, which does not mean for him what it means for
us. For him the word communism pointed to sacrifice and
cooperation, exemplified by Christian monasticism. Church
and state need one another in order to prevent either from
going into distorting extremes. They live best when they live
together in that tension which preserves individuality and
community in a proper balance.

It was in terms of such an understanding that Maurice
became involved in the events of the time. One result of his
preaching and teaching at Lincoln's Inn and elsewhere during 1848 was the formation of the Christian socialist movement. He led this movement together with a young lawyer,
J. M. Ludlow, and a young priest, Charles Kingsley. Maurice
was the prophet, Ludlow the organizer, and Kingsley the
publicist. They began in 1848 with a series of weekly papers
called *Politics for the People*, aimed initially at the Chartist
crisis. Their major effort went into the cooperative movement
with the founding of the Tailors' Association and the organization of other worker-managed producers' cooperatives.

Maurice was reluctant to see the movement turn into a business operation. He preferred to work through already existing institutions. But in time he was brought around. Charles Kingsley assisted in this, writing his tract, *Cheap Clothes and Nasty*, in response to revelations concerning the debased conditions of the tailors. Kingsley suggested:

> Let . . . a dozen, or fifty, or a hundred journeymen say to one another: "It is competition that is ruining us, and competition is division, disunion, every man for himself, every man against his brother. The remedy must be in association, co-operation, self-sacrifice for the sake of one another. . . . Why should we not work and live together in our own workshops, or our own homes, for our own profit?[7]

Maurice responded:

> I do not see my way farther than this. Competition is put forth as the law of the universe. That is a lie. The time is come for us to declare that it is a lie by word and deed. I see no way but associating for work instead of for strikes.[8]

On this basis Maurice supported the Tailors' Association and the other associations which were to follow. In time it became evident that Maurice and Ludlow were not in agreement. The latter believed that only the reorganization of society along socialist lines could bring about the needed reform. Maurice could stomach no such radical resolution. He aimed at the transformation of the minds and hearts of the people who constitute society. The reform which he sought was basically theological and not political. One of his followers was to complain that Maurice's theology was "all door," incapable of leading anywhere.

By 1854 the Christian Socialist Movement as an organization of cooperative societies came to an end. The cooperative associations failed; it has been said that they failed because the people involved were not capable of meeting the moral demands placed upon them for cooperation and sacrifice. The cooperative movement did not, of course, end and the Christian Socialist Movement could be said to have changed course and continued on. Maurice's activities were directed toward education, first as a teacher at King's College, London, and then as a professor at Cambridge University. He founded Queen's College, London, in 1848, which initially trained governesses, but subsequently became a center for the higher education of women in general. In 1854, having been dismissed by King's College for "unorthodox" doctrinal teaching, Maurice founded and became principal of the Working Men's College, Great Ormond Street, London. Here a variety of courses were offered, literature and art, as well as Bible and theology. He explained that he was concerned for the education of persons in the broad sense. He was also convinced that the college as such was a training ground for meaningful life in contemporary England. It was a society of teachers and students, a corporate, stratified, and functional society grounded on the Christian faith. Here persons would learn to live by the law of sacrifice and be prepared to live as brothers and sisters in and for the world.

Maurice's vision extended beyond the college to the nation. He was convinced of the necessity of some scheme for national education and believed that it could only be done properly by the church. At the time education below the college level was conducted by parish churches, religious sects, and by women such as Hannah More working through their Charity Schools. The result seemed to be that those who were being taught were divided rather than united. The church—by which he meant the Church of England—would bind the people into a unity. In time Maurice was forced to recognize the impracticality of his convictions, given the conditions of nineteenth-century England, especially the divisions which separated Christians from one another. As a consequence, Maurice believed that the state must raise up a national education scheme itself.

F. D. Maurice was not universally admired in his own time. He spoke out bluntly, broke with common opinion too often, engaged in controversy, and offended many who wished to regard him with affection. He was no hero-saint; but he is memorable as one who viewed himself as a "digger," reflecting deeply on the world's sufferings and joys, seeking to understand. He believed that his task as a theologian and a Christian was not to give all the answers but to seek for the light of God and to witness to that light. Thus all questions loomed before him and no question was avoided or ruled unfit for investigation. In a typical fashion he lined up some of the most persistent and difficult questions confronting the Christian and the non-Christian:

> What do we worship? A dream, or a real being? One wholly removed from us, or one related to us? Is He a Preserver, or a Destroyer? Has death explained its meaning to us, or is it still a horrible riddle? Is it still uncertain whether Life or Death is master of the world, or how has the uncertainty been removed? What is the evil which I find in myself? Is it myself? Must I perish in order that it may perish, or can it be in any wise separated from me? Can I give myself up and yet live?[9]

Maurice dug and grubbed and wrestled and prayed. Indeed, he was a man who dug deeply into himself to find communion with God. His son tells us that in the morning Maurice might be discovered rising "hurriedly from his knees, his face reddened, and his eyes depressed by the intense pressure of his hands, the base of which had been driven and almost gouged into the eye-socket, the fingers and thumbs pressed down over forehead and head." His wife wrote in her notebook: "Whenever he woke in the night he was always praying. And in the *very* early morning I have often pretended to be asleep lest I should disturb him whilst he was pouring out his heart to God."[10] Such evidence is, perhaps, the strongest witness to the transformation of the man, transformation which involved humility and exaltation, the humiliation of one who has recognized that Christ—and not himself—is the Head of his life and of everyone, and exaltation which involved the realization that he had tasks to perform in service to the Head and for the sake of the members of Christ's body.

Maurice died neither in the arena, as did Ignatius, nor by burning, as did Cranmer, but of natural causes in 1872 at his home in Cambridge. According to Mrs. Maurice his last words, spoken with great effort, were these: "The knowledge of the love of God—the blessing of God Almighty, the Father, the Son, and the Holy Ghost be amongst *you*—amongst *us*—and remain with us for ever."[11]

The Church in the World: The Necessary Interaction

There is a necessary interaction between the church and the world. By "the church" we have meant thus far that holy community which acknowledges the Lordship of Christ and is sent bearing the Good News to the world. The world, as Maurice reminds us, is that reality which does not acknowledge the Lordship of Christ. The world might properly be said to include all of reality, the inanimate and the animate, on planet earth. The Christian tradition, however, usually means by "the world" the realm of human activity existing apart from God, toward which the church is directed. The world for which Christ died is humanity pursuing its various ends, selfishly ignoring its true foundations and desperately struggling for survival. In the struggle, power, wealth, and brains seem to be all that ultimately counts. It is important to keep this definition in mind and to realize that thinking this way about the church and the world does not deny the fact that the church is the world defined as the totality of the inanimate and animate on earth. Nor are we denying the truth which Maurice expressed when writing: "The world contains the elements of which the church is composed."

The appropriate image is that conveyed by Jesus sending the seventy disciples "on ahead of him, two by two, into every town and place where he himself was to come." They were to go out into the hostile world, "as lambs amidst wolves." They were to bring in the harvest of souls, not caring for themselves, their security or safety, but caring for those to whom they were sent (Luke 10:1–9). Jesus, in the highpriestly prayer of the Gospel of John 17:14–19 speaks of his disciples in a saying which reflects the church's understanding of its mission.

I have given them my word; and the world has hated them
because they are not of the world, even as I am not of the world.
I do not pray that thou shouldst take them out of the world,
but that thou shouldst keep them from the evil one. They are
not of the world, even as I am not of the world. Sanctify them in
the truth; thy word is truth. As thou didst send me into the
world, so I have sent them into the world. And for their sake I
consecrate myself, that they also may be consecrated in truth.

There is a very real tension. The followers are sent into the
world. They are sent as strangers into a hostile environment.
They are sent not to wage warfare against it, however, and
not to be agents of divine wrath, but rather to be ministers of
reconciliation (2 Cor. 5:18), agents of God's saving love, serving the needs of those to whom they are sent.

The history of the church is the history of this encounter of
the holy community with the world. It is also the history of
ever-changing relationships between the church and the
world. Once given the biblical injunctions for the church's
mission, Christians are left to wrestle with the details in relation to the concrete, historical situation at any particular time
or place.

H. Richard Niebuhr (1894–1962), professor of ethics at the
Yale Divinity School, in his book *Christ and Culture*, considered the various types of relationship which have existed
between the church and the world. For "world" he substi-
tuted the word "culture," meaning that which the New Testament means by "world." He defined culture as "the 'artificial, secondary environment' which man superimposes on
the natural. It comprises language, habits, ideas, beliefs, customs, social organization, inherited artifacts, technical processes, and values."[12]

Niebuhr argues that given the initial thrust of the church
into the world there have been five types of relationship between Christ (acting through the church) and culture: (1)
There has been opposition. Christ is depicted as standing
over against culture, confronting the world with an either/or
decision: either you choose Christ or you choose the world,
salvation or damnation. In the early church Tertullian was a

forceful exponent of this view. In our times it is expressed by those who react strongly against the contemporary world and its refusal of the Gospel. (2) There is agreement. Christ is viewed as a kind of cultural superman, the epitome of the culture's achievements and values. He is a part of the cultural heritage to be transmitted along with other elements of the heritage that the perpetuation of the society may be assured. Gnostics represent this type in the early church. In our day it is expressed by "Culture Christianity." At its best it may lend a sense of ultimate authority to the highest aspirations of a society. At its worst it may deify race prejudice, sexism, and economic banditry.

The first two types stand at extremes to one another. The last three provide intermediate solutions to that which must now be recognized as a problem. (3) There is Christ above culture. This type is often associated with the High Middle Ages, with the theology of Thomas Aquinas, cathedrals such as Chartres, and Dante's *Divine Comedy*. That is to say, Christ is recognized as the fulfillment of the culture's aspirations and yet he is not identified altogether with the culture: he is above culture. To put it another way, culture can lead to Christ in a preliminary way. A leap of faith is necessary, made possible by revelation from above. Depending on how one focuses attention, the emphasis in the medieval synthesis can fall either on the human scene or on the revelation of God in Christ channeled through the divine agencies of the church.

(4) There is also Christ and culture in tension. In this type, both Christ and culture are valued, but culture does not lead to Christ, even in some preliminary fashion. Rather, the opposition between them is acknowledged. The Christian must come to grips with both, obedient to the demands of the state and also to the will of God. There is no way in which this can be done without sin and error. Both realms make their demands at the same time and are often in conflict with one another. Whatever hope there is for the sinner lies beyond history where the opposition is overcome. This type is dualistic and can be found in the two-kingdoms concept of Martin

Luther and in the teachings of Roger Williams on the separation of church and state.

(5) Finally, there is the view which Niebuhr calls "Christ the Transformer of Culture." In this type the opposition between Christ and culture is recognized, yet this opposition does not lead to separation. Christ is viewed as one who transforms or converts culture. The chief example here is F. D. Maurice, concerning whom Niebuhr writes:

> In Maurice the conversionist idea is more clearly expressed than in any other modern Christian thinker and leader. His attitude toward culture is affirmative throughout, because he takes most seriously the conviction that nothing exists without the Word. It is thoroughly conversionist and never accommodating, because he is most sensitive to the perversion of human culture, as well in its religious as in its political and economic aspects. It is never dualistic; because he has cast off all ideas about the corruption of spirit through body, and about the separation of mankind into redeemed and condemned. Furthermore, he is consistent in rejecting negative action against sin; and always calls for positive, confessional, God-oriented practice in church and community.[13]

The conversion theme is also strong in the Gospel of John, which Maurice so admired, and in the writings of St. Augustine of Hippo.

Insofar as we are here considering types which emerge from the careful study of the relation between Christ and culture, there is no wish to assert preferences in any dogmatic fashion. But insofar as we are at the same time considering strategies for the church we shall be forced to choose a type or some combination of types. Niebuhr seems to prefer the type associated with the words "conversion" and "transformation" and identified with Augustine, Maurice, and the Gospel of John. As a profound theologian greatly influenced by the discipline of Christian ethics, Niebuhr checks himself, however, with the knowledge that the truth is in the midst of the types, in the dialogue, or interaction of those who pursue differing visions.

We must keep all of this in mind as we proceed to explore

church-state relations through history. The relations of church and state at various turning points must not be isolated from the larger concern of the relation between Christ and culture, with all that it involves. The condition of the church and the nature of the state at different times must be taken into account. Differing views of reality affect human understanding. Within the limits of space established here, we cannot do all that we ought to do. In truth we should be considering, alongside church-state relations, the relation between Christ and culture in terms of art, music, and literature, modes of thought, world views, life-styles, and much else. But church-state relations illuminate the larger subject and parallel matters. Church-state relations are important in history and have a bearing upon us in the present.

For the sake of clarity, we shall be considering church-state relations with a pattern in mind: (1) The age of persecution and martyrdom when church and state stood in opposition to each other (up to A.D. 311); (2) the age of Constantine and after, when the Roman Emperors sought to dominate the church (up to the sixth century and the Emperor Justinian); (3) the so-called Middle Ages, when the hierarchical view of culture buttressed by papal theory led to the uneasy domination of the states of Western Europe by the church (up to Pope Boniface VIII and 1305); (4) the time of the Renaissance and Reformation when princes of the new nation states asserted their domination, not without opposition (up to the Peace of Westphalia in 1648); and (5) the times from Westphalia to the near present. This last will command attention out of proportion to the rest and will concern the rejection of the claims of the church by the state, accompanied at different times by persecution, indifference, or absorption into the general ethos. Finally (6), we shall end confronting our own times, the problem of secularism and the nature of the Christian witness in this post-Christian, scientific/technological age.

The pattern is cyclical: rejection, domination by state, domination by church, domination by state, rejection. But this is deceiving, for in any of the periods listed above we can find a complex pattern of interactions between two or more of the types described by Niebuhr. Furthermore, the stage upon which the human drama occurs moves, shifting and changing, into the future. Thus the opposition between church and state in the time preceding Constantine takes place against a background never to be repeated, making the similar rejection of the church by the state in our day different in many important ways. With these words of caution we turn now to consider church and state through history.

Persecution and Martyrdom: The First Phase in Church-State Relations

In the year 202 a group of those who confessed the name of Christ were slain in the amphitheater at Carthage in Africa. They went to their deaths, so the eyewitness account tells us, rejoicing that they were privileged to follow their Savior in his sufferings. Enthusiastic converts, in training for full membership in the church, Perpetua and her companions, the slaves Felicitas and Revocatus, together with Saturninus, Secundus, and somewhat later Saturus, were seized by the authorities and thrown into prison to await trial. Vibia Perpetua was the mother of an infant child. Felicitas was in an advanced stage of pregnancy. Perpetua's father, who did not share her faith in Christ, pled with her to consider her folly and save her life. It was at the trial before Hilarian, procurator of the province, that her father made a final, desperate attempt. Perpetua tells us, in her diary:

> All who were interrogated before me confessed boldly Jesus Christ. When it came to my turn, my father instantly appeared with my infant. He drew me a little aside, conjuring in the most tender manner not to be insensible to the misery I should bring on that innocent creature to which I had given life. The president Hilarian joined with my father, and said: "What! will neither the gray hairs of a father you are going to make miserable, nor the tender innocence of a child, which your death will leave an orphan, move you? Sacrifice for the prosperity of the emperor." I replied, "I will not do it." "Are you then a Christian?" said Hilarian. I answered: "Yes, I am."[14]

The father then attempted to seize his daughter, but Hilarian had him beaten off and pronounced the sentence of death.

Thus Perpetua rejected idolatry and followed her Lord in his passion and death, herself a sacrifice showing to all who have eyes to see, the way, the truth, the life.

For over a century officials of the Roman Empire had been struggling to understand the Christians and to devise some way of accommodating them. Regarded by many as a desperate faction, composed of credulous women and the scum of Roman society, they were said to interfere with the established order of society, disrupting families, opposing popular amusements, refusing to participate in ordinary religious observances, avoiding military service, and seemingly averse to public office. Furthermore, they held secret meetings at night, where, according to rumor, the basest lusts were exercised, incest practiced, infant children slain, their flesh eaten, their blood consumed. They were, some said, dangerous to the state, guilty of sacrilege, worshipers of the sun, bearing the name of a common criminal who had been crucified.

It was largely on the basis of such rumors and the popular outcry they aroused that the Christians were brought to the attention of the officials. These officials, in turn, were compelled to correct every public offense. The usual procedure was quite simple. No investigation was made of the charges, but the accused were given the opportunity to renounce the name, Christian, and to sacrifice to the Roman gods for the prosperity of the emperor. This would be sufficient to prove that they were not enemies of the state. If they refused, justice was administered quickly.

An insight into the official attitude is to be found in a letter of the Emperor Trajan to the governor of the province of Bithynia in the year 112. This governor, Pliny the Younger, had written for advice, having reported that he asked the accused if they were Christians and, when necessary, had put the question three times. If they confessed that they were Christians, he sentenced them to death, if only on account of their obstinacy and perversity. Trajan replied:

> You have adopted the proper course . . . in your examination of the cases of those who were accused to you as Christians, for indeed nothing can be laid down as a general ruling involving something like a set form of procedure. They are not to be

sought out; but if they are accused and convicted, they must be punished—yet on this condition, that whoso denies himself to be a Christian, and makes the fact plain by his action, that is by worshipping our gods, shall obtain pardon on his repentance, however suspicious his past conduct may be.[15]

Defenders of the faith, such as Justin Martyr, protested against the false accusations and against being tried not on the truth or falsity of the accusations but on the confession of the name alone. In spite of their protestations, however, the Christians were at odds with the empire. We have noted how their self-understanding as a new people set them apart. They did, in fact, refuse to participate in the worship of the gods and to make sacrifices before the statue of the emperor. They might attempt to reconcile the teachings of Plato with those of Scripture, but they seemingly could not reconcile the worship of the one true God with the worship of the empire. In this they were identified with the Jews, who had long held a special exemption on account of their national religion. The Christians could claim no such privilege.

Church and state thus stood opposed and their opposition was marked by widely scattered persecutions. We have seen in the letters of Ignatius of Antioch how one Christian went to his death rejoicing in the opportunity to be a witness to Christ with his life. As the numbers of Christians increased, the confession of the name became more widespread. The pressures to renounce the name also grew and some did indeed renounce Christ and make sacrifices to the gods. But a great many became confessors and martyrs, going to their deaths crying out "I am a Christian!" The picture of Perpetua enduring the attacks of a "wild cow" and the clumsy thrusts of a gladiator's sword in a kind of ecstasy, as though Heaven had already opened up to admit her, was to Augustine and others a sign of her victory over Satan and all his furies. The result of persecution was not the defeat of the church and its gradual disappearance, but rather its victory and continuing growth. The latter was due in part to the witness of the martyrs. Their steadfastness and courage worked on the hearts and minds of many who were at first bitterly set against them. They did not behave like criminals or traitors. Tertullian pointed out that the behavior of the Christians revealed no guilt or shame. "If he is denounced (as a Christian), he glories in it; if he is accused, he does not defend himself; when he is questioned, he confesses without any pressure; when he is condemned, he renders thanks."[16] To some, such behavior would be evidence of insanity, but to others it was proof of the authenticity of the Christian faith. The blood of the martyrs was indeed the seed of the church.

The turning point in the course of persecution occurred about the time of the Emperor Maximinus Thrax in A.D. 235. The empire was in the throes of a military and economic crisis and, in an effort to consolidate his control, the new emperor ruled with brutal force, putting to death anyone who stood in his way. In the turmoil, accompanied by such natural disasters as earthquakes in Cappadocia and Pontus, Christians became scapegoats and the persecutions intensified. In 249 the Emperor Decius assumed control and under him the first truly general persecution of Christians began. In an effort to lend support to the old religion and root out subversive elements in society, an edict was promulgated requiring all persons to appear before special officers and there to declare their allegiance to the Roman gods and to signify their belief by offering sacrifices. The Christians, refusing to comply, were quickly separated out. The church was under attack. Fabian, Bishop of Rome, was put to death on January 20, A.D. 250, to be followed by the bishops of Antioch and Jerusalem. Some, such as Cyprian of Carthage, went into hiding and escaped for the time being. Many, including some bishops, recanted their faith and made sacrifices to the gods. Those who thus lapsed and subsequently sought reentry were to pose one of the most difficult problems to the early church.

The Emperor Valerian, who came next in 257, was personally well disposed toward the Christians. He attempted to pursue a conciliatory policy, publishing an edict which ordered Christians at least to participate in the ceremonies of the official religion. The policy failed and a general persecution followed in which Cyprian was martyred. At the same time, the troubles of the empire were intensifying. There were rebellions in the army and the Persians were once more moving against the empire. Valerian led an army to stave off the invaders, was taken prisoner, and died in captivity.

After a struggle, Valerian's son seized power and decreed:

> The Emperor Caesar Publius Licinius Gallienus Pius Felix Augustus to Dionysius and Pinnas and Demetrius and other bishops. I have given order that the benefit of my bounty should be published throughout all the world, to the intent that the places of worship should be given up, and therefore you also may use the ordinance contained in my rescript, so that none may molest you. And this thing which it is within your power to accomplish has long since been conceded by me; and therefore Aurelius Quirinius, who is in charge of the Exchequer, will observe the ordinance given by me.[17]

This very formal statement issued in 261 marks another turning point and the beginning of the peace of the church. Christianity was to be a legally allowed religious society.

There was to be a further desperate attempt to placate the Roman gods by persecuting the Christians, this under the Emperor Diocletian, from 303 to 305. In 311 an Edict of Toleration was issued by the Emperor of the East, Galerius, and in 313 the so-called Edict of Milan was issued. By this latter act the Co-Emperors Constantine and Licinius agreed to allow the Christians complete freedom to practice their religion. This did not mean that all persecution ceased or that all emperors were tolerant or favorably inclined toward the Christians. The Emperor Julian sought to restore paganism, to displace Jesus with Helios. But the age of persecutions was at an end and the progress of Christianity was begun and assured—it grew from being an allowed religion in 261, to becoming a privileged religion under the Emperor Constantine, a professed Christian, to being acknowledged as *the* religion of the empire by the Emperor Theodosius I by 381.

From Constantine to Justinian: Imperial Control of the Church

The end of the age of persecutions came with the conversion of the Emperor Constantine at the Battle of Milvian Bridge in 312 and the Edict of Toleration promulgated by Constantine and Licinius in 313. These events were understood by the Christians to be directed by God. The Emperor Constantine, who was sole emperor by 325, was revered by Christians. Eusebius, Bishop of Caesarea, wrote just before Constantine's death in 325:

> The only begotten Word of God reigns, from ages which had no beginning, to infinite and endless ages, the partner of his Father's kingdom. And our emperor ever beloved by him, who derives the source of imperial authority from above, and is strong in the power of his sacred title, has controlled the empire of the world for a long period of years.[18]

This control involved the church, for it was inconceivable that there should be any autonomy in religion.

The Eusebian view of church and state assumes their interdependence and leans toward the domination of the church by the state, or Caesaropapism. As the ruler empowered from above, Constantine viewed himself as the protector of the church. He labored on its behalf, making evident his intention to foster Christianity as the preferred religion of the empire. Laws were decreed for the observance of Sunday as a day of rest (although this might be interpreted as honoring the sun god). The church's high view of celibacy was reflected in laws alleviating hardships worked upon unmarried persons in Roman society. Gladiatorial spectacles were forbidden, although the ban was not altogether effective. Divorce was made more difficult and could be punished by exile. Constantine built Christian churches, the greatest being the Church of the Holy Sepulchre in Jerusalem, the most notable being the Church of St. Peter in Rome. At Constantinople, the New Rome, he built churches dedicated to the Apostles and to Peace. Constantine dabbled in theology and intervened in theological disputes. He called into being the Council of Nicaea in 325, presiding over it and evidently participating in its deliberations. To his mind bishops were commissioned to care for the inner life of the church while he was a bishop to care for its external affairs. He was not always inclined to limit his authority, however. More than once he intervened in the internal affairs of the Christian community.

This he did when he felt that the internal squabbles of the church jeopardized the peace and security of the empire. If the Christian church was to be of the greatest assistance to the empire it must be united itself. Thus, to be a conscientious and effective ruler, Constantine must exercise dominion over the church as over a very important element of the entire society.

The Eusebian adulation of the emperor as divinely appointed was not shared by everyone. Chief amongst the early protestors was Athanasius of Alexandria in Egypt, a staunch defender of the Nicene faith. Athanasius began as an enthusiastic supporter of Constantine, viewing him as God's representative. As time passed and the violent disputes concerning the Trinity proceeded, Athanasius became distressed. Constantine, and then his son Constantius, appeared to support the heretics. At first he blamed the emperor's advisors, but by 358 he called the Arian Constantius the forerunner of Antichrist, or the image of Antichrist.

Athanasius, through numerous periods of exile, became the champion of the church's freedom. In his *History of the Arians*, he wrote:

> Where is there a canon [law] that a bishop should be appointed from court? Where is there a canon which permits soldiers to invade churches? What tradition is there allowing counts and ignorant eunuchs to exercise authority in ecclesiastical matters? . . . When did a judgement of the church receive its validity from the emperor, or when was his decree ever recognized by the church? There have been many councils, and many judgements passed by the church; but the fathers never sought the consent of the emperor thereto, nor did the emperor busy himself with the affairs of the church. The Apostle Paul had friends among them of Caesar's household . . . but he never took them as his associates in ecclesiastical judgements. . . . Where is there now a church which enjoys the privilege of worshipping Christ freely?[19]

Athanasius was not altogether accurate in his protest, but his outburst was expressive of his general perception. The church was in danger of losing its freedom. It was in danger of being altogether dominated by the emperor and his minions. Its policies and activities, its teachings and its liturgy were in danger of being influenced more by political necessities and whims than by the Gospel.

Athanasius was not alone. Liberius, bishop of Rome, was his staunch defender against the imperial court. Hosius, bishop of Cordoba in Spain, who was present at the Council of Nicaea as Constantine's ecclesiastical advisor, accepted the dualistic theory, along with a growing number of the church's leaders. He addressed Constantine in this manner:

> Remember that you are a mortal man. Fear the day of judgment. Do your best to appear there pure and without blame. Do not interfere in ecclesiastical affairs. Issue no commands about them. Learn rather from us what you ought to believe. God has given you the government of the Empire, and to us that of the church. Whoever dares to attack our authority is setting himself against the divine order.[20]

The classic instance of the collision of two widely different viewpoints is that involving the Emperor Theodosius I and Ambrose, bishop of Milan. In 388 a Christian mob at the town of Callinicum in the East went on a rampage during which a Jewish synagogue and a Gnostic church were destroyed. The Jews being under the protection of the empire, Theodosius felt that he must retaliate. He ordered the Christians to restore the synagogue. This they felt they could not do, for it was forbidden to them to contribute toward the erection of a building for a false religion. Ambrose supported the Christians, and when the emperor was present at the Eucharist, the bishop directed his sermon against him, declaring that he could not proceed to offer the sacrifice of the Eucharist until the emperor rescinded his order. The emperor complied. In 390 the imperial commander, Botheric, executed a man in Thessalonica for a crime which the people did not believe warranted so extreme a penalty. Botheric was murdered by a mob. Theodosius ordered a general massacre of those guilty. It is said that seven thousand people died at the hands of the soldiers. We cannot be absolutely certain as to what transpired then. One account tells of how the emperor, having absented himself from the church for months, tried to enter it on Christmas Day. He was met by Ambrose who refused him admission, not allowing him to be present at the Eucharist until he had done penance and had enacted a law ordering that no felon should be put to death until thirty days after sentence had been pronounced. From Ambrose we have assurance that the emperor did penance.

Theodosius, who did much to enforce the faith of the Nicene Creed and to suppress paganism, strove in a time of great disruption to establish and maintain a unified society, the central pillar of which was to be the orthodox Christian faith. To achieve this aim, the emperor, of necessity, exerted authority in and over the church. It was inconceivable to him as emperor that the religion of the empire should be independent of imperial power. Ambrose, on the other hand, was concerned to vindicate the autonomy of the church. By autonomy he meant the right of the church as a corporate body to self-determination, and the freedom of its ministers as representatives of the church to speak and act as they deemed necessary. This could be costly, but Ambrose recognized the corrupting effects of public endowment or government subsidies. The church was increasing in wealth due to imperial favor, but in accepting such favor it was indebted to the emperor and was allowing itself to be treated on a level with the pagan sects. Ambrose disdained the jeopardized wealth, saying: "The wealth of the church is what it spends on the poor."[21] Freed of its bondage to the state, the church could fulfill its prophetic role, reminding the people that the state is not absolute, is prone to corruption, and must be reformed.

Ambrose has been identified with the Augustinian view of the church as a higher and independent society by comparison to the state, while Theodosius is identified with the Eusebian view involving imperial control of the church. Ambrose is thus in line with the development of church and state in the West, while Theodosius is in the tradition which developed and persisted in the East. Concerning the latter, the Emperor Justinian is especially important. Justinian became emperor in 527, the last Roman to occupy the Eastern throne. Ruling over almost the entire Mediterranean area, he was confronted by immense problems. The empire was divided politically. The barbarians, those nomadic people who swept down upon Roman civilization and settled down, ruled much of the West. The empire was also divided religiously between those adhering to the faith, as defined at Chalcedon in 451, and other significant Christian groups which stood in opposition to that faith. Justinian addressed himself to political disunity, crushing the Vandal kingdom in North Africa in 533, wresting Southeast Spain from the Visigoths, and defeating the Ostrogoths in central Italy in 553. These victories were costly chiefly in terms of the weakening of the defense of the empire in the East. The Persians, taking advantage of Justinian's preoccupation with the barbarians in the West, pillaged Antioch in 540 and forced a humiliating treaty on the Emperor in 562. In spite of setbacks, Justinian did much to reunite and strengthen the old Roman Empire. There was reform and consolidation of Roman Law in the Justinian Code; reorganization of justice; building of roads, aqueducts, and fortresses to defend the empire on its frontiers.

Justinian pursued his secular aims ever conscious of the divine source of his imperial authority. His pursuit of unity was holy. That unity was to be grounded in the one, true, Christian faith. Indeed, that faith constituted the theory of empire for Justinian. With such a conviction, he renewed his attack on the pagans, depriving them of the right to teach and closing the famed Academy in Athens in 529. He also intervened in the church's internal affairs, siding with the orthodox (those accepting the decisions of the first four General Councils) while seeking to reconcile the heretics, some of whom had the support of his consort, Theodora. He was not altogether successful in his aim to restore unity to the church. The disagreements among Christians were deep and persistent.

Justinian exercised his authority over the church with vigor. Popes and patriarchs he regarded as his servants. In matters of belief and ritual, final decisions rested with the emperor. He wrote theological treatises, composed hymns, and summoned councils of bishops. He sent edicts out to instruct patriarchs, or bishops of the chief sees, including those of Rome and Constantinople. In the East the patriarchs were nominated by the government and elected by the church. In the West, Romans elected the pope but the elections had to be ratified by the emperor.

All of this is difficult to comprehend without some understanding of the relationship which was believed to exist between God and the emperor. The old Hellenistic view of the emperor as divine could not be countenanced. Nevertheless, he was regarded as divinely appointed to be God's representative on earth. There was one God, thus there was one emperor who would in the fullness of time enjoy dominion over the entire world. The rights and responsibilities of the emperor were defined in biblical terms; for instance, comparing him with St. Peter. Justinian himself wrote: "Since God handed over to us the sovereignty of the Empire, as was His good pleasure he also . . . commanded us, as He commanded Peter the supreme head of the apostles, to feed His most faithful flock."[22] The Eastern view of church and state is summarized in the life, deeds, and writings of the Emperor Justinian.

The Middle Ages: Church above State in a Hierarchical Society

There were two different views of church-state relationships during the Middle Ages, attached to two different theories of government. There was (1) the Descending theory of government, very much a part of the hierarchical world view, associated with the teachings of St. Augustine of Hippo, and reaching its most extreme formulation with Pope Boniface VIII in his papal bull or decree of 1302, *Unam Sanctam*. This theory was based on the assumption that all power is lodged in one supreme being. From this source of power all other powers are derived and proceed down through a God-given hierarchy from the powerful leaders of society to the most humble peasant. Add to this the conviction that the emperor stands at the pinnacle of earthly power, appointed by God to be the channel of authority to all the earth, and we have the

Eusebian view of church and state exemplified by Justinian in the sixth century. But with the assertion that all earthly power was transmitted by God through Christ to Peter and from Peter to the bishops of Rome, there is quite another view. It is in fact the view which papal theorists, including some popes, sought to promulgate. This papal doctrine, in process of formation from the time of Leo I in the fifth century, assumes that the church is one and that there is no salvation outside it. Its oneness is postulated on the assertion that there is one Lord, one faith, one Baptism. Pope Boniface put it this way:

> Of this one and only Church there is one body and one head—not two heads, like a monster—namely Christ, and Christ's vicar is Peter, and Peter's successor, for the Lord said to Peter himself, "Feed my sheep."[23]

Furthermore, there are lodged in this one church the "two swords, the spiritual and the temporal," and thus "he who denies that the temporal sword is in the power of Peter, misunderstands the words of the Lord, 'Put up your sword into its sheath.'" Both swords are thus lodged in the pope, but only the one, the sacred, is wielded by him. The other or temporal sword is to be wielded on behalf of the church "by captains and kings but at the will and by the permission of the priest."

There was also (2) the Ascending theory of government which assumed that all power was derived from below, that is from the base of the hierarchical pyramid or from the people at large. This view came into vogue in some quarters as a result of the rediscovery of Aristotle in the twelfth century, and in particular his *Politics* and *Ethics*. Thus the state originated from nature for the most practical reasons, as individuals combined in families, families banded together into cities, and cities into nations. In the later Middle Ages, the Ascending theory found expression in the teachings of Marsiglio of Padua, whose most influential work, *The Defender of the Peace,* appeared in 1324. He found no evidence to prove that God had created any human government. The state was thus to be viewed as autonomous and the sacred and the temporal were found to be completely separate. We shall encounter this theory again, for in some ways it is the basis for the modern understanding of church and state.

Finally, there was (3) the Mediating theory of government; mediating, that is, between the Descending and Ascending theories. The chief figure here is Thomas Aquinas (1225–1274), one of the greatest of the medieval theologians. According to Thomas, nature is potentially good. But because it aims at fulfillment beyond itself in the divine, it requires something beyond that which it already possesses in order that it may be truly good and complete. Just as the human being has body and soul, with the soul providing the necessary motivating force, so human society has an earthly existence and subsequently a heavenly. At the beginning the community exists to care for the material or temporal requirements of people. Thomas accepts Aristotle's dictum concerning the basis of government in the human necessity for community. But the ultimate end of earthly community is heavenly beatitude. Civil government is therefore potential and unfinished. It is the spiritual government instituted by Christ and held by Peter and his successors, the popes of Rome, which alone can guide human beings and governments beyond their earthly limits. Papal government perfects civil government, making actual that which is potential in the natural order, and realizing the fulfillment toward which all earthly things drive. That this view was incapable of holding in abeyance the Ascending theory of government, with its logical conclusions concerning the autonomy of the natural state, is evident from the knowledge we have of subsequent history. But here, as in other areas of human concern, Thomas demonstrated his amazing ability to comprehend widely different points of view.

We are chiefly concerned in this section with the first of the three views, the Descending theory of government, hierarchical in nature, assuming the fullness of power under God to be lodged in the popes of Rome. We are concerned for this theory now as we witness the growth of papal power, rooted in theory and exercised through particular events. This consideration is accompanied by the knowledge that throughout the years from 800 to 1300 there were recurrent clashes between representatives of temporal and ecclesiastical power. The struggles were not concerned with differing views of reality. There was no view as yet of the autonomy of church and state, sacred and secular. The distinctions between the two began to be made toward the end of the Middle Ages and are fundamentally "modern." The struggle, given the Descending theory of government and the hierarchical view of the universe, concerned who should govern and what the proper relationship should be between those empowered to govern.

The historical pattern begins with the coronation of Charlemagne on Christmas Day, 800. On that day at St. Peter's in Rome, Pope Leo III crowned Charlemagne, already King of the Franks, as Emperor of the Romans. According to Einhard, the Dwarfling, Charlemagne exclaimed as he left the church, "If I had known what Leo meant to do I would never have set foot in this church, even on this holy day."[24] It had been Charlemagne's intention to take the crown, placing it on his own head with his own hands. Instead, Leo seized it and did the deed. The newly crowned emperor, an adherent of the Eusebian view of church and state, saw himself as another Justinian, in whom imperial and priestly powers were united. Responsive to the divine will, he supervised the day-to-day activities of the church in his lands, called councils, and took an active part in doctrinal controversies. Leo III, on the other hand, viewed the Roman Church as the head of the Christian universe which creates through the pope a universal protector, the emperor of the Romans. This being the case, Charlemagne could not rightly "control" the church.

The struggle continued for control of the church through the long investiture controversy, to which reference has been made. Investiture involved the appointment of ecclesiastical officials, bishops and others, who ruled as feudal lords and whose lands and arms were of vital importance to the civil rulers. The question was whether these appointments should be made by civil authorities or by ecclesiastical. The controversy was but one ingredient in the church-state struggle, however. There was also the need for reform of a morally corrupt ecclesiastical hierarchy, which paved the way for the German emperors to assert authority over the church.

Henry III (1039–1056), Holy Roman Emperor, had good cause to exercise his claim to being able to depose popes, being confronted as he was by the depraved Benedict IX. It was then that Pope Gregory VII, Hildebrand, came onto the scene, further developing papal theory, reforming the church, exerting his command over the entire church in the West, issuing a decree against lay investiture, and finally challenging the authority of the emperor. Hildebrand excommunicated Emperor Henry IV (1056–1106). Having done so, the pope traveled north from Rome to attend a council of German nobles at Augsburg in 1077. On his way he stopped at Canossa. The emperor, realizing that his noblemen were deserting him, arrived at Canossa and for three days stood in the snow, seemingly humiliated and defeated, pleading for mercy. Hildebrand viewed the event as a victory, vindicating his policy against lay investiture and buttressing his claims to power, including the power to depose emperors. The pope viewed society as the body of Christ of which the church is the soul and the temporal realm the body. There was no question as to which rightly ruled the other. In fact, Canossa was no victory for Hildebrand. What happened at that time worked to the emperor's advantage. In 1081 Henry invaded Italy and forced the pope into exile where he died in 1085. The struggle continued.

The investiture controversy came to an end, technically, at Worms in 1122 with an agreement by which the rights of investiture were to be shared, with the papacy seemingly gaining the upper hand. But then, too, the agreement meant little to Emperor Frederick "Barbarossa" (1152–1190), who sought to emulate Charlemagne and declared: "Since by Divine Providence I call myself and am Emperor of the Romans, I have but the shadow of power unless I govern Rome."[25]

In 1198 Lothair of Segni, Innocent III, ascended Peter's throne. At his consecration he said:

> Only St. Peter was invested with the plenitude of power. See
> then what manner of servant this is, appointed over the house-
> hold [God's household]; he is the vicar of Jesus Christ, the suc-
> cessor of Peter, the Lord's anointed . . . set in the midst be-
> tween man and God . . . less than God but greater than man,
> judge of all men and judged by none.[26]

In the second chapter we considered something of the basis
for this claim, and something of the result which accrued to
the great benefit of the medieval church. Here we must be
reminded of the extent to which Innocent was able to carry
out his claims in the day-to-day world. One example concerns his treatment of King John of England. There had been
a dispute over the election of the archbishop of Canterbury.
The monks elected someone without consulting the king. The
king nominated another man of his own choosing. The pope
then chose a third man, Stephen Langton, without consulting
the king. King John wrote in anger to the pope and Innocent
replied in a mild tone of self-confidence, defending his action
and informing the king that he was determined to proceed
with the matter "for in the end He must win, 'to whom every
knee bows, of things in heaven, and things in earth, and
things under the earth,' whose power, however unworthily,
we as Vicar exercise on earth."[27]

Langton was consecrated in 1207 but John refused to recognize him as archbishop. In 1208 Innocent placed England
under interdict, involving the suspension of all ecclesiastical
rites. Services in the churches ceased. Burials were per-
functory. Marriages were not solemnized in the churches.
Baptism took place behind locked doors. Sermons could only
be preached on Sundays and then only outside the church.
King John pretended not to be concerned, but then began to
seize church property. In 1209 Innocent threatened to excommunicate King John and efforts were made to depose
him. King Philip of France prepared an invasion in 1212. The
next year King John capitulated, surrendering the realm of
England into the hands of the pope, to receive it back again
as a fief. Innocent then wrote to his vassal:

> Lo! You now hold your kingdoms by a more exalted and surer
> title than before, for the kingdom is become a royal priesthood

and the priesthood a kingdom of priests as stated by Peter in the epistle and Moses in the law.[28]

It is of course true that future kings of England would not regard their land as a fiefdom held from the pope. Once again the subsequent historical events prove how impossible it was for the papacy to put into practice that which it held in theory. The struggle continued. The final scene involves Pope Boniface VIII, who in his *Unam Sanctam* set forth the Descending theory of government with the most extreme claims for papal power. At the time the pope was engaged in a bitter contest with Philip IV of France (1285–1314) and Edward I of England (1272–1307). Both monarchs had attempted to raise funds from their clergy for war against the Duchy of Gascony. Boniface forbade the clergy of any nation to pay taxes to the civil government without permission of the pope. For a time, confronted by an enraged King Philip, the pope backed down, but then he issued the *Unam Sanctam* and followed this in 1303 with a threat to excommunicate Philip. It was then that Philip struck. False charges were made against the pope: he was a heretic, a sorcerer, a prisoner of ecclesiastical officials, and he kept mistresses to conceal the fact that he was a homosexual. One of the pope's greatest foes, Sciara Colonna, was enlisted, and a band of men was recruited in the vicinity of Rome. They marched to Anagni where the pope resided, seized and humiliated him. The French king, who was constantly abridging the rights of the church, seemed victorious. Having captured the pope, he retained the papacy under his control. For seventy-two years the seat of the pope was not at Rome but at Avignon, under the "protection" of the French monarch. A new age was dawning.

Beneath the play of events involving kings and popes, the medieval vision of the organic unity of all society was being realized to varying degrees. This vision informed the governmental theories of kings and popes, and also the art and architecture, philosophy and theology, liturgy and spirituality of the times. Few understood the vision as fully as Ailred (?1109–1167), abbot of the Cistercian monastery of Rievaulx. In the north of England Ailred ruled over 650 monks gathered from all parts of the world, a mixed lot drawn from virtually every vocation, including laborers who worked the monastery fields. In part they were drawn to Rievaulx by the kindness and compassion of its abbot. In part they were attracted by the community which he nourished there. The monastery was meant to realize as nearly as could be on earth the beatitude of that community which is the Blessed Trinity.

At the heart of all there is Love, who "by unswerving and unfathomable transcendence of its presence, controls, enfolds, penetrates all things, uniting them no matter how they differ . . . giving each a share in assured peace." It is God's intention "that all creation should be at one and in peace, reflecting, though faintly, the unity of the sovereignly absolute Being. Hence nothing has been left in isolation."[29] Community is thus both a natural instinct and God's will. The religious, monks and nuns, learn through that community which is the monastery to fulfill a natural instinct and to obey God's will. They do this not only for themselves but preeminently for others, demonstrating, for the sake of those outside, the truth of both human instinct and divine will. More than that, Ailred gave over to his monks the care of all people:

> Take the whole world to your loving heart. Think of honest folk and rejoice; of the wicked and grieve. Pity those in any way afflicted and depressed: the wretched poor, the lonely orphan, the helpless widow, the unsuccored mourner, the homeless vagrant, the discontented maiden; the peril of those at sea, the temptations of the monks. . . .[30]

Contemporary witnesses testify to the high degree to which Ailred succeeded at Rievaulx in achieving that unity and solidarity of all people which was the aim of medieval theorists and politicians, kings and popes. A newcomer to Rievaulx was reported to say:

> So great is the community and unanimity of the brethren that no one seems to have anything of his own, while each one seems to own the whole place. What strikes me most favorably is that there are no preferences; high birth does not count. The needs and infirmities of individuals are the only sources of difference and exception.[31]

The study of church-state relationships is deficient when it ignores the Ailreds of history.

Renaissance and Reformation: The Age of Royal Supremacy

The fourteenth and fifteenth centuries in western Europe are characterized by two persistent movements. One is the loss of power and prestige on the part of the papacy. In terms of power, the control of the papacy by the French kings through much of the fourteenth century, and the subsequent papal schism when there were two and then three popes where there could be but one, were signs of decline. In terms of prestige, the emergence of the Conciliarists with their application of the Ascending theory of government to the church undercut papal claims. Conciliarism involved attempts at solving the papal schism (1378–1417) based on the assumption that a general council of the church was superior to any pope, and that sovereign power was located in the holy community, exercised through a representative body, the general council. The pope and the curia were regarded as the executive arms of the body. Conciliarism did not altogether succeed in the achievement of its aims. The papacy rebounded once the schism was repaired. An important example is to be found in Pope Pius II, Aeneas Sylvius Piccolomini, a former liberal humanist and conciliar theorist who in 1460 pronounced as heretical all appeals to a general council. Papal monarchy was restored, but great damage had been done and ideas set loose which would not die.

The second movement has been described as the emergence of the new nation states. It is necessary to exercise some caution here, for the situation in Europe was not everywhere the same. The political realities differed greatly from the Germanies to the Swiss Cantons, to the Italian city-states, and to the monarchies of France, England, and Spain. Each case needs to be considered. But having given this warning, it is also possible to observe from the latter part of the thirteenth century on, the several factors which contribute in the end to the emergence of the autonomous and absolute secular state. The bubonic plague, the Black Death, diminished population in most parts of Europe by one third during the two centuries following its outbreak in 1348, disrupting society. Feudalism was disintegrating while a new middle class of merchants, industrialists, bankers, and skilled artisans was forming. They were situated in commercial towns and looked to the central government for protection against the aristocracy, highwaymen, and the like.

More important in some ways were the changes in human perception and feeling. The rise of the new nation states was associated with the growth of national sentiment, involving the development of a common national language and literature. The state as a body politic, with a life beyond the lives of the individuals who compose it, requiring the suspension of private conscience when the welfare of the nation demands it, was discovered at this time. During the Middle Ages the word "state" referred to the duties and privileges of a prince, or the "estate" of kings. The word was also used in relation to the "status" or condition of something. Niccolo Machiavelli (1469–1527) was one of the first to use the word "state" as we have been using it in considering church and state. He was one of the first to justify anything, whether criminal, immoral, or cruel, which a ruler might do, not for himself but for the sake of the common good, the good of the state. Thus the concept of Christendom, involving all of Europe, all peoples under the leadership of pope and emperor, began to wane and to be displaced by the concept of the nation state.

The force of this change was apparent in England where, after the distresses of the Wars of the Roses a strong monarchy was established by the Tudor monarchs, beginning in 1485 with King Henry VII. During the time of Henry VIII events both contributed to the strengthening of royal power and qualified its use. The severance of ties between England and the Church of Rome was at least in part a political event. It made possible the realization of the doctrine of royal supremacy over the church as well as the commonwealth. There was *one* ruler in England over all estates of the realm, including the clergy. In relation to the clergy, he was acknowledged to be their protector and supreme head, although initially the clergy added "so far as the law of Christ allows." But most important of all, the monarch was becoming the personal embodiment of the nation. Anointed under God to rule as a David, a Constantine, a Justinian, the King of England was, to use Pope Innocent III's words, "less than God but greater than man." Queen Elizabeth was surrounded by a royal mystique. She was England's Judith, Deborah, Diana, Eliza, sent by God to bring prosperity to her people and to protect them from their enemies. She represented the symbol of the nation who referred to herself as "mere English" and in her Golden Speech of 1601, nearing the end of her life, spoke of being made queen by God that she might be God's "instrument to preserve you from every peril, dishonour, shame, tyranny and oppression."[32] The Queen as the symbol of unity, was the guarantor of the wholeness and prosperity of all the diverse estates composing the nation. Church and state (or commonwealth) are one, thus, under the godly and beneficent rule of the queen, striving together for the good of the commonwealth, the entire people of England.

There were many who labored this theme during the sixteenth century in England. None is more interesting than Richard Hooker, best known as the author of one of the most important books of the Elizabethan Age, *Of the Laws of Ecclesiastical Polity* (1593, 1597). Book VIII of this work was published posthumously and has thus been the cause of considerable scholarly concern over the years. In it Hooker deals with royal supremacy. It is evident that he places a major emphasis on the matter of unity, the unity of a national people. He is also concerned to avoid the disunity which comes from differentiating too strongly between church and state as both Roman Catholics and Puritans tend to do. Thus he writes:

our estate is according to the pattern of God's own ancient elect people, which people was not part of them the commonwealth [state], and part of them the Church of God, but the selfsame people whole and entire under one chief Governor, on whose supreme authority they did all depend.[33]

It did not seem to matter from whence royal supremacy came, whether from above (Descending) or from below (Ascending). If it came from the generality of people, it was ratified by God. The governor of the nation thus rules by divine right. A major assumption here, of course, is that the inhabitants of the nation are all Christians, at least nominally.

Hooker did not espouse the absolute power of the Queen without qualifications, however. In particular royal power is qualified by law. Thus he wrote:

> Happier that people whose law is their king in the greatest things, than that whose king is himself their law. Where the king doth guide the state, and the law the king, that commonwealth is like an harp or melodious instrument, the strings whereof are tuned and handled all by one, following as laws the rules and canons of muscial science.[34]

Such an elevation of law above the king would not be pleasing to the most avid defenders of royal supremacy, nor to James I who is reported to have said, "I am above the law. I am the law." For the general thrust was toward the absolute power of the national state and the unqualified sovereignty of the royal personage who ruled by divine right. Much of the history of the West from the sixteenth century on concerns the contest between those who assert royal power by divine right and those who oppose it. The revolutions which resulted from the struggles opposed royal power with a brand of nationalism that had no room for a king. Some counteracted royal sovereignty with liberal or democratic forms of government. Others, despairing of any other solutions, fled into anarchy.

There were, of course, those in sixteenth-century England who did not support royal supremacy. There were Roman Catholics and Calvinist Puritans who resisted submission to the king. In the name of papal supremacy, the Roman Catholic Church encouraged Catholic Spain to attack England. In 1588 the Spanish Armada was defeated but the political and theological reasons for it continued. Thomas Cartwright (1535–1603), a leading spokesman for the Puritan cause in the Church of England, wrote:

It is true that we ought to be obedient unto the civil magistrate which governeth the church of God in that office which is committed unto him, and according to that calling. But it must be remembered that civil magistrates must govern it according to the rules of God prescribed in his word, and that as they are nurses [caring for the commonwealth] so they be servants unto the church, and as they rule in the church so they must remember to subject themselves unto the church, to submit their sceptres, to throw down their crowns, before the church, yes, as the prophet speaketh, to lick the dust of the feet of the church.[35]

The Puritans followed the way prepared by the magisterial reformers of continental Protestantism. Both Luther and Calvin strove to ensure the independence of the church, and thus its ability to function meaningfully in relation to the state. Luther discussed his political views in the context of the two-kingdoms theory, which divided people into two classes:

the first belonged to the kingdom of God, the second to the kingdom of the world. Those belonging to the kingdom of God are all true believers in Christ and are subject to Christ. For Christ is the King and Lord in the kingdom of God . . . Now observe, these people need no secular sword or law. And if all the world were composed of real Christians, that is, true believers, no prince, king, sword, or law would be needed.[36]

But most people are not true believers. For them God provided the civil state. The two kingdoms are intrinsically different, therefore, but not opposed, for both are God's creation. There is a strong element of paradox in Luther's theory. In practice, however, German Lutheranism very much depended on the civil magistrate. Indeed the Lutheran churches became national churches, largely existing under political control. Passive obedience to the ruler was taught, although in theory Luther limited such obedience to those areas where the state operated properly. He looked upon the church as the critic of the state and justified civil disobedience in some circumstances. For Luther, church and state existed in permanent tension with one another.

John Calvin (1509–1564), the French Reformer of the Swiss canton of Geneva, was very much concerned to assure the independence of the church but in practice worked for the transformation or conversion of society as a whole. Examples are to be found in Geneva, where Calvin was dominant, and in Massachusetts where only church members were accorded the rights of citizenship. The relationship between church and state in Calvin's Geneva was very close. The church's independence was preserved in order that the civil authorities might be prevented from seizing control of the Reformation and diverting it to their own selfish interests. With the church exercising great power, at least in part through its conduct of discipline in overseeing the morals of the citizenry, Geneva was on the way toward being transformed into the Kingdom of God. That which was the ideal achieved by a few religious persons of the medieval church, was now applied to the entire population. The city became the monastery and the daily occupations of the citizens became the work of God.

It must be noted, however, that while Calvin taught passive obedience to the commands of the magistrates in Geneva, Calvinism as an international movement, confronting hostile governments in Scotland and France, and elsewhere, developed a theory of civil disobedience. It was in Scotland and in France, where the Calvinists were severely persecuted, that the distinction between church and state was greatest, mirroring the distinction in Calvin's theology between the righteous omnipotence of the sovereign God and the utter depravity of human beings. Such a distinction was capable of supporting political theories which would never have occurred to Calvin.

Finally, mention must be made of those on the left wing of the Reformation, sects extending from the Zwickau prophets and the Münsterites, to the more peaceful and moderate Schwenkfeldians and Mennonites. While it is impossible to speak of these diverse groups as of one body, it can be said that where they acknowledged that the civil ruler was ordained by God, they argued that such rulers were provided for the sake of non-Christians and not for Christians. God has concern for justice and order in the world, but the world and the church do not mix. The Christian must not participate in the civil government or benefit from it: Christians are as sheep for the slaughter.

Behind such convictions there was a general viewpoint which may be put this way: With their understanding of the Gospel as planted within each individual, these radical reformers looked to the world and saw that it did not conform to the Gospel. They looked to the church and saw, be it Roman Catholic or Protestant, that it did not conform to the example set by the church of the New Testament. This New Testament church they located not so much in the letter of the Scripture as in the spirit. They then sought to recover the true church, to establish the kingdom of God in purity. This church would be holy and righteous, acceptable to God, standing ready as the last days of earthly history approached. The urgency of the matter, a spiritual and temporal urgency, forced them to the conclusion that the world, and in particular the state, must be rejected. It is clearly no instrument of salvation. The example of the New Testament church teaches that the state has never been anything other than an impediment to Christianity. Therefore, they conclude, let us restore, reconstitute the true church, expecting and welcoming persecution and martyrdom.

There were, thus, seeds being sown, preparing the church for what was to come and was already beginning. Royal supremacy was doomed. The true prophets were the revolutionary Calvinists and the radical reformers of the left wing of the Reformation.

Christianity and the Secular State: From the 17th to the 20th Century

In 1648—after thirty years of war had laid waste the land; destroyed its economic structures; impoverished its people; marked the end of the Holy Roman Empire, its prestige and power—the Treaty of Westphalia was signed. It is widely regarded as an important symbol, the turning point between the old age and the new, the Middle Ages and the so-called Modern Era. For there at Westphalia representatives of Germany, France, and other nations, came to the conclusion that the affairs of state could no longer be discussed or settled on religious bases. The Thirty Years War had begun as a struggle between Protestant and Roman Catholic princes. It was a religious war concerned with the defence of "saving truth." But it was also a highly political war exacerbated by the religious concerns of its combatants. In 1648 it was agreed that the saving truth as held by one branch of the Christian church could not be expected to triumph over the views of other branches. Christianity seemingly could not be reunited. There would be a diversity of churches and governments would have to accommodate such ecclesiastical pluralism. Thus there would have to be toleration for the sake of the peace and prosperity of the nation states.

It is probably wrong to place too much emphasis on what came to be known as the Peace of Westphalia. One should certainly take into account the growth of toleration in broader terms. In England, for instance, where after decades of struggle in which first Anglicans, then Puritans and Separatists, and then Anglicans again sought to enforce religious uniformity and failed, the upshot was a bloodless revolution in 1688 and the passage in parliament of a Toleration Act in 1689. In England and elsewhere leaders and followers seemed to give up the struggle. Their nations were worn out. Peace was of greater value than religious or dogmatic truth. Toleration was the wisest policy. Religious indifference was both a cause and a result.

Contributing to this attitude there was the Enlightenment with its emphasis, especially in Germany and England, upon reason and nature. Religious revelation was subjected to the judgment of the most widely held societal moral standards and to that minimal religious awareness which seemed common to all. Enlightenment religion was simple, emphasizing the existence of a Supreme Deity, creator and overseer of the universe, who desired that people should worship him through their good deeds and who enforced this desire with rewards and punishments now and in the world to come. This religious expression was optimistic, emphasizing human free will, and opposing the Calvinist doctrines of depravity and predestination. It was a religion of moral behavior for whom Jesus was the supreme example. The sacraments were not highly regarded. Individuals were of greater concern than communities, although Enlightenment religion aimed at preparing better citizens for this world rather than reconciling sinners to a righteous God.

Traditional Christian faith as expressed in the ecumenical creeds and in the Thirty-Nine Articles of Religion was under attack. It is not surprising that some of the attackers believed that they were defending the church. Michel de Montaigne (1533–1592) began the process whereby universal moral principles came to displace the Ten Commandments as the measures by which human actions were judged. In politics Machievelli, as we have observed, argued that at times reasons of state required the suspension of the individual conscience; and Hugo Grotius (1583–1645) posited international law as the law of nature. In philosophy deism and pantheism displaced revealed Christian dogma. True religion was said to be reasonable, its laws apparent in nature. In natural science the theory of the classical cosmos as finite was destroyed by the discovery that the universe is infinite and self-subsisting. Moreover, this cosmos was believed to be devoid of any personal creator or sustainer. The new cosmology tended to be materialistic and mechanistic. Where in the Middle Ages the salvation of humanity was the goal, now human beings became matter in motion, God and humankind being pushed out of the center of things.

Nicholas Copernicus (1473–1543) instigated a revolution. Heretofore the earth was believed to be stationary, the unmoving center of the universe, consisting of spheres with an outer limit, all moving around the earth, which was at the center. Now Copernicus suggested:

The stations of the planets, their retrogressions and progressions, seem to be motions, not of those planets, but of the earth. And the sun is thought to possess the center of the universe; all of which things we are taught by the order of succession in which those phenomena follow each other, and by the harmony of the whole world, if we will only, as they say, look at the matter with both eyes.[37]

The revolution occurred and grew as more and more scientists and philosophers and those they influenced opened their eyes. Each new discovery in astronomy, physics, biology, anthropology, and geology required the rethinking of basic assumptions and seemed to result in the weakening of the inherited Christian tradition.

Or so it seemed. There were those who welcomed the discoveries as freeing the holy community from its enslavement to a passing culture, something which we shall have cause to consider further as we proceed. For the moment we must try to absorb the fact that this was a new age, different from any which preceded it. Traditional Christianity as expressed in the churches was no longer accepted by an increasing number of people as the basis for making large decisions, waging wars, or controlling economies. Religion was more and more a private concern. Thus dethroned, it was to be regarded by nation states in differing ways. It could be rejected, as it was in France at the time of the revolution and in Stalin's Russia. It could be absorbed or so conditioned by the culture that the line dividing Christianity from the prevailing moral values of the nation state would be blurred if not obliterated. Such was the case, to a certain extent, in Nazi Germany, and at times it has seemed to be true of the United States of America. Religion could be regarded as a parallel but separate agency operating for the good of society, as has been the case in some Western European nations and, at times, in the United States. The church itself—or perhaps we should more accurately say, the churches—could regard its function in society and in relation to the state in various ways, in part determined by the attitudes expressed by the states themselves. It could accept its independence of the state and work out its mission in a relationship characterized by tension. This is one way to describe the American solution to the problem of church and state.

The story of the pursuit of religious liberty, involving separation of church and state, in America is a forceful example of the new situation. One of the key documents in the story is Thomas Jefferson's "Bill for Establishing Religious Freedom," passed by the Virginia House of Delegates in 1785. It must be recalled that the Church of England had been established in the Virginia Colony. During the eighteenth century its privileged position was challenged by dissenting groups, principally Baptists and Presbyterians, who were eager to obtain freedom for themselves and full benefit of the civil franchise. The establishment was also challenged by the general impact of the Enlightenment with its insistence on toleration and its proclamation of a simple creed. The impulse for religious liberty was partly due to such influences, but more important were the leaders of the Virginia Colony, who were nominally members of the Church of England and of the Episcopal Church which succeeded it. These included George Mason, Thomas Jefferson, and James Madison, all powerful advocates of civil liberty and profound believers in religious liberty. James Madison (1751–1836), whose education included study of Justinian's *Institutes* and John Locke's treatises on contract, would not settle for toleration. He demanded liberty. He therefore succeeded in having the Virginia Bill of Rights of 1776 modified to read: "all men are equally entitled to the free exercise of religion, according to the dictates of conscience." From that moment his hands were on the reins as he labored for full religious freedom and the disestablishment of the Church of England in the Virginia Colony.

The Virginia Bill of Rights was significant, preceding as it did similar actions in the French Constituent Assembly, and in the federal government of the United States. Step by step events progressed toward the crucial debate in 1784–1785 over Patrick Henry's religious assessments act, requiring that taxes gathered for religious purposes be divided among the denominations. The act was defeated, with Madison leading the fight. In 1785 there was adopted Thomas Jefferson's "Bill for Establishing Religious Freedom," the passage of which was of great importance for the future. This bill did not succeed in fully separating church and state. Full separation was not achieved until 1802 when all laws relating to the privileges of the Protestant Episcopal Church were repealed. Nevertheless, Jefferson's statute and the passage of it by the Virginia House of Delegates was the crucial event leading to full separation. The pertinent section reads:

> We, the General Assembly, do enact, That no man shall be
> compelled to frequent or support any religious worship, place,
> or ministry whatsoever, nor shall be enforced, restrained,
> molested, or burthened in his body or goods, nor shall oth-
> erwise suffer, on account of his religious opinions or belief; but
> that all men shall be free to profess, and by argument to main-
> tain, their opinion in matters of religion, and that the same
> shall in no wise diminish, enlarge, or affect their civil
> capacities.

The delegates confidently asserted something which is altogether in tune with Enlightenment religion and the actual
situation in America:

> we are free to declare, and do declare, that the rights hereby
> asserted are of the natural rights of mankind, and that if any act
> shall be hereafter passed to repeal the present or to narrow its
> operation, such act will be an infringement of natural right.[38]

So it was that Virginia led the way, having considerable influence on the development of the Constitution and Bill of
Rights.

The road to the first amendment to the Constitution stating
that "Congress shall make no law respecting an establishment of religion, or prohibiting the free exercise thereof,"
was a long one, involving much discussion and debate. The
enforcement of it took longer still. For the founding fathers
were concerned for the religious disposition of the nation and
were not intentionally seeking to destroy the churches. The
resolutions of Congress concerning the Bible, the provision of
congressional chaplains, the Thanksgiving Day proclamation
of 1789, and official addresses by the President—these and
numerous other incidents serve to demonstrate the conviction of Washington, Jefferson, Madison, Adams, and others
that the new government could not succeed without the benefit of religion. The Declaration of Independence stated that
all people are "created equal" and "endowed by their Creator
with certain inalienable rights." A lively remembrance of
this fact was considered by many to be vital to the very being
of the nation. Religious occasions were to be encouraged. The
churches were to be regarded as assets to the national well

being. And yet it was not the place of government to decide matters of religious belief or practice, nor should it impose religious observances on its people. There must be provisions made to guarantee the rights of religious-minded persons to express their convictions and to engage in activities which conformed to their convictions, so long as they did not impose their views on other citizens by unjust means of coercion. The right of the people to choose that which they will believe must be protected. True religion has no need for governmental interference and, indeed, is opposed to such interference, which in the past has resulted in the distortion of the truth to suit the state's mundane purposes. Such was the trend of thought in the late eighteenth and early nineteenth centuries.

The separation of church and state, therefore, had a positive aspect and could be not only accepted but fostered by most churches. The separation could also be the source of continuous debate concerning the drawing of the line between the separate spheres of influence and responsibility. Should the state be allowed to coerce its citizens into military service which is against the dictates of a religiously informed conscience? Should the state materially assist educational institutions which serve the national purpose but are run by religious bodies? Such questions have exposed the problems and the dangers inherent in the relationship of church and state in America. This relationship has otherwise been considered beneficent and necessary.

In the meantime, the churches had to work out their relationship to the society at large. Given the separation of church and state, what should be the place of the church, or more properly churches, in the society? It is to this question and some answers to it that we turn next.

Church and Society: The Social Gospel in America

The separation of church and state in an age of secularism can result in the withdrawal or isolation of the church from the affairs of the state and of the wider society. Christianity can be regarded as a most useful therapeutic aid to individuals in the midst of the stresses and conflicts of daily life in industrial society. But insofar as the holy community is itself by definition a social entity and is sent with the Gospel into the world—to the societies of mankind—it will by necessity become involved in the affairs of the state and of the culture. Karl Barth (1896–1968), the great modern Swiss theologian, speaks of the profoundly social nature of the church and its mission:

> Service is not just one of the determinations of the being of the community [the church]. It is its being in all its functions. Nothing that is done or takes place can escape the question whether and how far within it the community serves its Lord and His work in the world, and its members serve one another by mutual liberation for participation in the service of the whole.[39]

The salvation of the individual is to be viewed in terms of the corporate life of the holy community and the social nature of the Gospel.

In realizing its vocation to the society, the church in this secular age labors under certain grave handicaps. In particular its efforts toward the realization of the Gospel in society may be met with indifference or hostility. The truth it speaks may be ignored or denied, not because it has been investigated but because it comes from the church whose proper sphere of operation is seen to be limited to dealing with individuals and families and their personal crises.

There is, however, an advantage in this age of separation of church and state, for the church now exists as differentiated from the state. With this freedom it can consider its mission to the society with candor and take its stance, now speaking against the culture, now affirming the culture, now wrestling in painful tension with the culture, now working for its transformation. History can be written and studied from this perspective, as, indeed, H. Richard Niebuhr has suggested in his book, *Christ and Culture*. We shall now turn to one example: the Social Gospel in America, its achievements and frustrations, and finally its virtual demise.

That which we call the Social Gospel was a movement, largely involving prominent clergy and laity in America from about 1865 to the 1930s. It grew out of the American religious ferment of revivalism, voluntary societies for the alleviation of the sufferings of the poor and other victims of society, and liberalism in theology. There were also nonecclesiastical influences such as the populist and progressive movements in politics and developments in the physical and social sciences, including social Darwinism and doctrinaire socialism. Liberal theology was placing great emphasis on the personality and teachings of the historical Jesus, while de-emphasizing the traditional dogmas of the church. The movement was also influenced by the Christian Socialist Movement in England and the writings of Frederick Denison Maurice.

The Social Gospel movement began in relation to ideas and events which were prominent in nineteenth-century America. There was, for instance, the "Gospel of Wealth." As elaborated by Andrew Carnegie (1835–1919), one of the great industrialists and a prominent Protestant philanthropist, the "Gospel of Wealth" was based on the conviction that the gifts of management operating in a free competition for property would assure the survival of the fittest in American society. There would be a price to pay. Many would suffer, but their suffering would be justified by the resulting general prosperity. William Lawrence (1850–1941), Bishop of Massachusetts, believed that the so-called gifts of management were the result of moral attitudes and habits and that "in the long run it is only to the man of morality that wealth comes." These men of wealth should know, as John D. Rockefeller acknowledged, that God gave them their money and that they were stewards of their wealth, responsible for deeds of charity and for the development of philanthropic enterprises. This doctrine, which associated poverty with sin, was widely taught from the pulpits of the land. Horace Bushnell (1802–1876), the prominent pastor of North Church, Hartford, Connecticut, so preached, and the social message coming through his sermons was not altogether exceptional. The "Gospel of Wealth" which provided momentum for the economic expansion of the United States, could and often did provide the rationale for social and economic injustice, for racism and sexism.

At the same time there were violent social eruptions. The Knights of Labor were organized in 1867. In 1877 there were strikes against the railroads on which all industry depended. Riots followed, with battles between strikers and police and military units. The threat of anarchy was felt after a bomb was thrown into the midst of a protest meeting in Chicago. The Homestead steel strike in 1892 resulted in pitched battles, ten deaths and at least sixty wounded. In 1894 two thousand troops were sent to guard the mails during the Pullman strike in Chicago. Violence, bloodshed, and confusion marked the American industrial scene. There were, as might be expected, conservative reactions to the upheaval. Neither the government nor big business was prepared to make concessions to the troublemakers. Injunctions were issued against labor unions. Suppression was the rule of the day. And yet it was evident to the wise that suppression would not work and that compromise was necessary.

Not all of the churches during this time of troubles condoned the "Gospel of Wealth" and its practitioners. An example of concern expressed for the poor and the laborers is to be found in the rise of the so-called institutional churches, closely allied to the foundation of the settlement and neighborhood houses. A prominent and influential figure is that of Jane Addams (1860–1935) founder of Hull House in Chicago, dedicated to helping the poor in the neighborhood. Among the institutional churches were Berkeley Temple, Boston; the Baptist Temple, Philadelphia; and the Metropolitan Temple, New York. All major denominations were involved in this work in the 1890s, but the pioneer and best example was to be found in New York, beginning in 1882, at St. George's Church, under the leadership of an Episcopal priest, William Rainsford. J. P. Morgan was St. George's senior warden, developing its philanthropic activities until by 1889 this one parish had spent well over two million dollars on the poor of New York. The parish program involved social welfare, recreation, and education. In 1906 its staff numbered thirteen full-time employees. In 1882 Rainsford explained his vision, the kind of church he wished to build:

It should be a teaching house and a dancing house; a reading house and a playing house; and because it was these, it should be a preaching house, bidding the neighborhood look for, strive for, and believe in a better manhood for a better day.[40]

The spirit expressed here was shared with the social gospelers. But the latter tended to regard the work of the institutional churches as good but not good enough, as supportive of the philanthropic side of the "Gospel of Wealth" but not dedicated sufficiently to attacking and solving the problem of society at its heart: the "Gospel of Wealth" itself.

The undergirding ideas of the Social Gospel movement stemmed from various places. Most important for us here were the theological roots. These can be found in their most profound expression in the teachings of Walter Rauschenbusch (1861–1918), the son of German immigrants, a Baptist who as a young man experienced a conversion and subsequently studied theology. At twenty-five he became the pastor of New York's German Baptist Church, a small congregation of poverty stricken people located on the edge of Hell's Kitchen, a notorious slum area. Profoundly affected by what he saw there, Rauschenbusch claimed that he experienced another conversion:

It came from outside. It came through personal contact with poverty, and when I saw how men toiled all their life long, hard toilsome lives, and at the end had almost nothing to show for it; how strong men begged for work and could not get it in hard times; how little children died—oh, the children's funerals! They gripped my heart.[41]

Through the years that followed he labored to understand the mission of the church to a society which produced such suffering. In time he developed a theology, set forth in an immensely influential book published in 1917 as *A Theology of the Social Gospel.*

Rauschenbusch began with historical analysis. The heart of Jesus' teaching was the Kingdom of God, the Kingdom which is fundamentally a fellowship of righteousness in which love and justice reign. At an early period, the Kingdom motif waned and when it ceased to be the dominating concept the church itself became the supreme good. Moral restraints were removed from the ecclesiastical realm so that the major concern was for the power of the church and its domination of the state. Without the ethical dynamic of the Kingdom motif, unjust social conditions developed and the day-to-day activities of the church were narrowly self-serving. Theology became preoccupied with issues which were either irrelevant to the Gospel or to the society the Gospel was meant to serve. Rauschenbusch spoke out boldly: "The Kingdom of God breeds prophets; the Church breeds priests and theologians."[42]

What is this Kingdom of God? It comes from God himself, initiated by Jesus Christ and carried on through the operation of the will of God. It is to be brought in the end to fulfillment by God. The Kingdom is concerned not for the preservation of doctrines or rites, but for the overcoming of resistance to its in-breaking and the achievement of its great ends. The Kingdom is both a present reality and a future possibility. It can be called the energy of God realizing itself in human life, and as such it is forever pressing in on the present, arousing immediate action, but at the same time drawing us forward, for it is always coming. Jesus is at the very heart of the Kingdom, it is his view of it which moderns must grasp and not the views of those who came before him. Then too, the Kingdom can be described as humanity organized according to the will of God. As such it tends toward a social order which will guarantee to all people their fullest, freest, and highest development. Rauschenbusch writes:

> This involves the redemption of social life from the cramping influence of religious bigotry, from the repression of self-assertion in the relation of upper and lower classes, and from all forms of slavery in which human beings are treated as mere means to serve the ends of others.[43]

This Kingdom must be the end for which the church exists. Apart from the Kingdom of God it can become an anti-Christian power. Personal salvation and the Kingdom of God must be viewed together, they must not be torn apart, as seems to have happened so often in the church. And lastly, the Kingdom is not confined to the church. It embraces all of existence. It is the transformation of the social order. Thus the church is but one organization, alongside the family, the industrial society, and the state, in which the Kingdom lives and realizes itself. This fact must be grasped by the churches.

Rauschenbusch's theology for the Social Gospel was imbued with a sense of urgency concerning the present social crisis. The appointed time had arrived. The spirit of ante-Nicene Christianity was moving again. The Kingdom was once more being perceived as a potent force which could eventuate in social reconstruction through the infant science of sociology. The goal was clearly the implementation of Jesus' teaching, the realization of love in society for which the religious symbol was the Kingdom. Rauschenbusch had a serious doctrine of human sin, but in the end his theology was optimistic, in tune with the optimism of his age. He made contact with various influential forces in American society: among them nascent sociology, belief in progress, and outrage against American capitalism. Like F. D. Maurice, Social Gospel advocates spoke out against those who held that competition was the central economic principle and emphasized cooperation instead. They spoke against the violation of the natural right of contract and against profit making which was harmful to human welfare. They provided a prophetic and critical voice in a time of tumult.

What did the Social Gospel movement accomplish? There was certainly no revolutionary change in American society as a result of its devotees' activities. The principle of competition was not supplanted by that of cooperation. The Kingdom of God did not come in its fulness. And yet things did happen. Chiefly, the Social Gospel movement aroused the consciences of many in the church and in the industrial society. The practical consequences of this arousal are virtually impossible to measure or analyze. Where the church was concerned, the Social Gospel movement influenced the ecumenical movement in the United States and abroad.

Where the Social Gospel and the churches are concerned, the Episcopal Church can be said to have led the way. This is not surprising when we consider the influence of the Christian Socialists in England on many of the leading Episcopalians. It was in 1887 that the Church Association for the Advancement of the Interests of Labor, commonly called C.A.I.L., was begun. One of its leaders was the social radical, James O. S. Huntington, founder of the Order of the Holy Cross. Its president from 1887 to 1904 was Father Huntington's father, Bishop F. D. Huntington. The society was formed of men of various church groups and parties and illustrates the fact that by this time Maurice's Christian Socialism was permeating Anglo-Catholicism. C.A.I.L. mediated industrial disputes, Father Huntington at one time being influential in settling a coal strike in Illinois. It attacked the abuses of sweatshops and tenement houses, worked for the greater recognition of organized labor, and brought its influence to bear upon General Convention. It worked for the appointment of a commission on the relation of capital and labor at the General Convention of 1901, at which time C.A.I.L. boasted of having seventy-five bishops as vice-presidents.

In 1889 W. D. P. Bliss founded the Society of Christian Socialists: "to awaken members of the Christian Churches to the fact that the teachings of Jesus Christ lead directly to some specific form or forms of Socialism." In 1891 the Christian Social Union was founded, after the pattern of a similar group in England, and took for its special field the study rather than the treatment of industrial conditions. The Church Socialist League began in 1901 under the leadership of priest-theologian Bernard Iddings Bell. The Church League for Social and Industrial Democracy was founded in 1919 to deal with postwar conditions, to foster the substitution of "fraternal cooperation for mastery in industry and life," and "to give moral and practical support to those who shall clearly be seen to have incurred persecution through advocacy of social change." All of these were largely unofficial, voluntary societies associated with the Episcopal Church, but in 1901 the General Convention had committed the church to serious consideration of the problems faced by capital and labor. The commission authorized at that time was later to become a joint commission on social service and to have a full-time field secretary in 1911. When the National

Council of the Episcopal Church was formed in 1919 a department of Christian Social Service was established and began to absorb some of the concerns and activities of the voluntary societies.

The postwar period of the 1920s marked another turning point as the crisis of the Social Gospel movement developed, eventuating in its virtual demise. The question was, how to bring in the Kingdom of God and to effect a union between righteousness and power, the Word and politics? Some thought that the combination would happen automatically. Others were troubled and uncertain. The quest for means ended in painful frustration. The problem seemed to be that of uniting capitalism (which had escaped the church), labor (which the church had never won), and Christianity (estranged from both and in danger of losing its own true identity). Social gospellers concentrated their efforts on capital in reaching out to big business, by and large ignoring the middle class which was most deeply involved in the church's day-to-day life. They had some success, as with Arthur "Golden Rule" Nash in the textile business, W. P. Hagood of the Columbia Conserve Company, and J. J. Eagan of American Cast Iron Pipe. These business leaders sought to fashion their lives and adapt their enterprises to the teachings of Jesus. But none of them fostered a more humane behavior toward their employees on the basis of the Social Gospel alone. Christianity was found to make business prosper and profits increase.

In the 1930s harsh realities dealt body blows to the Social Gospel movement. The great depression, disillusionment concerning doctrinaire socialism, especially in Russia, and the rise of Hitler and the Nazis in Germany—all challenged the optimism, humanism, and fundamental pacificism of the Social gospellers. Furthermore, the fusion or synthesis of the Gospel and secular society seemed to many to be idealistic and unrealizable, and to some thoroughly wrong.

One of those who came to object most strenuously to the Social Gospel was Reinhold Niebuhr (1892–1970) who had been a member of the Fellowship of Reconciliation, a pacifist Social Gospel organization. Possessing an intimate knowledge of that which he attacked, Niebuhr saw tension where others saw a developing synthesis. His political morality was based on the crisis of civilization flirting with disaster. With a pessimistic view of human groups—they are all essentially predatory—Niebuhr argued that religion and politics were not to be confused, and certainly not to be identified with one another. They were often in opposition and always in tension. Christians must realize that they cannot transform society and that the Gospel principle of love is not pragmatic: it is foolishness. The Christian, in seeking to implement justice as an end, may be forced to use methods which would be denounced by other Christians. In much of this Niebuhr was reacting to the naïveté of the Social Gospel liberals and their optimistic views of Christianity and society. But he still believed that Christians should be involved in politics and in social action. They must enter the struggle and endure the "nicely calculated less and more" of history and politics.

Niebuhr knew of no easy solutions. His thought was dialectical, as when writing of the desirable synthesis of Renaissance and Reformation, by which he meant, not the melding of the two into something else but the perpetual dialectic of pretension and humility. He believed in the necessity of both, although recognizing that the modern predicament in the West was largely the fruit of Renaissance elements and that these elements had to be kept in check by Reformation humility.[44] "Renaissance pretension" came under heavy criticism in Niebuhr's time, but it is evident to the student of the historical dimension of human existence that without pretension—that is, without creative imagination—the truth conveyed by the Reformation is empty. Christianity, Niebuhr understood, is not the source of culture. Human beings are, and Christianity is the means by which humanity remains that source to the end of time. The problem posed, from Niebuhr's point of view, was how people could be won over from those of their illusions which are rooted in the Renaissance and are propelling them and their politics toward disaster. The answer was, in part at least, through encouraging Renaissance pretension, knowing that the result is the destruction of the pretenders by their own pretension. In a sense he viewed catastrophe as inevitable. But catastrophe is a means of grace, for in its midst the self repents and is renewed with humility displacing pretension.

Paul Tillich (1886–1965) appeared on the American scene in the 1930s, a refugee from Hitler's Germany. He drove criticism of industrial society beyond the economic and political levels to the foundations of culture and indeed into the personal self. The crisis for the Social Gospel had been the depression and it had been met by capitalist institutions working together with the agencies of the state. The New Deal appeared to succeed, although the economic recovery it spurred was greatly assisted by the advent of World War II. Where then was the crisis now? According to Tillich it was in the self; that is to say, in the disintegration of the consciousness-centered personality. The Social Gospel could be faulted not only for its naïveté but also for its ignoring of the self and those areas of culture which are concerned with the personal, such as family life, school, church, art, play, and the healing sciences. Most glaringly, it did not deal with issues which were emerging as major concerns for the future. Racism and sexism are two major examples, both being deeply concerned with the personal as well as with the society.

With this we approach our own day and our own personal experiences. It is tempting to pursue the historical thread and show that the emphasis on the personal bore much good fruit during the decade following World War II. But it also carried with it considerable dangers in succeeding years and was met by the challenge of the civil rights and anti-war movements of the 1950s and 1960s. In such movements there was a return to emphasis on the social, a refurbished Social Gospel appeared, and social action programs were devised in most of the American churches and in their ecumenical agencies. Indeed, we can observe, by careful historical analysis and through personal experience, the dialectic in operation between the personal and the social, the quest for selfhood and the struggle for a just society. The struggle is characterized by tension, recurrent crises, and constant change as the emphasis falls on one and then on the other.

On the level of nations and cultures, a similar condition

exists. Where nations are concerned, the relationship between church and state seems to be dynamic, ever changing,
and full of tension, with no final solution, at least not in our
time. The pattern we have observed through history suggests
various possible relationships, some dependent upon external circumstances, all with advantages and disadvantages.
Where cultures are concerned, the relationship of Christ to
culture, or church to culture, varies. H. Richard Niebuhr
suggested five possibilities, preferring that relationship
which is identified as "Christ transforming culture." And
even though he has a preference, as anyone should, he
realizes that none of the possible relationships is absolute. It
would seem that the major lesson in all of this concerns not a
particular, dogmatic way of relating Christ and culture or
church and state, endowing that way with divine authority.
What we seem to learn is that there is interaction and that the
interaction between Christ and culture, church and state is
vital to both. The culture of which church and state are important elements depends upon their complementary contributions. The church needs the state, for it is to the state
that it is sent. Without the state it cannot fulfill its mission.
The state needs the church to save it from self-destruction.

· 5 ·

The Mission of the Community: "To Every Kindred and Tongue"

Charles Henry Brent and the Nature of Mission

Charles Henry Brent (1862–1929) was in many ways a typical representative of the early twentieth century. A naturalized American citizen, he spent enough of his life in Canada, the Far East, and Europe to qualify as a citizen of the world. We cannot, therefore, begin with a description of a particular place, an Antioch, a Cambridge, or a London, for Brent was not to be tied down. Travel was characteristic of his life, and if we picture him anywhere it might be on board a ship playing deck hockey or writing one of his many books while crossing the Indian Ocean. Or we might imagine him proceeding by foot and by horseback through the mountainous terrain of Luzon in the Philippines. We might contrast the bishop driving his car at breakneck speed over some highway in northern New York or climbing up the steep incline of a mountain in Switzerland. Having been in so many places, having seen so much, Brent came to regard all the world as his concern and, although he was proud to be an American,

191

Charles Henry Brent, 1862–1929

he acknowledged that as a member of the Christian community his earthly loyalties were ultimately supranational. The whole earth was for him the focus of the Church's mission. Every part was responsible to every other part to witness to the greatness of God's love and to cause the glory of God, and of his Christ, "to be praised" (Eph. 1:11–14).

It was with this global vision and with a sense of responsibility stretching beyond the place where at any given moment he happened to be, that Brent labored in a city mission (St. Stephen's, South End of Boston), in a "foreign mission field" (the Philippine Islands), and in a mission to the churches of all nations through the Ecumenical Movement, from the World Missionary Conference at Edinburgh, Scotland, in 1910, to the first World Conference on Faith and Order at Lausanne, Switzerland, in 1927.

Charles Henry Brent was born at Newcastle, Ontario, Canada, in 1862, and was ordained deacon by the Bishop of Toronto in 1886. The next year, while in charge of St. Andrew's Mission, Buffalo, New York, he was ordained priest. Having disagreed with the bishop of his New York diocese concerning a matter of ceremonial use, Brent went to live with the Cowley fathers in Cambridge, Massachusetts. This was at a house of the Society of St. John the Evangelist, founded in 1865 by R. M. Benson at Cowley, near Oxford, in England. Here Brent lived under a monastic rule and regarded himself as an Anglo-Catholic. He was ready to take the vows of a novice in the order when once more an altercation occurred to change the direction of his life. The Superior of the Cowley fathers in Cambridge, A. C. A. Hall, as a member of the Standing Committee of the Diocese of Massachusetts, signed the certificate ratifying the election of Phillips Brooks, the noted Broad Churchman, as the new diocesan bishop. With party strife still strong, Hall was expected to oppose this election to the bitter end. This he would not do and as a consequence was recalled to England by the father superior of the order. Brent, who greatly admired Hall and remained his close friend for years, left Cambridge, the Cowley fathers, and the pursuit of the religious life as a monk.

Brent labored for the next decade (1891–1901) at St. Stephen's Church and House in a depressed area of Boston's South End. In 1900 he summarized the work of this urban mission in these words:

> Nine fleet years have sped their way since we took possession of this field—years full of differentiations which we hope are signs of progress. Various societies and guilds have sprung into life and are flourishing with more or less vigor; the Mission Room with its Lodging House and woodyard is quite an old story; the house at 5 Garland Street is the taming ground of many sturdy representatives of boyhood; St. Stephen's House hides various phrases of energy; and St. Anne's House is a valuable adjunct to

our parochial establishment. But the evolution still proceeds with its differentiations. This Fall saw the opening of St. Stephen's Neighborhood House at 3 Garland Street, under the supervision of an earnest committee and a competent corps of workers. The Neighborhood House is the development of a modest little venture known as the Children's Laundry, begun many years back, and so zealously mothered by Mrs. Wethern as to burst its swathing bands and break out fresh on Garland Street. Under its roof child life is tutored in the simple household arts and brought into touch with the beautiful and the good.[1]

No mention is made here of the church's liturgical routine or of the pastoral work directed to the needs of individuals. Both were vitally important to Brent and were fostered with great care.

In 1895 Brent reported once more on his work, indicating the nature of the church's mission in the community and laying down principles which he took with him to the Philippines and which remained with him for the rest of his life. (1) The missionary must go into a community without preconceived plans, work with the already existing organizations there, and learn of the people and their conditions before setting new policies. (2) Realizing that they must minister to the entire community and not to a select few, missionaries must adapt their services of worship to the needs of the people and not always insist on the Book of Common Prayer. "The Liturgy is less intelligible than Hebrew to the ordinary run of the uninstructed, the Godless and the indifferent." (3) They must work to develop the moral conscience of the people around them and not seek to make them church members before they are ready and able. (4) The missionaries must commit themselves to their work and not look upon it as a stepping-stone to something "better." (5) Organizations are necessary but secondary to the work of making the influence of Christ felt in the lives of people. Sympathy, character, and Christian devotion are more needed than institutional machinery.

In 1901 Brent was elected bishop of the Philippine Islands. That is to say, he was sent as a bishop by the Protestant Episcopal Church in the United States of America to the islands recently brought under American rule after centuries of Spanish domination. The Roman Catholic Church was dominant, but there was a growing population of non-Roman, English speaking people and there were native Igorots and Moros beyond the reach of the Spanish missionaries.

Brent accepted his election after much thought and struggle within himself. He was consecrated two months later and set out for the Philippines in May of 1902 after much work establishing the necessary personal and financial support for his mission. He was far from certain that he could fulfill the expectations of his friends, and of his Lord:

> May I keep my motive pure. Now I am single-minded. I have but one desire—to serve God and my country. If I do this it makes little difference whether life is long or short, whether I am here or there. Time is eternity; here is there.[2]

When his episcopacy in the Philippines came to an end in 1917, the record of Brent's accomplishments testified to the steadfastness of his service. Not that he was without fault. Indeed, he more than once demonstrated his inability to judge the true nature of those he chose to serve as missionaries. There was a certain simplicity and credulousness about him. There was also criticism concerning his long absences in Europe and America, absences justified in terms of his responsibility to keep the Philippine mission alive to those who were its chief support. His faults were overshadowed, however, by the long-lasting results of his work.

First, he made it clear that he was not in the Philippines to compete with or to convert the Roman Catholics. His primary duty was to Americans and other English speaking non-Romans. In fulfillment of this responsibility he established a cathedral church, with a parish and a ministry to the souls and bodies of those drawn to it. Brent's personal influence was felt by the American officials from the governor general down, the bishop being regarded by many as the conscience of the rulers. He labored against their inclinations to exploit their subjects and for Philippine self-rule, which he knew must come in time.

Secondly, Brent reached out to Filipino and Chinese natives not ministered to by the Roman Catholic Church. But especially, he labored among the Igorots of the northern islands of Luzon and the Moros in the far south, at Zamboanga and Jolo. This work required sensitivity and patience. Following the principle which he had established in the South End of Boston, Brent sought to live among the Igorots and Moros and there to listen, watch, understand, and be influenced by them. He rejected the widely held view that missionaries to such people must strike fast. The bishop strove, rather, to nurture people in the Christian faith and life. He wrote:

> The purpose of Christianity is to create and sustain an abiding, worthy purpose. Emotional religion can create but not sustain. What is needed is something that will fill life—intellectual, moral, spiritual.[3]

Such an approach necessitated one's being not only adaptable but also secure in one's own beliefs. Brent did not, for instance, regard the religion of the native Filipinos with hostility. His attitude toward other religions was positive. He saw God working through them and at times wondered whether the New Testament ought to be bound up with the Old Testament or with passages from other religious classics—at least for use in the mission fields. His approach led him to establish schools and clinics and hospitals to care for the people and to provide for their nurture. In the process it could be hoped that the example of the missionaries, and in time of the Christian laity, would do more to commend the faith than any sermons or arguments.

Brent's work was not restricted to such activities. He is remembered in the Far East for his leadership in bringing the opium traffic under control. In spending time and energy as an official American delegate to international conferences aimed at the elimination of the many abuses of the opium trade, Brent saw himself engaged in a vital humanitarian and Christian cause. Such work was not irrelevant to his missionary vocation, but rather at the very heart of it, for opium was destroying many of those to whom the Gospel was sent. It would be folly and worse to ignore the social evils affecting the lives of the Filipinos.

Brent's work on the Opium Committee, beginning with his appointment by William Howard Taft in 1903 and extending to the international conference in Geneva in 1924, was the beginning of his involvement in international affairs. In 1917 the United States entered the war then raging in Europe and Brent was plunged into its midst, becoming in 1918 the Senior Headquarters' chaplain of the American Expeditionary Forces in France. His attitude toward war itself was clear:

> War is hell—this is the verdict of those who know it best. The word hell is among the most used along the battle front. It is not merely the crimson hate, the busy death, the brazen fury of the trenches. At the base camps, at the camps in England, war is hell. Lust rages and reigns. Bodies are corrupted with a corruption worse than death. But human nature has discovered new power in this hell—power to dare and do at all costs which we didn't dream it possessed, power to suffer on the waves, in the trenches, on the road, in the hospitals, beyond all that we imagined. It is for us all to tax ourselves in a search for that same power and to put it into effect to hasten the end, to mitigate the evil, to destroy the power of this infamous, hideous war.[4]

In spite of his convictions concerning war, Brent was no pacifist. He did his part, combating that which he knew to be evil, reforming the American military chaplaincy and ministering to the troops, from General Pershing, his close friend, to the lowliest doughboy. His experience in the war, together with his experience in the Far East, led Brent to believe that the unity of mankind was imperative and that church unity was essential. Although he left the Philippines and became bishop of Western New York, Brent devoted the rest of his life to the cause of peace and unity among nations and churches.

The beginnings of his participation in the Ecumenical Movement are related to his involvement in the World Missionary Conference at Edinburgh in 1910. There he became convinced that the church's mission required the reunion of the church. He set his mind on a plan which came to him at the General Convention in the same year at Cincinnati: a world conference to deal with matters of faith and order separating the churches. Having placed the idea before the convention and receiving support, he set about—with the assistance of many people in various churches—to organize the conference. It was to be concerned with issues involving both belief and organization on which Christians disagreed. The quest would be to discover the points of fundamental belief on which all could agree and make the basis for their life together.

The story is long and complex. The way was made difficult by the stubborn resistance of many who were convinced that they alone possessed the truth. It was aided by world events, the organization of the League of Nations after World War I, and the meeting of the Universal Conference for Life and Work at Stockholm in 1925. In 1927 Brent's dream was realized. There gathered at Lausanne, under his chairmanship, representatives from one hundred twenty-seven churches, from all parts of the world. Brent opened a session saying:

> You and I must put ourselves in the right relation to God. I am as strongly convinced on many subjects as the rest of you, but I am anxious to get rid of prejudice and ignorance, and it is for us, in a way that perhaps we have never done before, to put ourselves at the disposal of God, to give our minds and our hearts and our judgments into His hands that He may sway us whither He will.[5]

Lausanne was a beginning. In time there would come more conferences. Leaders such as William Temple (1881–1944), who was to be archbishop of Canterbury; John R. Mott (1865–1955), the American Methodist layman; and Vedanayakam Samuel Azariah (1874–1945), bishop of Dornakal in India, emerged. In 1948 the World Council of Churches held its first great meeting in Amsterdam. Brent was dead by then, but he was remembered there as one of those who led the way.

Brent's final thoughts about many things, and principally about the mission of the Christian community, are preserved in a book which began as a series of lectures delivered in Scotland in 1921. He was revising these lectures for publication when he died in Lausanne in 1929. Here, acknowledging that "Christianity is in extreme peril,"[6] civilization in ruins, the church divided and its witness feeble, Brent painted a picture of what he chose to call the great Commonwealth, which others called the Kingdom of God. He understood the Commonwealth at first in terms of considerable breadth. It is "that joint possession of all human aspiration and achievement which the world contains, all the world's raw material, spiritual, moral, and material, embracing both the unwon things of to-morrow as well as the inheritance of the past."[7] It was a vision of wholeness, of which the unifying principle is fellowship and the means forgiveness. Forgiveness was of central importance to Brent, finding its fullest expression in Christ's command that we love our enemies. It is in the light of this that he wrote:

> The missionary ideal is the one great motive and effort of the human race that, ideally at any rate, has never known the limitation of race or country, but would appeal to all men on the basis of a common manhood with a common Fatherhood. From the very beginning there was no definite rule as to where missionary endeavour should begin or stop; the desire was to give the Commonwealth of God to the human race.[8]

Brent was no pessimist. As grim as the signs of the breakup of western civilization might be, he was convinced that "a mental awakening" was occurring, a sense of brotherhood emerging "through sorrow for common suffering and for irreparable mutual injuries."[9] Furthermore, he detected signs that the universe was shrinking. "It shrinks as we get to know more about the far limits of space and it expands as beyond the boundaries of the known, new fields of exploration open up." The unity of the human race is accentuated by the advance of technology. Such realities provide opportunities to realize the wholeness of existence more fully. The accumulated experience of the mission fields, moreover, makes its demands for wholeness, for a unified church, and for good will and peace among nations. Experience also makes its claim upon Christians for a higher form of Christian character.

The church as the instrument of God for the establishment

of the Commonwealth of God must be reformed and purified.

> The idea of the Church has become so identified with the agencies and instruments in its employ that its essential character is lost to view; indeed, it needs deliberate effort to think of the Church independently of architecture, sacred edifices, parish houses, and organizations for this and that good end; whereas, not one of these is necessary to the Church's life. Were they all swept away, leaving no vestige behind, the Church might even gain by the loss.[10]

This is so because the "Church is an edifice or temple of human beings in organic relationship to God and to one another." As such its function

> is to make available for successive generations of mankind the particular Christian boon of salvation. It must keep clear its sole purpose of perpetuating the work begun by its Founder, whose body it is for our times in as real a fashion as human flesh and blood were His body for the days of His mortality. The Church must seek the most unimpeded and perfect way in which to accomplish its responsibility. The only failure of the Church which is not shameful is failure of the sort suffered by our Lord, that which is due to the refusal of the gift offered by those who have been given full opportunity to know the value of the gift. At first sight it seems contradictory that the Church should win her way by being refused by those for whom she exists, but the paradox is solved when we remember that our Lord said, "And I, if I be lifted up, . . . will draw all men unto me."[11]

Such was the vision expressed in words. We cannot sufficiently recall the voice, gestures, personality of Brent.

William Temple wrote of Brent chairing the Lausanne conference:

> His position as the pivotal person of the Conference was plain, and his quiet, firm and often humorous control of the discussions was most effective. I particularly remember his delight on one occasion when two most respected members of the Conference, Bishop Gore and William Adams Brown, were fiercely resisting one another while each was sure that the other must really agree with him. Bishop Brent saw the humor of the situation, inadvertently let loose a whoop of laughter to the as-

tonishment of the earnest disputants, and by his humorous interjections quickly restored peace and goodwill.[12]

This was the sort of incident many remembered, but which loses much in the retelling. The point in the retelling lies in the conviction that the person of Brent was itself a witness to the Gospel.

Charles Henry Brent died in his sleep while passing through Lausanne in 1929. The cause of his death sounds altogether modern: overexertion, digestive disturbance, and in the end heart fibrillations. He died with confidence in that which was to come. Such confidence he expressed when he wrote:

> The fullest vision of Him of which we are now capable is only an earnest of that which is to be. But in this we can rest secure that in future manifestations of Himself God will not surprise us by suddenly showing Himself to be something contrary to the basic revelation of His character. The groundwork of the Cross holds all the rest in its safe keeping. And all the comings of Jesus Christ in, and at the close of, time will be in loving self-giving even though they be in clouds and great glory. For His glorious Majesty, too, will bear the sign of the Cross.[13]

Mission: Christ and the Church

In our day when the world is so rapidly changing and the inherited concepts of missions, missionaries, and missionary work seem outmoded, we hear much questioning: "Why missions?" "What's the true story about missions? Did missionaries in the past do some good or did they do more harm than good?" "If missions have validity what should they be like now?" Such questions suggest the need to go back through the years to the roots of Christian missionary activity in history, to examine the course of events from the beginning to the present, and to consider ways in which the church should be reformed for mission in the years ahead. There are hints and suggestions in the life of Charles Henry Brent. These occur most clearly where he spoke of the church as the instrument of God for the establishing of the Commonwealth of God.

On the most basic (and biblical) level we are taught that missions are rooted in mission and that mission is not correctly understood if we think solely of the missions of the church. Such misunderstanding focusing on the church has been at the root of much frustration and evil. Mission is the mission of Christ to the world. At the World Missionary Conference in Willingen, Germany, in 1952, one group made a great impact on the conference by criticizing its motto: "The Missionary Obligation of the Church." They asserted that mission has its source in the triune God, not in the church, and stated:

> Out of the depths of his love for us, the Father has sent forth his own beloved Son to reconcile all things to himself, that we and all men might, through the Spirit, be made one in him with the Father in that perfect love which is the very nature of God.[14]

Canon Max A. C. Warren, the head of the Church Missionary Society and an Anglican, indicated the heart of the matter in an address at Willingen, proclaiming that the decisive act of God, the fulfillment of the divine missionary will, is the Cross of Christ.

> The Cross is the illuminating center of the mystery of God's redemptive purpose. It is there that we begin to look into the heart of God, begin to believe that some understanding is possible, even for us, of the mystery of redemption. And it is by way of the Cross that we are compelled to see both the necessity for showing forth that redemption and also the manner of the showing.[15]

Here we are reminded of the intimate relationship of renewal and reform and mission, mission being the external expression of internal renewal in Christ. We are also reminded that the church is both the object of Christ's mission and the instrument by which that mission reaches into the world. The focus is thus on God and on the church only to the degree to which it participates in the divine mission of salvation for the world. This participation is the one great purpose of the church.

The church is the object of Christ's mission. Isaiah portrays for us the elevation of Zion, as upon a great mountain, the nations of the world (not just one chosen nation) flowing up to it:

> and many peoples shall come, and say:
> "Come, let us go up to the mountain of the Lord,
>   to the house of the God of Jacob;
> that he may teach us his ways
>   and that we may walk in his paths" (Is. 2:3).

That which was a promise in Isaiah was beginning to happen by the time of the Epistle to the Ephesians where the gentiles of Ephesus are told:

> . . . remember that you were at that time separated from Christ, alienated from the commonwealth of Israel, and strangers to the covenants of promise, having no hope and without God in the world. But now in Christ Jesus you who once were far off have been brought near in the blood of Christ (Eph. 2:12–13).

The church is gathered to be dispersed, its members sent out to witness to new life in Christ. The governing thought is embodied in St. Paul's statement: "For what we preach is not ourselves, but Jesus Christ as Lord, with ourselves as your servants [your slaves] for Jesus' sake" (2 Cor 4:5). The church, as the gathered people on mission, is composed of those who die to self that they may be the means by which the Lord— and new life in him—is made known. This means that the desires of the witnesses are always subordinate to the needs of those to whom they are sent. The relationship is that of the servant to the master. In such witness God's love is proclaimed and those illuminated by it are drawn to the mountain, gathered in by God, from thence to be sent out by the power of the Spirit to witness to divine love in the cross of Christ.

In the knowledge of this, those who are the church are humbled and penitent. There are many pitfalls along the way. Christians have often witnessed not to Christ but to something else: nation, race, class, self. They can become so concerned for the "success" of the church as an institution that they end up competing with other witnesses for glory and converts. They often focus attention on the self's need for fulfillment, enrichment, identity, security, forgetting the mission and losing sight of the fact that as they witness, forgetful of self, they find their true selves in Christ. They are often afraid, unwilling, or unable to adjust to new circumstances, ashamed to speak Christ's name for fear that they will be laughed at or denounced. All such equivocations have existed and exist.

The history of the church presents to our view a record which is very mixed. There are examples of faithful witness, true participation in Christ's mission to the world. There are examples of works good in themselves but misdirected and inappropriate to the mission. There are examples of apostasy and evil masquerading as expressions of Christian witness. By now we should not be surprised. The Church is not identical with the Kingdom of God (Brent's Commonwealth of God). It serves that Kingdom, is the instrument of its coming, and is human and fallible. It is composed of people on a pilgrimage, certain of their destiny but not yet arrived. Humiliated and penitent, they are renewed for participation in Christ's mission.

We shall have occasion to observe the true and the false, love and hatred, faithful witness and apostasy as we quickly review the history of the missionary activity of the church. In that which follows we shall take note of the rapid expansion of the church, beginning from Jerusalem, during the first five centuries after Christ. Then we shall consider the Middle Ages when the church of western Europe struggled to survive against the threats of the Muslims to the south and the barbarians to the north. By then expansion had ceased, although there was dramatic evidence of missions stemming from Ireland and Britain to convert the barbarian nations. Expansion began again at the end of the fifteenth century when the explorers set out, to the east and to the west, circumnavigating the world, taking their Christianity with them. During this period missions were established in far-flung places and converts were made, but the activities of the missionaries were qualified and limited by the lack of motivating power on the part of many and by the control exercised over them by European governments more concerned for economic gain than for Christ's mission. The nineteenth century has been called the "Great Century" of Protestant missions. Between 1789 and 1914 missionary societies (not governments or commercial companies) led the way, sending out thousands of witnesses, chiefly from Britain and America, founding churches, preaching widely, starting schools and hospitals, colliding with other religions, and at times entering into vigorous competition with other Christians. After 1914 the expansion of the church slowed down and seemed to cease in some places. Somber realities dampened missionary spirits. Twentieth-century observers pointed out how superficial much of the work of the nineteenth century had been. Europe, which had so patronizingly exported its brand of culture-Christianity, became a missionary field itself. The "receiving" or "younger" churches in the mission fields outside of Europe seized control, many of them just in time as new nations expelled the "colonizing intruders." As a result people found themselves questioning the nature of the Christian mission and the validity of missions. Involved in this questioning were seeds sown by the Ecumenical Movement, which owed its existence to missionaries who rejected competition as a major element in missionary activities and thus sought for cooperation and even organic unity among Christians in missionary fields. And so it is that we shall end with some consideration of the Ecumenical Movement as the instrument for much rethinking concerning the nature of the church, of Christ, and of mission.

We now traverse the centuries to observe the participation of the Christian community in Christ's mission to the world.

From Christ to Justinian: The First Expansion of the Church

The Christian mission, beginning from Jerusalem, reached out through the Mediterranean Sea with dramatic speed in the first two centuries after Christ. We know of substantial Christian communities in Antioch on the Orontes; in Ephesus and other places of Asia Minor; in Philippi and Thessalonica; in Nicopolis and Athens on the Greek Peninsula; in Rhegium, Rome, in Puteoli in Italy; in Syracuse in Sicily; in numerous places across the Alps and in modern France, including Lugdunum and Vienne; in Spain and in North Africa with a great center at Carthage; further east in Cyrene; in Alexandria in Egypt; and, of course, in Palestine. The most considerable Christian populations were in Asia Minor and in the regions around Carthage in Africa. Missions both in North Africa and in Gaul (modern France) seem to have stemmed in part from Asia Minor. It is estimated that by A.D. 313 the population of the Roman Empire stood at about fifty million, ten percent being identified with the Christian faith.

What we know of this early missionary expansion is limited to the writings of Christians and their opponents, and in some instances to archeological remains. For instance, there are the New Testament accounts of Luke in Acts and the letters of Paul detailing the movement north and west from Antioch as far as Greece, not to mention the details of Paul's journey to Rome and his letter to the Christians there preceding his arrival. We know very little of the origins of the church in Egypt, although we do know about the founding of a Christian school there, with which the names of Clement (c. 150–215) and Origen (185–254) are linked. The Christian mission reached beyond the great metropolis of Alexandria into the desert areas and by the middle of the third century the Coptic Church was forming, developing its own linguistic and cultural Christian traditions. The church in Ethiopia is one of the oldest and is connected with the story of Frumentis, a young Christian from Tyre. Frumentis was shipwrecked and made a slave by the king of Axum. There, with a companion, he preached and won great favor. In time Frumentis was made a bishop by Athanasius and assumed the title Abba Salāma (the father of peace). So goes the legend.

Another intriguing legend concerns India. We know very little concerning the spread of Christianity to the east from Jerusalem. In an earlier chapter mention was made of the

Armenian Church, established in the third century by a missionary from Cappadocia—Gregory the Illuminator—and becoming one of the first Christian kingdoms with the conversion of King Tidrates. There is evidence that the Christian witness went from Edessa into Mesopotamia in this early period. Identified with this movement of the faith is Syriac-speaking Christianity, which is critical of Greek-speaking Christians and which developed a character, including literature, such as the *Acts of Thomas* dating from the third century. Here we have a clue as to the arrival of Christianity in India. The *Acts of Thomas* relate the Apostle Thomas to the Indian Mar Thoma Church, a church which exists today with the conviction that it was founded by the apostle. The possibility of this ought not to be denied. Modern investigations have revealed the usefulness of the monsoon, the great wind capable of propelling sailing ships from the Red Sea to the south coast of India where the Mar Thoma Church is found.

How do we account for this rapid spread of Christianity? Many causes have been suggested. There was a remarkable system of roads which bound the Roman Empire together and there were trade routes criss-crossing the Mediterranean Sea. This great communications network was possible because of the control of this vast area by Rome, control maintained by a large and skilled bureaucracy and by the Roman armies. Christianity traveled along established routes and found bases for its operation in the communities of Jews which thrived in the major population centers. From the Jewish communities Christians reached out to the gentiles and responded to anxieties and needs expressed in the society at large. There was, for instance, widespread anxiety concerning death: Christians preached the resurrection of the dead. There was a widespread yearning for inclusive community: Christians preached "one Lord, one faith, one Baptism" and labored to destroy those cultural and religious prejudices which divided people from one another. There were those among the pagans who longed for holiness of life and recognized in Christianity a way out of the licentiousness and cruelty of their society. And there was the ardent zeal of those first followers of Christ. Eusebius of Caesarea, whom we have encountered before, put it this way:

> At the time [about the beginning of the second century] many
> Christians felt their souls inspired by the holy word with a
> passionate desire for perfection. Their first action, in obedience
> to the instructions of the Saviour, was to sell their goods and to
> distribute them to the poor. Then, leaving their homes, they set
> out to fulfil the work of an evangelist, making it their ambition
> to preach the word of the faith to those who as yet had heard
> nothing of it, and to commit to them books of the divine
> Gospels. They were content simply to lay the foundations of the
> faith among these foreign peoples: they then appointed other
> pastors, and committed to them the responsibility for building
> up those whom they had merely brought to the faith. Then they
> passed on to other countries and nations with the grace and
> help of God.[16]

We must not think that all Christians exemplified holiness or
possessed such zeal for the Gospel. But holiness and zeal set
the tone of the community and characterized its witness.
Martyrs were among the leaders in this respect.

The earliest Christians scattered through the Roman Empire were largely, but not exclusively, from the lower classes
of the society. Thus Celsus (c. 180), who wrote against the
Christians and was answered by Origen, stated:

> Far from us, say the Christians, be any man possessed of any
> culture or wisdom or judgement; their aim is to convince only
> worthless and contemptible people, idiots, slaves, poor
> women, and children. They behave like mountebanks and beg-
> gars; they would not dare to address an audience of intelligent
> men.[17]

There were people of remarkable intelligence who took great
risks in joining the Christian tradition in those first centuries.
One such was Justin Martyr (c. 100–165) who, like Clement
and Origen during the third century, worked to interpret the
Christian message in the context of Greek thought. In an
irenic passage, Justin wrote:

> I confess that I both boast and with all my strength strive to be
> found a Christian; not because the teachings of Plato are differ-
> ent from those of Christ, but because they are not in all respects
> similar, as neither are those of the others, Stoics, and poets and
> historians. For each man spoke well in proportion to the share
> he had of the generative word (or reason).[18]

It is true, of course, that for Justin all leads to Christ who is the Word, "who is from the Unbegotten and Ineffable God, since also he became man for our sakes, that becoming a partaker of our sufferings, He might also bring us healing."[19] The earliest Christianity did not, thus, appeal to one type or class of people. Philosophers and slaves mingled in the one body.

The process whereby the Gospel was related to the dominant philosophical and religious traditions of the time must also be considered an important part of the history of missions, for the Gospel came to be viewed by many as the fulfillment of other ways to God and not their destroyer. This was a principle, not always adhered to, which was to be of profound importance. We can see it as we observe not only the encounter of the Gospel with the Greeks, but also with the Armenians, the Romans, the Copts, the Indians, and many others.

The expansion of Christianity not only continued with the advent of the Emperor Constantine and the Edict of Milan (313) but was accelerated. In every area the church grew in numbers and in inclusiveness. There were moments when paganism seemed to be resurgent, as during the rule of the Emperor Julian (361–363), but it was never sufficient to stop the onward thrust of Christian expansion during the fourth and fifth centuries. We have observed in previous chapters the main lines of the period from Constantine to Justinian. It must suffice here to acknowledge that along with the acceptance of Christianity there were dangers. The advocating of the Christian faith by the emperors at times compromised the church's necessary freedom and integrity. The adoption of Christianity by masses of people could, and at times did, weaken commitment and qualify the character of the Christian life, so that reform was needed. But the fact is that in spite of these dangers, and in spite of the internal and external threats to the survival of the empire and those to the stability of ordinary life, Christianity not only continued, but grew.

Rome was sacked in 410 by Alaric and his Gothic army. It was not the first time nor would it be the last, but it prompted

St. Jerome to cry out, "If Rome can perish, what is safe?" The answer came from Augustine of Hippo:

> You are surprised that the world is losing its grip? that the world is grown old? Think of a man: he is born, he grows up, he becomes old. Old age has its many complaints: coughing, shaking, failing eyesight, anxious, terribly tired. A man grows old; he is full of complaints. The world is old; it is full of pressing tribulations. . . . Do not hold on to the old man, the world; do not refuse to regain your youth in Christ, who says to you: "The world is passing away, the world is losing its grip, the world is short of breath. Do not fear, *Thy youth shall be renewed as an eagle.*"[20]

Christianity was the wellspring of youth. It could not help but persist and grow, rising above spent empires and cultures. The truth was that Christianity was universal in time as well as space. It belonged to the future as well to the past and present.

From the fourth to the sixth centuries, Christianity moved beyond the old empire into the territories of its enemies. The barbarians, sweeping in waves from the north and the east to the frontiers of the empire and then penetrating into it, took Christians as prisoners. Some probably broke under the pressure and renounced Christ, others died for the faith, and still others survived to witness to Christ, converting the antagonistic barbarians. Ulfilas (c. 311–383) capitalized on the barbarian incursions and became one of the greatest Christian missionaries. From 340 until his death, Ulfilas labored among the Goths (it was said that his mother was one of them) converting many and reproducing spoken Gothic in written form so that the Bible might be made available to the people.

During these years missions among the people of France were led by the soldier-monk, St. Martin of Tours (c. 316–397), but the greatest advances were made when Clovis, the king of the Frankish people (one of the barbarian tribes), was baptized in 496. Three thousand of his troops were said to have been baptized with him.

Finally, mention must be made of the conversion of the Celtic people in Ireland. St. Patrick (c. 389–461) is customarily associated with this event. When Patrick (whose life and activities are shrouded in legend) began his missionary activities in Ireland about 441 the people there were almost entirely heathen. In spite of great hardship and vigorous opposition, Patrick persisted so that at the time of his death the Irish were largely Christian. Patrick was trained as a monk in France, but the Irish Christians—as a people related to Celts everywhere, on the continent, in Wales, and in Scotland—developed their own understanding of Christianity. For instance, although there were bishops, monasteries practicing the most severe asceticism were the primary centers of Christianity and the abbots the most powerful ecclesiastics, acting as clan chieftains. Furthermore, a unique Celtic Christian culture developed, reflected in the legends of Patrick, St. Bridgit, and others, in the art—such as that of the *Book of Kells*—and in the words of Patrick's breastplate. This latter has the characteristics of a pagan charm, the triune God standing between the faithful and the evil powers all around:

> I bind unto myself to-day
>   The strong Name of the Trinity,
> By invocation of the same,
>   The Three in One, and One in Three. . . .
> I bind unto myself to-day
>   The power of God to hold and lead,
> His eye to watch, his might to stay,
>   His ear to hearken to my need;
> The wisdom of my God to teach,
>   His hand to guide, his shield to ward;
> The word of God to give me speech,
>   His heavenly host to be my guard.
> Christ be with me, Christ within me,
>   Christ behind me, Christ before me,
> Christ beside me, Christ to win me,
>   Christ to comfort and restore me,
> Christ beneath me, Christ above me,
>   Christ in quiet, Christ in danger,
> Christ in hearts of all that love me,
>   Christ in mouth of friend and stranger.[21]

Surrounded by Christ, the Christian was safe. The effectiveness of the invocation of the name in providing protection against evil had been tested and its power acknowledged. Thus Christianity pushed beyond the sophisticated empire into darker and in some ways more spiritually attuned places.

The Middle Ages: Barbarians and Crusades

Two historical events of great importance indicate that the thousand years from A.D. 500 to 1500 were, on the whole, years of constriction and confinement for the Christian community in Europe. The first of these events was one which extended through the entire period. From the third century on, waves of migrations out of central Asia into the European continent disrupted the weakening Roman unity and provided serious obstacles to the Christian mission. Migrations of nomadic, sometimes warlike people, extended, with intervening periods of peace, from Alaric's sack of Rome in 410 to the Tartars of the fifteenth century who, since the days of Ghengis Khan (d. 1227), had been causing disruption and devastation in the east. It was not until 1480 that Ivan III liberated Moscow from Tartar domination.

The second main inhibiting event was the rise of Islam. This began with Mohammed (c. 570–632), "the praised one" of Mecca in Arabia. He seized hold upon the pagan worship of Allah, principal deity of Mecca, reformed it and used it as a means of reforming the society as a whole. His intention was to do away with idolatry, organize an effective government, put an end to infanticide, and prohibit certain kinds of sexual promiscuity. Turned out of Mecca by those who resented his dictatorial methods, he fled with his disciples to Medina and there established a power base, enlisting the support of pagans and Jews. Those who resisted him were slain. He returned to Mecca in triumph and from thence Islam spread to Spain in the west by the early eighth century and to Constantinople and eastern Europe by the fifteenth.

The religion of Mohammed emphasized the God who is

One, the all powerful creator of the universe who presides over the final judgment, providing rich rewards for those who are obedient, and terrible punishments for those who are not. This teaching was conveyed through a sacred book, the Koran, which repudiated the Christian doctrine of the Trinity and spoke of Jesus as a prophet and no more. Alongside belief in the one God (with Mohammed as his prophet), Islam taught the brotherhood of all people, regardless of race. Religion and the state were viewed as one in God, in the prophet, and in the prophet's successors. The necessity to reach out to the whole world with the message of the brotherhood of all under the fatherhood of God was asserted. Islam involved stringent personal discipline, with a strict moral code, regular prayer, and meritorious pilgrimages to Mecca. For those who refused to turn toward Mecca and worship Allah, there was subjugation and death.

The Muslim tide flowed out of Arabia felling nations and destroying Christian centers. The reasons given for their swift and relentless success are many and not limited to considerations of weakness on the part of those they approached. The incursions into western Europe were brought to a halt in 732 by Charles Martel and his Frankish army when Abd-er-Rahman was defeated in a battle between Tours and Poitiers. In the east matters could not be solved so simply. Pressure was applied and maintained by the Muslims, diverted for a time by the Tartars and by the Crusades. Christian efforts to convert the Muslims were not successful. The Crusades were never actually effective in converting the inhabitants of the Holy Land. Even St. Francis of Assisi, who went to the east to persuade and not to coerce, was unable to convert the Sultan of Egypt with whom he met.

It can be argued that the ineffectiveness of Christianity against the Muslims was due to the superiority of the religion of Islam with its emphasis on the one God and on universal brotherhood. Islam was commended to Europeans by outstanding Arabic philosophers, the product of a highly developed civilization in Islamic lands. The threat they posed was acknowledged by some philosophers and theologians in Europe who recognized the great difference between the Islamic view of the one God, far removed from his creation, and the Christian view of the triune God who bridged the gulf between deity and humanity by sending to earth Jesus Christ, both God and man. It was St. Thomas Aquinas (1225–1274), who opposed the Crusades arguing that infidels have natural rights which must be respected, and who mounted the intellectual counterattack upon the Arabic intellectuals. Speaking in their terms, Thomas insisted that God was made man in Christ Jesus, that in the Incarnation God proclaimed his love of humanity, and that God is not distant and vindictive, but near and gracious. The Crusades seemed to deny this divine love, but they had their own rationale, which we shall encounter later on.

The Christian mission was much more successful in reaching and converting the barbarians. Indeed, the most vivid stories concerning the mission and missionaries have to do with the conversion of the Jutes, Angles, Saxons, Danes, Vikings, Franks, Lombards, Alamanni, and the like. As we have noted, there were successive waves of conquest. Each seemed to end in the settling down of the barbarians and their eventual conversion. The history is lengthy and complex. Here let us focus on the British Isles. A key date is 597, marking the arrival of St. Augustine of Canterbury in the kingdom of Kent. Christianity had come to those islands during the first century A.D., but we know little about it. What little we do know about Christianity in Britain prior to Augustine leads us to suspect that the area we know today as England had been evangelized much more thoroughly than we have been led to believe by subsequent historians who served the Roman mission of St. Augustine and his successors. The early British Christians seem to have been pushed by invading Jutes, Angles, and Saxons into the west where they were isolated behind Offa's wall in Wales. There were, as we have observed, Christians in Ireland and the Celtic brand of Christianity there had been transmitted across the sea to Scotland by St. Columba (521–597) who made his home on the island of Iona. Christianity had been introduced to the Picts of Scotland by St. Ninian (d. 432?), but this original planting of Christianity received a boost from Columba and his compan-

ions. In time the Celtic Christians of Scotland moved south-
ward into the kingdom of Northumbria, and beyond, led by
remarkable monks such as the great St. Aidan (d. 651) who
established his base at Lindisfarne and proceeded to the conversion of king and people. Lindisfarne, an island at high
tide, was not only a base for the missionary activity of the
Celts in England, but also a great center of monastic civilization exercising considerable influence for many years.

St. Augustine of Canterbury, along with his monks, was
sent by Pope Gregory the Great (590–604). It is of interest to
note that Augustine and his companions attempted to abort
the mission but then bowed to Gregory's demand that they
proceed. Thus began the Roman mission which succeeded in
converting the Kentish King Ethelbert (c. 560–616)—whose
wife Bertha was already a Christian—and with him all his
people. The mission then moved northward through various
kingdoms until the Roman and Celtic missions met and
clashed. They differed concerning various practices, such as
the date of Easter and the sort of haircut the clergy should
have. Beneath such issues there was the question of who
possessed authority to decide such matters. The issue was set
before the Synod of Whitby in 663–664. Whitby was a double
monastic house of men and women over whom the Abbess
Hilda ruled. Appreciative of both Roman and Celtic traditions, she acted as a mediator and reconciler at the synod. But
the outcome was in the hands of the king of Northumbria
who decided in favor of Roman custom. The Celtic mission
suffered a defeat but did not entirely disappear. Nevertheless, under the leadership of Augustine's successor, Theodore
of Tarsus (602–690), the church in what we now know as
England was organized in Roman style, dioceses were
formed and synods held.

The ideals of the victorious Roman mission were expressed
by Pope Gregory in answer to certain questions put to him
by Augustine. He indicated the need for flexibility in dealing
with non-Christians and Christians alike, a willingness to
accommodate some of the practices of those being converted.
Furthermore, Augustine was instructed to compile a liturgy
patterned after that of Rome, but, wrote Gregory:

> . . . it pleases me, that if you have found anything, either in the Roman [church] or [that] of the Gauls, or any other Church, which may be more acceptable to Almighty God, you carefully make choice of the same and sedulously teach the Church of the English.[22]

The universal church, Gregory was saying, had room for variety based upon local needs as interpreted by sensitive leaders. It was an ideal which he expressed, although not always followed, but it helps to account for the rapid spread of such a mission as that of Augustine of Canterbury and his successors.

It was from Britain and Ireland that the missions for the conversion of the barbarian peoples of northern Europe in the seventh and eighth centuries came. Columban (550–615) was among the first, crossing from Ireland to Gaul in 585, founding the monastery of Bobbio in Lombardy, working to convert the Arian Lombards until his death. The beginning of the missions to the pagan tribes of Frisia, Denmark, Hesse, Bavaria, and Thuringia began with the arrival of Willibrord (658–739), a monk of Ripon in the present England, with eleven companions in 690. With the strong support of the Frankish king and the blessing of Pope Sergius I (d. 701) who appointed him an archbishop, Willibrord, from his base at Utrecht preached the Gospel, founded churches, and established communities of monks and nuns among the Frisians.

In the eighth century, Wynfrith, better known as Boniface (680–755), monk of Nursling near Southampton in England, obtained the support of Pope Gregory II (d. 731) who made him a missionary in the papal service and proceeded to Thuringia in the present Germany near Erfurt. In a remarkable career, Boniface labored with Willibrord in Frisia and from thence went to Hesse where he enjoyed immediate success. He was consecrated bishop for all Germany east of the Rhine river. In a letter written between 723 and 725, Daniel, bishop of Winchester (d. 745), wrote to Boniface advising him on missionary methods, saying that the missionary should aim at the converting of the heathen intellectually. Boniface, however, with his considerable experience in the field, knew that the non-Christians must be met on their own grounds.

There is, for instance, the story of the felling of the sacred oak tree of Geismar, from whose wood Boniface built a church dedicated to St. Peter. This was no mere destruction of a heathen shrine. It was a contest of the gods. The heathen fully expected that Boniface would be struck down for his sacrilegious act. When he was not harmed at all—when nothing at all seemed to happen—it was clear that the Christian God had won and should be served. In time Boniface was made archbishop of Mainz and spent his last years organizing the church in southern Germany, reforming the Frankish church, and working among the Frisians. He died a martyr's death being slain by a mob of angry heathen.

The Crusades have been mentioned in relation to the conquests of the Muslim armies. There were eight Crusades, extending from 1095 to 1270. They had as their ostensible purpose not the spread of the Gospel among non-Christians, but the recovery from the Muslims of the sacred places of the Holy Land associated with the life of Christ. This they accomplished, a Latin feudal kingdom being established and the holy places secured. In 1099, when Jerusalem was taken, one of the crusaders, Raymond of Agiles, wrote: "When the city was taken it was worth the whole long labour to witness the devotion of the pilgrims to the sepulchre of the Lord, how they clapped their hands, exulted, and sang a new song unto the Lord."[23]

The winning of the Holy Land was not the only motive behind the Crusades, however. There were military reasons and powerful commercial interests. Indeed, the Crusades often degenerated into rampaging mobs of soldiers and others bent on loot and glory. The low point came in 1204 when the armies of the fourth Crusade looted Constantinople. This atrocity turned the Crusades into a war against Eastern Christendom. A Latin empire was established at Constantinople and a Venetian was installed as Patriarch, or head of the church there. It did not last, of course. The final remnant of the Crusader territories in Palestine was lost in 1291 and Latin control of Constantinople lasted but sixty years in all.

The Crusades provide a dismal chapter in the history of missions. What can be said more positively concerning the later Middle Ages? Mention should be made of great individuals: John of Monte Corvino, who reached Khanbalik (Peking) in China about 1293, and Ramon Lull, who witnessed to Christ among the Muslims and died of injuries received at their hands in 1315. It was Lull who wrote: "Missionaries will convert the world by preaching, but also through the shedding of tears and blood with great labour, and through bitter death."[24]

The Expansion of Europe: The Beginning of Modern Missions

In the year 1454 Pope Nicholas V (d. 1455) issued a decree to the king of Portugal concerning the "plan for the Indies." In the previous year Constantinople had fallen to the Muslims (the Ottoman Turks), Europe was enclosed by non-Christian enemies and increasingly dependent upon Venetian merchants with their exorbitant charges for goods from India and elsewhere in the east, including the precious spices which were much in demand. In addition a new source of slaves seemed necessary, slaves who had previously been taken from Slavic Europe. Now the pope encouraged the Portuguese to find new sea routes circumventing the obstacles to the east. In the process it would be expected that non-Christians would be converted and that contact would be made with Christians in far distant places, with the possibility of further alliances against the Muslims. At the same time, the papacy, sitting in judgment on the affairs of the world, divided any new lands discovered between Portugal and Spain, drawing an imaginary line down the Atlantic Ocean, awarding Africa, Asia, and Brazil to Portugal and all lands westward, North, Central, and most of South America, to Spain.

The Portuguese led the way with their superior ships and their navigational and map-making skills. Inspired by Prince Henry, named the Navigator (1394–1460), they pushed down the west coast of Africa. The black people of tropical Africa were contacted about 1444, in 1482 the conquest of the Congo was begun, and in 1487 Bartholomew Diaz rounded the Cape of Good Hope. In 1498 Vasco da Gama reached the west coast of the Indian subcontinent at Calicut, and the Portuguese colonization of India was begun. By 1517 Fernan de Andrade reached China at Canton and three years later there was a Portuguese ambassador at the court of the emperor of China. In the process, the explorers did indeed outwit both the Muslims and the Venetians, and they took priests with them as chaplains and as missionaries to the people they met and subdued.

Spain began its serious involvement in expansion with the expulsion of the last remnant of Muslim (or Moorish) territorial control in Spain, at Granada. In that same year, one of the two rulers of Spain, Isabella of Castile, consented to the plan of the Italian explorer, Christopher Columbus, "to make for India through the seas of the [Atlantic] Ocean with three armed caravelles." Convinced that the eastern shores of Asia lay westward across the Atlantic, Columbus set forth with a letter to the ruler of China. He first landed on one of the islands of the Bahamas and called it San Salvador. From the outset, Columbus rejoiced in the opportunities both for the Christian faith and for the increase of Spain's wealth.

In quest of gold and converts, soldiers and friars, Franciscans and Dominicans (the Jesuits soon followed), pressed steadily on. In 1513 Balboa reached through Central America to "the Great South Sea"—the Pacific Ocean—and dreamed of a land called Peru with its mountains of gold, "more gold than there was iron in Biscay." In 1519 Cortez began the swift conquest of Mexico, destroying the weakened Aztec civilization. In 1531 Pizarro confirmed Balboa's dream and began the conquest of Peru. The mines of Peru were worked by the surviving Incas under the harsh supervision of the Spanish masters, and gold began to flow across the Atlantic enhancing the wealth and power of Spain. The Spaniards were also to penetrate the present United States in an attempt to establish a mission in Florida in 1527. A permanent settlement was made there in 1565 and lasted under Spanish control until the beginning of the eighteenth century.

It is important to realize that through this entire period, from the beginning of the sixteenth century to the latter part of the eighteenth, Christianity accompanied the explorers, soldiers, early European traders and settlers, and the colonial officials, and was regarded as identical to the nationalities of the westerners. For instance, in seventeenth-century India Parava Christians let it be known that to be converted and baptized was to be incorporated into the caste of the Parangis, that is, to be made Portuguese. Missionaries might well, and often did, vehemently deny such an equation of religion with nationality, but they could not deny their subordination to the civil rulers who oversaw their work. In Spanish America the far distant Spanish rulers appointed bishops and no papal decree could be acknowledged without royal approval. Thus, the faith and the wealth of nations were intimately related. It was just here, however, that the trouble began. For that which was deemed economically sound (for instance, the buying and holding of Africans as slaves and the economic exploitation of Latin America) offended consciences and aroused the desire for reform.

The Dominican missionary, Bartholomew de Las Casas (1474–1566) was angered by the treatment the Indians received from their landlords in Santa Domingo and Cuba. Convinced that force ought not to be used against the Indians he inveighed against those who treated them as dumb beasts:

> The Indian race is not that barbaric, nor are they dull witted or stupid, but they are easy to teach and very talented in learning all the liberal arts, and very ready to accept, honor, and observe the Christian religion.[25]

He struggled against overwhelming odds to protect the Indians against abuse and to convert them to "Christianity by the methods of Christ." His work in Guatemala and Nicaragua, evangelizing Indians who had withstood the Spanish onslaught, bore fruit. In time there came a decree from Pope Paul III (1534–1549) which said:

> We, who, though unworthy, exercise on earth the power of our Lord and seek with all our might to bring those sheep of His flock who are outside into the fold committed to our charge,

consider . . . that the Indians are truly men and that they are not only capable of understanding the catholic faith but, according to our information, they desire exceedingly to receive it. . . . We define and declare . . . that, notwithstanding whatever may have been or may be said to the contrary, the said Indians and all other people who may later be discovered by Christians, are by no means to be deprived of their liberty or the possession of their property, even though they be outside the faith of Jesus Christ . . . nor should they be in any way enslaved.[26]

The ideal was clear, but it was difficult to realize in relation to people and nations lusting for gold and cheap labor.

Beyond simple justice due to human beings, there was sensitivity to other cultures and religions. If there was little of the former, there was less of the latter. The people whom the explorers encountered were characterized as savages and heathen. There were exceptions. Chief among the exceptions were certain Jesuits, members of the Society of Jesus. This society was founded by the Spaniard, Ignatius of Loyola (1491–1556) and authorized by the papacy in 1540. The Jesuits formed an army of spiritual shock troops doing battle against the Protestants. They also made important contributions to university education, the formulation of modern Roman Catholic theology, and to missions.

The first and foremost Jesuit missionary was Francis Xavier (1506–1552). He went to India in 1542 and to Japan in 1549, where he opened a Christian mission in a land virtually untouched by the west. In India Francis exhibited his sensitivity to the importance of caste (the social stratification of Indian society) and the necessity to respect the cultural conditions of the fisher folk of South India among whom he worked. It was in Japan, however, that Francis came to believe that there was much of value in the culture of these non-Christian people and that missionaries should build on the good that already existed. It was wrong, he believed, to reject as worthless a civilization which bred nobility in people and contained a basic understanding of God.

Matthew Ricci (1552–1610), another Jesuit, entered the seemingly impenetrable China where he won favor with the emperor by his ability to repair clocks. His success, limited although it was, was connected with his patience and his careful use of Chinese words and images to denote God (*T'ien Chu*, "Lord of Heaven") and the holy (*Sheng*, "the venerable"). The Chinese teacher Confucius was called St. Confucius by Ricci. There is also the example of Robert de Nobili (1577–1656), missionary to Madurai, India, the center of Tamil culture. Robert "went native" adopting Brahman dress and eating habits. He mastered the language and separated himself from everything western. As a *guru*, religious teacher, he gained a following and aroused much controversy, for there were those convinced that Christianity must not condone the caste system but must break down all barriers which separate people. In a positive sense, accommodation involved adoption of cultural symbols and the adaptation of liturgy to local custom and languages. But it also involved risk. The papacy recognized the risk, in particular that the distinctive nature of the Christian Gospel might be lost, and in 1742 and 1744 decreed an end to all efforts at accommodation, requiring that everything be done in India and China and elsewhere as it was done in Rome. The great experiment was seemingly at an end; it remained inoperative for two centuries.

In the seventeenth century the domination of Portugal and Spain yielded before the French who quickly established footholds around the world, and effected an area of dominance in the present Canada and the valley of the Mississippi River. The history of New France extends from 1608, when Samuel Champlain began a trading post at the present city of Quebec, to 1763 when at the end of the French and Indian wars they surrendered their lands in North America to England and Spain. Caught in the conflict between peoples such as the Iroquois and the Hurons, the French struggled to be accommodating and ended by aggravating the suicidal conflict which was wearing down all involved.

By the seventeenth century non-Roman Catholic powers entered the contest for new lands. The impulse was not primarily religious, Protestants lacking interest in missions at the time. The English and the Dutch were most prominent, the former reaching eastward to India and westward to North America. The Dutch went as far east as Indonesia and in the west settled in New Amsterdam (the present New York), among other places.

The first permanent English colony in what is now the continental United States was begun in 1607 as a commercial venture of the London Company in Virginia. It was chartered by King James I and the charter made it clear that the missionary motive was secondary. Alexander Whitaker (1585–1617), minister of Henrico, in *Good News from Virginia* (1613), wrote back to England pleading:

> Let the miserable condition of these naked slaves of the divill move you to compassion toward them. They acknowledge that there is a great good God, but know him not, having the eyes of their understanding as yet blinded: wherefore they serve the divell for feare, after a most base manner . . . . Let me advise you to be liberall in adventure hither, and I dare affirme, that by Gods assistance, your profitable returnes shall be of more certainty, and much shorter expectation.[27]

This was the general attitude of the Puritans as well as the Anglicans and worked to the detriment of the church's mission and to the discredit of the Christian faith among a proud and deeply religious people.

Again, there were exceptions. John Eliot (1604–1690) of Massachusetts learned the language of the Pequot tribe of the Iroquois nation, translated the Bible, and treated converts with great care. David Brainerd (1718–1747) labored among the Indians and became for many the model missionary. The Anglican Society for the Propagation of the Gospel in Foreign Parts made its contribution to work among the Indians during the eighteenth century. But by and large the story during colonial times is one of deep tragedy for the native Americans, perpetrated by intruders who brought with them disease, liquor, and firearms. Such Christians seemed not devout but rather enemies of the God known to many as Atachocan, creator of the world, or Messou, who restored the world after the great flood and gave the gift of immortality.

There is much more which deserves attention: the conversion of Russia following the fall of Constantinople in 1453 and the declaration of Moscow as the Third Rome, the head of the Orthodox East; the British East India Company and the employment by Anglicans of German Pietists to work in South India; and the important missionary enterprises of the Scandinavians during this time. Two things are impressive: (1) the spread of Christianity around the world with the expansion of western European power, and (2) the thinness with which it was spread, the tenuousness of much of the missionary work, and the repeated compromising of the Gospel through western prejudices and lusts.

Too often the missionaries were under orders of military, political, and commercial interests, insensitive to the conditions of the people to whom they were sent, viewing them as less than human, devoid of civilization and religion. More often than we can bear to enumerate, missionaries rationalized the inhumanity of soldiers and merchants, neglecting to establish indigenous leadership, so that when reactions set in against foreigners, missionaries were expelled and missions collapsed. It could be said that Christians were learning and that persons such as St. Francis Xavier, Robert Nobili, and David Brainerd were on the cutting edge of what would be when the Spirit took command.

The Great Century of Protestant Missions: 1789–1914

Roman Catholic missions experienced a revival in the nineteenth century. This involved greater participation by the laity in Europe, greater independence from the Roman Catholic governments which had controlled the missions since 1500, and the adoption of different methods. They deemphasized mass conversions and concentrated on a slower but seemingly more effective appeal to individuals and families. But the story of missions in the nineteenth century is dominated by Protestantism (and, one should add, Anglicanism), because this period marks the real beginning of Protestant world missions and because the results were apparently so dramatic. From meager beginnings, some of which we observed in the last section, Protestant missions by 1900 involved 13,600 overseas missionaries in every part of the world. By 1914 there were 22,000, half of them women.

Women were prominent in the history of modern missions. Examples range from Mary Fisher, the Quaker who sought to convert Sultan Mohammed IV in 1658, to Dr. Fanny Butler, the medical missionary who arrived in India in 1880, to Helen Willis of the Plymouth Brethren, the last Protestant missionary to leave China in 1959. Quaker women left their mark on New England, Mary Fisher and Ann Austin arriving in Boston in 1656, Mary Dyer suffering martyrdom for the faith as she knew it in 1660. During the nineteenth century women served in various capacities, as wives of missionaries but also as leaders in educational and medical missions.

The rise of Protestant missionary concern in the late eighteenth century was a product of Evangelical revivals in Britain and the United States. These revivals were influenced by German Pietism with its evangelical intensity and missionary zeal. The revivals also involved attitudes which were to be reflected in subsequent missionary activities. These included a considerable independence from control by the civil government and a relatively freer attitude toward ecclesiastical institutions enabling the missionaries to adjust to differing local situations to a degree virtually unknown to their Protestant predecessors or their Roman Catholic contemporaries.

In both Britain and America the renewal of concern for mission took place in voluntary societies. We have noted such societies before and now observe that alongside societies concerned with issues of public and private morality (such as slavery and temperance) and those devoted to charitable causes, there were societies concerned with specifically religious needs, such as the Bible societies and those devoted to missions. The societies were characterized by disinterested benevolence, derived in America in part from the natural rights philosophy embodied in the Declaration of Independence and in part from the assertion of human worth over against the Calvanist emphasis on human depravity. Thus the same elements which inspired Christian Socialism and the Social Gospel were there in the origins of the modern missionary movement.

In addition to disinterested benevolence and human worth, there was the conviction shared by many that the end of the world was near and that before the end the Gospel must be made known to all people. The urgency of this belief was imbued with a sense of optimism in such a way that sufficient motive power was generated to set the machinery of the church going. It would be erroneous to speak of this movement solely in terms of "foreign" missions, although for some that was where the emphasis properly belonged. The mounting enthusiasm for missions involved all aspects of church life, with missionary services in local churches, and with "home" missions as well as "foreign" or overseas missions.

In Britain the most prominent Bible society was known as the British and Foreign Bible Society (1804) with associations and auxiliaries which became agents for the missionary movement in England as well as overseas. In America the American Home Missionary Society, founded in 1826, was an agency of Presbyterian, Congregationalist, Dutch Reformed, and Associated Reformed churches. By 1850 it employed 1,065 missionaries founding churches in new communities which were then provided with financial assistance. In the Episcopal Church home missions were the work of outstanding bishops such as Alexander Viets Griswold (1766–1843) in New England; John Henry Hobart (1775–1830) in New York State; Philander Chase (1775–1852) in Ohio, Michigan, and Illinois; Jackson Kemper (1789–1870), the church's first designated missionary bishop who labored in the mid-West; James Hervey Otey (1800–1863) in the deep South; and others. Such individual efforts were enhanced in 1820 by the creation of the Domestic and Foreign Missionary Society, referred to in the second chapter. From 1820 on into the twentieth century home missions would be a major concern of the Episcopal Church.

The beginnings of "foreign" missions in nineteenth century Britain go back to the remarkable William Carey

(1761–1834). A shoemaker from Northamptonshire, Carey became a Baptist minister. Along the way he was influenced by Captain Cook's *Voyages*, by geographical and ethnological research, and by the examples of John Eliot and David Brainerd among the American Indians. He was also impressed by the great Roman Catholic and Pietist missionaries and influenced by the evangelical preaching of the Anglican Thomas Scott (1747–1821). As a result Carey focused his life on launching a mission to all humanity. In 1792 the Particular Baptist Society for the Propagation of the Gospel amongst the Heathen was founded to support Carey. In the next year Carey was sent to India. There in Bengal he worked to support himself and his wife, studied the local language, and translated the Bible into several Indian tongues. He began to train Indians for ministry to their own people and he actively stimulated social reforms. An accomplished linguist and also a botanist with a good reputation in the field, Carey became well known and admired in India and in Europe, and for years after his death was looked to as a model missionary.

One result of Carey's inspiration was the founding of the London Missionary Society in 1795. This society was interdenominational and became a major instrument for Protestant missions in the nineteenth century. Four years later the Church Missionary Society (CMS) was founded by Anglican Evangelicals. For the next century it exercised great influence at home and abroad in places such as India, Africa, New Zealand, Canada, the West Indies, China, Japan, and among the Muslims. The CMS was not alone, of course, for the Society for Promoting Christian Knowledge (1698) and the Society for the Propagation of the Gospel (1701) long preceded it. But the CMS was the major conduit in Anglicanism for the evangelical zeal which was arousing Protestantism at the time. In addition to societies there were outstanding individuals. Indeed, some of the best Anglican leadership went into overseas missions during the period. Among the many who might be mentioned, there were Reginald Heber (1783–1826) in India, Edward Bickersteth (1850–1897) in Japan, David Livingstone (1813–1873), and Alexander Mackay (1849–1890) in Africa.

Henry Martyn (1781–1812) occupies a special place in the story of Anglican missions. Fellow of St. John's College, Cambridge, Martyn heard of William Carey from the evangelical churchman Charles Simeon and read a life of David Brainerd. He then studied for ordination and was ordained in 1803. In 1805 he set out for India as a chaplain of the East India Company. His ministry in India was brief, but in a relatively short time he achieved much. He conducted services among the people in their own dialect, established schools, translated the New Testament into Hindustani and then translated it into Persian. Planning an edition of the New Testament in Arabic, Martyn died of a fever in Tokat, Turkey.

In America the modern missionary movement began at Williams College in Massachusetts about 1808 under the leadership of Samuel J. Mills, Jr., a student much affected by the second Great Awakening. Mills was instrumental in the formation of a society called "The Brethren," concerned "to effect in the persons of its members a mission or missions to the heathen." At Andover Seminary this secret society expanded, adding, among others, Adoniram Judson, Jr. In 1810 some of the Brethren offered themselves to the Congregational Society of Massachusetts, which created the American Board of Commissioners for Foreign Missions, sending Judson, Luther Rice, and three others to the Orient. On the way out, Judson and Rice became Baptists and were involved in the founding of the General Missionary Convention of the Baptists in 1814.

The American Board had in mind the establishment of missions among nonbelievers and the translation and publication of the Bible in "languages spoken by unevangelized nations." In an appeal published in 1812, as the first missionaries left for the Orient, the clergy of the American churches were exhorted to join in the evangelization of the world. It was to be a great cooperative effort

> to bring about this event in the shortest time. All the power and influence of the whole Christian world must be put in requisition, during the course of those beneficent labors which will precede the millennium. . . . The utmost exertion of every

Christian now living, so far as his other duties will permit, is required in this glorious service. How boundless must be the field of labor which admits, and will continue to admit, the labors of all benevolent persons, in every region of the habitable globe![28]

Missionaries did indeed go out to all the earth from America to convert the heathen. Conversion, education, healing, distribution of the Bible in a multitude of languages, were expressive of the missionary zeal and benevolent spirit of American Protestantism.

The overseas work of the Episcopal Church, conducted through the Domestic and Foreign Missionary Society, began in Greece, newly liberated from the Ottoman Turks. John J. Robertson, John H. Hill and his wife, and Solomon Bingham, a printer, set sail in 1830 determined not to offend Greek Christians by seeming to proselytize and aiming to provide general education in a Christian context to meet apparent needs. This work, along with a mission to the Muslims, received little support and gradually waned.

The case was different in Liberia. Here the American Colonization Society had founded a nation for freed American slaves in 1817. The work of the Episcopal Church began there in 1835 when the black churchman James Thompson, secretary to the colonial agent in Cape Palmas, started a school with the assistance of his wife. In the next year Launcelot B. Minor, John Payne, and Thomas Savage, a physician, arrived. In 1850 Payne was bishop and there were fourteen mission stations, two hundred forty communicants, and fifteen schools. Education and evangelism went hand in hand to form there "a visible church of Christ . . . under the ordinances of the church." Another beginning for black missions occured in 1861 when the black priest, James T. Holly, led a group of black emigrants from the United States to Haiti. Holly founded the "Orthodox Apostolic Church of Haiti," with the approval of the American House of Bishops which entered into a covenant with it. There then began a remarkable story of courage which unfolded as Bishop Holly served his people against great odds, including repeated political and social disturbances, until his death in 1911. In 1912 Holly's Haitian church became a foreign missionary district of the Episcopal Church in the United States.

The permanent mission of the Episcopal Church to China is associated with the name of William J. Boone, a graduate of Virginia Seminary who in 1837 went to Java to study Chinese. In 1841 Boone and his wife established a mission at Amoy with plans for a hospital and a preaching hall. On the death of his wife in 1842, Boone returned to the United States and was elected the first overseas missionary bishop of the Episcopal Church in 1844. The next year Boone, with eight others, arrived in Shanghai. By 1850 the first church was consecrated there with twelve to thirteen hundred people present. The sermon was prepared by the bishop in English. He then translated it into the Amoy dialect and then with help into the speech of Shanghai. Language always seemed to provide a major challenge. In time the Episcopal Church had missions not only in Africa and Asia, but also in Central and South America. Such investment in overseas missions was considered vital to the Episcopal Church well into the twentieth century.

The detailed history of Christian missionary activity during the nineteenth century is vast and complex. Here we are limited to recording beginnings and to considering the general assessment of the movement during the century. In 1910 the first World Missionary Conference was held at Edinburgh. We have noted the presence of Charles Henry Brent, missionary bishop of the Philippines, and the conviction that the world mission required cooperation and, especially in the mission field, some degree at least of organic unity if the harmful competition between denominational groups was to be overcome. Edinburgh thus marks the turning point at which missions and ecumenicity are viewed together. The conference was imbued with enthusiasm for the missionary task and with optimism concerning its outcome. John R. Mott, who was its chairman, proclaimed: "The Evangelization of the World in this Generation." By this he intended the missionary imperative which confronts every generation, but some took him to mean the conversion of all people on earth in the next twenty to thirty years. The slogan expressed, as Bishop Stephen Neill, a missionary leader of our time, has put it, "the continually rising curve of missionary endeavour, and the hope that the curve might continue to rise similarly." Bishop Neill catalogues some of the achievements which supported such optimism:

1. Though some countries, such as Tibet and Afghanistan, remained closed, missionaries had been able to find a footing in every part of the known world.
2. The back of the pioneer work had been broken. Languages had been learned and reduced to writing; all the main living languages of the world had by now received at least the New Testament.
3. Tropical medicine had solved most of the problems of disease, and made possible the prolonged residence of the white man even in the most unfavourable climates.
4. Every religion in the world had yielded some converts as a result of missionary preaching.
5. No race of men had been found which was incapable of understanding the Gospel, though some were more ready to receive it than others.
6. The missionary no longer stood alone; an increasing army of nationals stood ready to assist him.
7. The younger Churches were beginning to produce leaders at least the equals of the missionary in intellectual gifts and spiritual stature.
8. The Churches had become engaged, as never before, in the support of the missionary enterprise.
9. Financial support had kept pace with the rapid expansion of the work in every part of the world.
10. The universities of the West were producing a steady stream of men and women of the highest potential for missionary work.
11. The influence of the Christian Gospel was spreading far beyond the ranks of those who had actually accepted it.
12. Intransigent opposition to the Gospel seemed in many countries, such as China and Japan, finally to have broken down.[29]

Twentieth Century Challenge: Repentance and Renewal

The vision of "The Evangelization of the World in this Generation" was dashed upon the rocks of hard realities from 1914 on. Two global wars, divided by a massive economic depression, not only disturbed the work of missionaries but raised serious questions concerning the validity of the missionary vision. The wars changed many things and contributed to the breaking up of the old colonial empires. Britain's withdrawal from India in 1947 was the beginning of the end of the once mighty British Empire. Such withdrawal took place in response to rising nationalism, a phenomenon rapidly spreading over Asia and Africa. In the process hatred against the oppressive Christian west was vented. The result was that where the Christian church was equated with the colonial powers the Gospel was rejected and missionaries expelled.

In Europe itself there were changes occurring which challenged Christianity and threatened the peaceful and prosperous continuance of the churches. In 1917 a revolution occurred in Russia, after which atheistic Marxism sought to control and then to eliminate Christianity. Soviet Communism in the early years saw to the execution of twenty-eight bishops and one thousand two hundred ninety priests of the Russian Orthodox Church. At the same time the Soviets launched an anti-god movement which held up all religion to ridicule and cast doubt on anyone who claimed to be Christian. By 1950 Communism had swept over China and down into Southeast Asia. In Europe it gained followings in several East European countries and was a power to be reckoned with in Italy and France. In addition to such forthright opposition, there was the steady diminution of the churches themselves. Church attendance in nations such as France and Britain dropped severely. Much talk was heard of the "Post-Christian Era," the paganization of Europe, and the insidious nature of creeping secularism.

Finally, note must be made of the emergence of a world culture. Whatever happened in one place in the world could have ramifications in any other place. A grain harvest fails in Russia causing large sales of wheat by the United States. These sales are accompanied by a rise in food costs and arouse housewives across the nation to strike. Meanwhile, in the Sudan, in Africa, a famine sets in. Grain is sought but has already been dispersed to Russia, and thousands upon thousands die. The consequences of growing interdependence among the nations of the world have only begun to emerge. As they emerge it is clear that Christianity faces a challenge involving issues of race, sex, nationality, religion, and culture. The new situation of instant electronic communication means that whatever Christians do will be more fully exposed to public scrutiny and the Christian record analyzed more rigorously.

From the vantage point of the last half of the twentieth century, with all the changes which have and shall occur, the so-called "Great Century" of Protestant missions is found to be one of both greatness and folly. As we have seen there were elements in the evangelical revivals which promised that the missionary movement influenced by them should be independent of governmental control and of narrow ecclesiastical traditions. As it happened, missionary activity has been criticized in the twentieth century for being the tool of Western imperialistic powers. It has been found so imbedded in Western churchly traditions that missionaries appeared bent on conquest rather than accommodation.

In India, Christian missionaries during the nineteenth century tended to view themselves as waging war against the moral darkness and idolatry of Hinduism. To a large extent this attitude was derived from Charles Grant's *Observations on the State of India among the Asiatic Subjects of Great Britain* (1792). Grant depicted Indian society as corrupt, its corruption stemming from the Hindu religion. Therefore, he argued, if there was to be good government, the Indian people must first be won away from Hinduism to Christianity. Britain's national interests in India were thus tied to Christian missionary work, an understanding which seemed to prevail up to the Indian Mutiny of 1857 which marked the end of any strong Christian influence on public policy in India. The mutiny was inspired in part by the fears of Muslims and Hindus that the whole population was about to be forcibly converted to Christianity.

In West Africa the racism of the modern missionary movement was exposed. Henry Venn, Secretary of the Church Missionary Society from 1842 to 1872, made an African,

Samuel Crowther, bishop of the Niger Mission. Crowther was consecrated by the archbishop of Canterbury and others in England and labored in Africa until his death in 1891. In the 1880s an inquisition against Bishop Crowther was begun. There were those who argued vehemently against the CMS program to create an indigenous African church. There now came missionaries far more extreme in their views, openly venting their racist prejudices. Crowther was vilified and stripped of much of his power. After his death no successor was appointed. When nationalism rose in the twentieth century and the whites were driven out of one place after another in Africa, Crowther was looked back upon as a powerful symbol of the black African's ability to evangelize and to rule in the church.

As revolution swept across Africa and Asia, the Christian churches worked frantically to make their missions self-supporting both financially and in terms of leadership. But in some places there was neither enough time nor enough patience. In Ethiopia David B. Vincent renounced his European name, became Majola Ageli, and was involved in the founding of the Native Baptist Church in 1888. He was proud to be black and African. The missionaries he viewed as having led in the exploitation of his land and people by whites. At one time he said:

> Prayer-books and Hymn-books, harmonium dedications, pew constructions, surpliced choirs, the white man's style, the white man's name, the white man's dress, are so many non-essentials, so many props and crutches affecting the religious manhood of the Christian African. Among the great essentials of religion are that the lame walk, the lepers are cleansed, the deaf hear, the dead are raised up, and the poor have the Gospel preached to them.[30]

The black African was in process of becoming the missionary to the white European and American churches, teaching them about things essential and nonessential, testing their devotion to the Lord.

Then too, the twentieth century has scrutinized the achievements of the nineteenth and is unimpressed by the statistical results. In the places where the missionaries went they ordinarily achieved footholds and little more. Christians numbered but two percent of the population in India, one percent in China, and one-half percent in Japan. In China the Christian faith, as embodied in ecclesiastical institutions, has been rejected again and again. Sierra Leone in Africa was established as a Christian land, a home for freed slaves. The work of the missionaries there was fostered by the government and has had a continuous existence of one hundred and seventy years. Indeed, for a time in the nineteenth century missionaries from Sierra Leone went to Ghana and Nigeria and were influential in the spread of Christianity in Africa. But today Christians constitute but five percent of the population and there is no evident missionary zeal. Of that five percent it is questionable how many deeply committed Christians there are. A survey made recently of the Mende people of Sierra Leone, among whom Christian missionaries worked for generations, discovered:

> Most chiefs who are professing Christians also have an ancestral shrine in their compounds. . . . A number of other individuals who are nominally Christians continue the ancestral practices at the same time. . . . Many of them turn instead to magic. They rely quite often on special talismans. Others are regular clients of medicine men whose help they seek in love affairs and to further personal careers.[31]

Not all African churches are like this. In the next chapter we shall note a striking exception in East Africa.

Most positively, the changing world of the twentieth century has provoked a number of different attitudes toward missions. There are, of course, those who retain a nineteenth century view of home and foreign missions. This is especially true of Pentecostal churches and their missions, which have experienced phenomenal growth around the world. Pentecostals emphasize the work of the Holy Spirit and "speaking with tongues." With zeal and simplicity they plunge into the most desperate situations of poverty and suffering, taking with them the Christian message of hope, along with food and medicines. In Latin America and Africa the Pentecostals provide a courageous witness.

In many places the older methods have been modified. The modern ecumenical movement has been important in this, the greatest change being from programs based upon missions sent from a superior to an inferior people, to programs based upon churches in different places working in partnership to meet the particular needs of each. We shall have cause to consider this more fully as we proceed, particularly in relation to the Toronto Conference of Anglicans in 1963. A further modification has to do with the waning power and influence of the church in the west. It is now clear to many leaders that mission applies not to separate missionary jurisdictions but to all people and to all human situations. To put it another way, Christ's mission involves coming to grips with the principalities and powers of this world. So spoke E. R. Wickham, founder of the Sheffield Industrial Mission and a bishop of the Church of England.

Some twenty years ago Bishop Wickham wrote:

> If some environments make response [to the Gospel] more probable and others more improbable, then it follows as night follows day that the Church must be acutely concerned with those conditioning factors, from the point of view of her missionary task, if for none other. There is Biblical precedent! The children of Israel, we are told, cried unto God by reason of their bondage in Egypt, yet "they hearkened not to Moses for anguish of spirit and for cruel bondage." . . . If men are "made" by their environment in the widest sense, as they so manifestly are, the Church's mission is not exhausted by mere awareness, but demands a direct impact on those institutions and within the culture pattern. It is the concern with what may be called "principalities and powers"—all-pervasive and determining factors that can enslave men or liberate them, stunt them or increase their stature as men, and which can be demonic or angelic.[32]

There have been many who have identified themselves as being involved in Christ's mission when struggling against apartheid in South Africa, fighting for justice in South America, striving for women's rights in society and church, working for a greater sense of responsibility toward a sorely taxed natural environment, laboring in industrial missions in Sheffield and Detroit, and marching in civil rights protests. There is a point at which social action and mission converge and for many it is the most viable form of Christian mission for the last quarter of the twentieth century.

Another way of mission in the present era involves dialogue with other religions. Canon Kenneth Cragg has been an eloquent advocate of such dialogue which begins with an awareness of common humanity under God. He has been particularly concerned with Islam, exploring likenesses as well as differences. In one place he has written:

> The Bible and the Qur'ān are full of the splendour and the mystery of the universe, the fidelities of nature, the strange entrustments of pregnancy and harvest. . . . The mercies of God in the different fields of prophet and Messiah, of revelation and Scriptures . . . still have mutual features we must be careful not to miss. The rule of God, the instrumentality of men, the moral of history, the care of time, the reckoning with death, are among them. The diagnosis of sin, despite the different laws, has elements in common.[33]

This does not mean that the many disagreements are ignored but rather that an effort is made to push beyond them to a higher level of mutual understanding. For John V. Taylor of the Church Missionary Society this way of meeting other faiths has involved an understanding of the Holy Spirit as universally present in the world, while

> *uniquely* present in Christ and, by extension, in the fellowship of his disciples. But even that unique presence is not enclosed, either in Christ or in his church, but exists between Christ and the other, between Christians and those who meet them. The centre is always on the circumference, yet it proves to be the circumference of *that* centre and not another.[34]

Finally, there is the attitude which accepts the servant character of the church and the hard realities of the present most seriously. Those who hold it do not flinch to speak of the humiliation of the church in the twentieth century. They regard that humiliation as being a means of restoring the true nature of the Christian mission in the world. In our day some express what is meant here in terms of waiting or patience. T. S. Eliot, the modern Anglican poet and dramatist, describes this waiting in his *Four Quartets:*

I said to my soul, be still, and let the dark come upon you
Which shall be the darkness of God . . .
I said to my soul, be still, and wait without hope
For hope would be hope for the wrong thing; wait without
   love
For love would be love of the wrong thing; there is yet faith
But the faith and the love and the hope are all in the
   waiting.
Wait without thought, for you are not ready for thought:
So the darkness shall be light, and the stillness the
   dancing.[35]

Another way of expressing this attitude is to speak of Christian presence such as that practiced by Père Charles de Foucald and the Little Brothers and Little Sisters of Jesus. They do not preach or found schools and hospitals or use other customary methods of modern missions. They simply live among the poor. They are found all over the world, among the Eskimos of Alaska, in a village of Papua, and on a houseboat with refugees at Hong Kong. Wherever they are they live lives of prayer and go out to work performing the same sorts of labor as their neighbors do. Foucald has said, "I wish to cry the gospel with my whole life." His followers seek to emulate him, separated from the ordinary externals of the church, praying, loving, working, being Christ present in the world. They are, of course, not alone. Perhaps the most effective participants in Christ's mission today are unknown except to those they serve.

A landmark for Anglicans in this new age was the Anglican Congress which met at Toronto, Canada, in 1963. The Anglican communion had made great strides by then. Composed of autonomous churches around the world related by a common history and filial ties through the see of Canterbury, the communion functioned through the Lambeth Conference of Bishops meeting every ten years, and through the Advisory Council on Missionary Strategy. The latter had been established in 1878 but did not function fully until 1948. Further progress was to be made in 1968 when Lambeth created the Anglican Consultative Council.

In 1959 Stephen F. Bayne, Jr., bishop of Olympia in the state of Washington, was made the first Executive Officer of the Anglican communion. He was the moving force of the Toronto Congress of some one thousand delegates from eighteen provinces and more than three hundred and forty dioceses. The delegates assembled in penitence for their sins of omission and commission and resolved to advance Christ's mission, putting aside all talk of missions and missionaries. The fruits of their deliberations were contained in a document called *Mutual Responsibility and Interdependence in the Body of Christ*. For a community of churches long divided between the "haves" and the "have nots," where economics was a concern, the document contained some revolutionary ideas. At the outset it was stated:

> The full communion in Christ which has been our traditional tie has suddenly taken on a totally new dimension. It is now irrelevant to talk of "giving" and "receiving" churches. The keynotes of our time are equality, interdependence, mutual responsibility.
>
> Three central truths at the heart of our faith command us in this:
>
> *The Church's mission is response to the living God Who in His love creates, reveals, judges, redeems, fulfills. It is He Who moves through our history to teach and to save, Who calls us to receive His love, to learn, to obey and to follow.*
>
> *Our unity in Christ, expressed in our full communion, is the most profound bond among us, in all our political and racial and cultural diversity.*
>
> *The time has fully come when this unity and interdependence must find a completely new level of expression and corporate obedience.*[36]

Interdependence meant the study of the actual needs and resources of the entire communion of churches and a commitment, concretely financial, which would constitute the beginning of action to end "the humiliation and beggary" among the newer provinces of the communion. It also involved establishing the administrative machinery needed to bring about a more radical commitment to mission. The document ended:

> We are aware that such a program as we propose, if it is seen in its true size and accepted, will mean the death of much that is familiar about our churches now. It will mean radical change in our priorities—even leading us to share with others at least as much as we spend on ourselves. It means the death of old isolations and inherited attitudes. It means a willingness to forego many desirable things, in every church.
>
> In substance, what we are really asking is the rebirth of the Anglican Communion, which means the death of many old things but—infinitely more—the birth of entirely new relationships. We regard this as the essential task before the churches of the Anglican Communion.[37]

The chief result of the program called Mutual Responsibility and Interdependence in the Body of Christ (MRI) was the creation of a Directory of Projects through which cooperation in mission was fostered as churches assisted one another in vital areas of need. But, as the Anglican Consultative Council meeting in Dublin, Ireland, in 1973, reported, MRI has "been too largely identified with the Directory of Projects, and this in turn has led to a 'shopping list' mentality." The high ideals expressed at Toronto were not realized, although valuable new relationships between the churches of the Anglican communion were established. With awareness of the failures of MRI the Dublin meeting of the Anglican Consultative Council initiated another program called "Partners in Mission." The aim was to recapture and emphasize the spiritual dimensions of the Toronto Congress indicated when in their report they called for "radical changes in our priorities." Thus, through a series of consultations in different parts of the world, churches with the assistance of partners from all sections of the Anglican communion would engage in the planning and fixing of priorities. The Episcopal Church held its consultations in the spring of 1977 in all eight of its provinces ending with a national consultation in Louisville, Kentucky. Dioceses, Provinces, and the Executive Council of the Episcopal Church were all called upon to examine themselves and their goals in the presence of partners from Africa, Asia, Europe and Latin America. The results were both exhilarating and painful.

In Province I (New England), for instance, the partners

from Ontario, Barbados, the Windward Islands, Malaysia, South America, and ecumenical representatives from the National Council of Churches recognized the high quality of leadership in the province but pointed to the lack of a sense of partnership, a crippling parochialism, and a loss of nerve where the mission of the church is concerned. At Louisville the Executive Council approved the continuation of the Partners in Mission process and acknowledged its responsibility in several areas including such matters as parochialism, urban work, stewardship, and evangelism. It recognized the centrality of worship, the necessity of new life-styles, and the importance of an examination of Church structures. With high hopes that the ideals expressed at Toronto in 1963 may now begin to be realized, they said:

> We, the members of the Executive Council, have been privileged to share a renewed vision of Christian partnership. We are mindful that the mission of the Gospel begins, continues, and ends in God. The Spirit of the Lord has been moving among us at every level of the church's life. For this we are deeply grateful.[38]

The Ecumenical Movement: "That they may be one."

The Ecumenical Movement began with a variety of movements which gradually merged to form the World Council of Churches. First, there were movements serving to coordinate existing functions. The World Student Christian Federation, founded in 1895, was one of these. John R. Mott, whom we have already met, announced:

> The Federation will . . . unite in spirit the students of the world . . . in doing this it will be achieving a yet more significant result—the hastening of the answer to our Lord's prayer "that they all may be one."[39]

The International Missionary Council, inspired in part by the Edinburgh Conference of 1910, came into being in 1921. It subsequently held world conferences at Oxford (1923), Jerusalem (1928), and Tambaram, India (1938). It was at Tambaram that the younger missionary churches gained entrance and began to make their influence felt. The council came to be the focal point and clearinghouse for many of the churches working in missionary fields.

The second category of movements consists of those which brought the Christian conscience to bear on issues affecting the modern world. The World Alliance for International Friendship through the Churches worked to prevent World War I. It continued its influence through the first World Conference on Life and Work at Stockholm, Sweden (1925). Avoiding matters of faith and order, this latter movement sought to apply the principles of the Gospel "to the solution of contemporary social and international problems." A second conference was held at Oxford in 1937.

The third category involves movements directly addressing the doctrinal differences separating the churches. Most important was the Faith and Order Movement of which Charles Henry Brent was the prime mover. Brent chaired the first conference at Lausanne (1927). William Temple, then archbishop of York, chaired the second at Edinburgh (1937); the third, held at Lund, Sweden (1952), was chaired by Yngve Brilioth, who was to be archbishop of Uppsala in Sweden. From the outset this movement evidenced concern not only for mutual understanding and cooperation, but also for organic union.

The separation of Life and Work from Faith and Order was artificial. In 1937, at their respective conferences, the two movements voted for merger, and at Utrecht (1938) plans were made for the founding of a World Council of Churches. A provisional body was formed, which existed throughout World War II with Archbishop Temple as its leader. During the war the World Council in Process of Formation, as the provisional body was called, engaged in heroic efforts on behalf of peace and justice through offices in Geneva and headquarters in London and New York. Finally in 1948 the First Assembly of the World Council was held at Amsterdam. Most of Protestantism, all of the churches of the Anglican communion, and some Orthodox churches were included in its membership. At the third Assembly in New Delhi, India (1961), the International Missionary Council was incorporated and the membership of the council was further broadened.

The Message of Amsterdam to the world signaled the deep intent of its framers:

> Christ has made us His own, and he is not divided. In seeking Him we find one another. Here at Amsterdam we have committed ourselves afresh to Him, and have covenanted with one another in constituting this World Council of Churches. We intend to stay together.[40]

On this basis the World Council moved into the future, ever expanding, promoting unity, and facilitating the church's mission to the world.

At the same time organic union between the divided churches began. The prime movers were in the missionary fields. In 1927 the Church of Christ in China was formed involving many Protestant churches but not the Lutherans and Anglicans. In Japan, as a result of government demands, the Church of Christ in Japan was formed. The Church of South India, in some ways the most influential and challenging, including Anglicans, Methodists, Congregationalists, and others, began in 1947 after twenty-eight years of negotiations. Subsequently plans for reunion were actively pursued in North India and Ceylon. Organic union seemed to many people to be the logical outcome of the ecumenical movement. This was an opinion not shared by all. There were those fearful of a mammoth international institution and content to realize unity through intercommunion, which is the coming together of different churches to share in one another's eucharistic celebration.

In the United States of America in 1885 there was formed an American Congress of Churches "to promote Christian union and advance the Kingdom of God by free discussion of the great religious, moral and social questions of the time." The Congress did not last and other efforts at cooperation were begun. In 1905 an Interchurch Congress on Federation came into being with the intent of founding a national federation of churches. A letter was drafted and sent out by a committee of Congregationalists, Presbyterians, Baptists, and Lutherans inviting all Protestant churches to send delegates. The purpose was stated thus:

> We believe that the great Christian bodies in our country should stand together and lead in the discussion of and give an impulse to all great movements that "make for righteousness." We believe that all questions like that of the saloon, marriage and divorce, sabbath desecration, the social evils, child labor, relations of capital and labor . . . indeed all great questions in which the voice of the church should be heard concern Christians of every name and demand their united and concerted action if the church is to lead effectively in the conquest of the world for Christ.[41]

The Federal Council of Churches was the result in 1908, from the outset emphasizing social action, careful of the independence of its members, and active through a large network of state and local councils. The Episcopal Church did not join the Federal Council until 1940. William Reed Huntington objected to the federative principle, preferring organic unity. Others were too conservative to approve of what appeared to be an instrument of American political and theological liberalism.

In 1950 a larger federation was achieved with the merging of various large interdenominational agencies with the Federal Council into a National Council of the Churches of Christ in the United States of America. Among the organizations involved were the International Council of Religious Education, the Foreign Missions Conference, the Home Missions Council, and the United Council of Church Women. Run by a biannual assembly and a general board, the Council had among its purposes:

> To manifest oneness in Jesus Christ as Divine Lord and Savior, by the creation of an inclusive cooperating agency of the Christian churches in the United States . . . to continue and extend the . . . general agencies of the churches, and to combine all their interests and functions.[42]

In the meantime, organic unions were occurring. The World Council estimates that between 1925 and 1964 some thirty-seven unions, involving one hundred and twenty-four churches took place around the world. We have mentioned some of these overseas. In the United States the reunion of the Presbyterian Church and the Cumberland Presbyterian Church took place in 1906 and marked the beginning of a series of intrafamily unions involving Presbyterians, Baptists, Lutherans, and others. Among the early interfamily unions were those that resulted in the United Congregational Christian Churches in 1931, the Evangelical and Reformed Church in 1934, and then the uniting of the Congregational Christian Churches and the Evangelical and Reformed Church in 1957 to form the United Church of Christ.

Other unions were made and various efforts at organic union begun and frustrated, but the most ambitious effort began as a result of a sermon by Eugene Carson Blake, stated clerk (chief executive officer) of the United Presbyterian Church, preached in Grace Cathedral, San Francisco, in December 1960. In May 1961 the General Assembly of the United Presbyterian Church urged the Episcopal Church to join it in issuing an invitation to the Methodist Church and the United Church of Christ "to explore the establishment of a united church truly catholic, truly reformed, and truly evangelical." The result was the Consultation on Church Union (COCU) which held a planning meeting in October, 1961, and was joined by the Disciples of Christ and the Evangelical United Brethren. In March of 1963 the first meeting of the now official COCU took place at Oberlin, Ohio. There a considerable degree of unity was found to be already in existence, but difficult problems were also acknowledged. In particular the consultation considered the many issues involved in "Scripture, Tradition, and the Guardians of Tradition." At Princeton, New Jersey, in 1964, ministry and sacraments were discussed. The delegation of the Episcopal Church made it clear that it would abide by the Lambeth Quadrilateral and its definitions of the sacraments and the historic episcopate. In the next year at Lexington, Kentucky, the church's ministry constituted the sole topic and, through careful negotiations, a sufficient degree of mutual understanding was achieved and a plan of government began to emerge.

In time for a meeting of the consultation in 1970 at St. Louis, Missouri, *A Plan of Union for the Church of Christ Uniting* was placed before the member churches for study and action. This document begins with a listing of the nine member churches, including the Episcopal Church, and then states that they,

> a company of the people of God celebrating the one God, Father, Son, and Holy Spirit, moving toward his coming kingdom and seeking in faithfulness to unite under the Gospel for Christ's mission and service in the world, open ourselves individually and corporately to renewal from the Holy Spirit, struggle against racism, poverty, and environmental blight, war, and other problems of the family of man, minister to the deep yearning of the human spirit for fullness of life, provide for the common use of the resources and gifts of many traditions, in a church catholic, evangelical, and reformed, do covenant together in this Plan of Union for the Church of Christ Uniting (C.C.U.)[43]

All that remained was for the member churches to adopt the plan, and for "The Service of Inauguration of the Church of Christ Uniting" to take place. Thus far the inauguration has not occurred.

At the very time the plan was placed before the churches it was evident to some that the momentum for its realization was waning. Over a decade earlier, Albert C. Outler, Professor of Theology at the Perkins School of Theology, Dallas, Texas, an important leader of the Ecumenical Movement, wrote:

> It is an open secret that the ecumenical movement has, in recent years, lost some of its earlier momentum—more because of the extreme difficulty of the residual problems it faces than from the failure of nerve among its devoted advocates. But these advocates are still too few—and they tend to be bunched somewhat too closely in a sort of ecumenical coterie. There are still vast segments of Protestant Christianity—denominational officials, pastors, laymen—who are not much more than nominally committed to the ecumenical movement and its aims.[44]

This lack of communication and commitment was long recognized as a major problem in an age where the consensus of people was required if any action was to be authenticated. The base of the ecumenical movement was too narrow.

There was more to the waning of momentum than that which Outler specified in 1958. In the 1960s things happened to change the perspective and atmosphere of the ecumenical movement and to direct it out of customary channels. On October 28, 1958, Angelo Giuseppe Roncalli, almost seventy-seven years old, was elected Pope John XXIII. He died on June 3, 1963. In his brief pontificate Pope John made a tremendous impression on Christianity and the world. Less than a year before his death he convened the Second Vatican Council, which was to achieve many things for the renewal and reform of the Roman Catholic Church. Included in its achievements was the *Decree on Ecumenism*, whereby the Roman Church entered a new era of ecumenical cooperation. In December 1960, Geoffrey Francis Fisher, archbishop of Canterbury, visited Pope John at the Vatican in an historic meeting, bringing together the leaders of the two worldwide communions for the first time. One result of that meeting was the creation of the Anglican-Roman Catholic International Commission. This commission proceeded to explore issues separating the churches and in time issued two major statements on the Eucharist and ministry.

Vatican II made its influence felt around the world, so much so that the impossible became possible, Roman Catholics and those who had stood in bitter opposition to them for generations began talking with one another and worshiping together in expectation of fuller unity to come. Concerning those who look to the future when Christ's prayer that "all may be one" will be realized, Alan C. Clark, Roman Catholic bishop of Elmham and cochairman of the Anglican-Roman Catholic International Commission, said: "The grace of ecumenism animates and energizes their ministry of reconciliation and, not unexpectedly, their encounter with the cross of separation."[45]

There is a sense in which Vatican II let loose the ecumenical spirit, heretofore confined within a movement and a bureaucracy, and in which that spirit cannot now be contained. It would seem that there were two kinds of reaction involved.

First of all there were those who became impatient for a fuller kind of fellowship and simply forged ahead ignoring the cumbersome processes of the ecumenical movement. This impatience was exacerbated in the United States by the civil rights movement, the anti-Vietnam movement, the charismatic movement and women's liberation movement. Secondly, there were those who had been lukewarm in their attitude toward the ecumenical movement and who now discerned, as if for the first time, the threat to their denominational identities. This in turn was influenced in the United States by a growing conservative reaction during the 1970s. Opposition to the ecumenical movement seemed to grow in proportion to the growth of conservatism in the country and in the churches.

It is possible, of course, that the ecumenical movement will be renewed and reinvigorated by the setbacks and challenges of the 1960s and '70s. After all, ecumenism, cooperation, interdependence, and mutuality are not considered dispensable by any church leaders. Furthermore, the World Council of Churches, the National Council, and the Consultation on Church Union continue laboring for the realization of Christianity's oneness, that the church may effectively participate in Christ's mission.

In meditating on John 17:11, "That they may be one," William Temple spoke of Jesus' cause resting on a little group of disciples. "If they fall apart, the cause is lost. What is essential is that they be united." The Book of Acts shows how their unity was tried and tested and survived. On the basis of that unity the Gospel was preached and the Lord's work done. Temple then went on to a deeper level, the point at which everything discussed in this chapter, and indeed the entire book, comes together:

> But the unity of the Church is precious not only for its utility in strengthening the Church as an evangelistic agent. It is itself in principle the consummation to which all history moves. The purpose of God in creation was, and is, to fashion a fellowship of free spirits knit together by a love of God—or, as St. Paul expresses it, to "sum up all things in Christ" (Ephesians 1:10).[46]

Further on Temple expanded his basic theme: that unity and fellowship which is in God.

> The unity of the Church is something much more than unity of the ecclesiastical structure, though it cannot be complete without this. It is the love of God in Christ possessing the hearts of men so as to unite them in itself—as the Father and the Son are united in that love of Each for Each which is the Holy Spirit. The unity which the Lord prays that His disciples may enjoy is that which is eternally characteristic of the Triune God. It is therefore something much more than a means to any end; it is itself the one worthy end of all human aspiration; it is the life of heaven.[47]

So meditated one of the great Christians of the twentieth century, one who understood the nature of Christ's mission in terms of reconciliation, unity in fellowship being not some great and impossible ideal, but rather that from which all came and toward which all goes, the deepest truth about creation.

· 6 ·

The Church in History: Concluding Reflections

Four Themes and Four Issues

In this study of the church in history we have explored four themes: (1) "The Christian Community," (2) "Renewal and Reform," (3) "Church and Culture," and (4) "The Mission of the Community." These themes have involved four issues in the form of questions that have confronted Christians in the past and confront them still: (1) What is the church and what constitutes its essential nature? (2) How is a church which is faltering and weak to be renewed and reformed? (3) How are Christ and culture, church and state related in history, and how ought they to be related now? and (4) What has been the church's self-understanding of its mission in history, and what ought it to be now and for the future?

As we have reviewed the history of the church in terms of each theme, answers to the questions have been encountered. Such answers have varied, as they must, with the changing times and places and with the succession of unique individuals who have struggled with the issues.

Ignatius of Antioch, at the beginning of the second century A.D. believed that the essential nature of the church rested in a people united in the one God, witnessing to the saving Gospel, professing faith in Jesus Christ, his cross and resurrection, worshiping in the one Eucharist under the one bishop who is the symbol of their unity and the agent by which their union with God is accomplished. From Ignatius to the Lambeth Quadrilateral of the late nineteenth century—with its belief that the visible unity of the church consists in its acceptance of Scripture, the Nicene and Apostles' Creeds, the sacraments of Baptism and Holy Communion, and a ministry rooted in the historic episcopacy—the struggle to preserve the essential nature of the church has persisted, and we have encountered something of that struggle here. What is remarkable is the degree of agreement which has existed concerning the essential nature of the church. This agreement is emphasized by the degree to which we can find the Lambeth Quadrilateral in Ignatius and Ignatius in the Quadrilateral.

Disagreement surfaces in part as people and churches emphasize one of the essential ingredients over all others. Thus it was that in the time of Pope Innocent III, during the thirteenth century in Europe, the ministry—as centered in the papacy and the curia, and the sacramental system centered on the Mass—had priority over other elements. During the sixteenth century, Martin Luther and those who came after him shifted the balance by emphasizing the authority of Scripture over all other authorities and the necessity of a justifying faith. Then too, it must be admitted that there have been times when nonessentials have been given undue weight in the affairs of the church. Cultural values, ceremonial, divisive prejudices, and the like have caused the church to deny its Lord. It seems clear that while there may be differences in the way in which the question concerning the essential nature of the church is answered, there is a limit for those who faithfully strive to follow Jesus Christ.

Thomas Cranmer, believing that the church had exceeded the limit and become disobedient to its Lord, sought to reform the church through external and internal means. He strove with others, including King Henry VIII, to separate the Church of England from what he saw to be a corrupt and unfaithful church, rejecting the papal claims to universal authority. In the process of achieving this separation he worked to purge the church of all idolatry and superstition. This was the largely negative side of the reform and it involved the destruction of the monasteries as well as the destruction of objects, statues and shrines, which people in their simplicity and superstition were led to worship. Then, following the example of the early church—the church of Ignatius— Cranmer promoted the means by which personal renewal and social reform could be encouraged and achieved. Thus an English Bible; Articles of Religion, defining the true faith over against dangerous errors; a Book of Common Prayer emphasizing Holy Communion in God and in the community; and an ordinal providing for the continuance of the ancient ministry of bishops, priests, and deacons were provided as circumstances allowed, but chiefly in the reign of King Edward VI. All was designed to promote the renewal of the people through the grace and mercy of God. Down through the ages Christians have recognized the necessity of reform and have labored in different ways, through various means, and with diverse results. We have taken note of the tension between the ascetics and the ecclesiastical officials in the early church. Both Evangelicals and Anglo-Catholics in England and America were intent upon reform in different ways and with considerable distrust of one another. While our study demonstrates that reform is a recurrent and necessary theme, such reforms as occur are never pure in motive or in activity. The question concerning how the church is to be renewed and reformed persists.

In the nineteenth century, Frederick Denison Maurice faced the question of the right relation of church and culture with the conviction that the church is "human society in its normal state; the World, that same society irregular and abnormal. The World is the Church without God; the Church is the World restored to its relation with God, taken back by Him into the state for which He created it." The aim was therefore the transformation of culture, recalling it to its true being in God. Where church and state were concerned, Maurice did not view them as opposed but as different, functioning together; the state forcefully eradicating all selfishness, preserving individual rights and property; the church obliterating selfishness in the minds and hearts of people, promoting cooperation and community. Maurice's views were not the only ones expressed in the nineteenth century. Indeed, we have observed various relationships between Christ and culture, church and state, proposed and acted upon. There have been those in history who have gone to extremes. Tertullian in the early church, and some on the left wing of the Reformation in the sixteenth century, have called for the complete separation of the church from culture. And those who utterly confuse Christianity with culture, with the morals and prejudices of their own society, appear time and again. But most of the time Christians seem to be concerned to find a proper balance between the church and the world to which it is sent. We have encountered those struggling to alter the balance: Ambrose of Milan and others in the early church seeking to recover the church's necessary independence of the culture and the state, the Christian Socialists in England and the Social Gospelers in America seeking to recover the church's necessary involvement in the affairs of the society as the arena of God's saving activity. The answers differ; the question remains to be answered by each generation.

Charles Henry Brent in the twentieth century was clear in his own mind that the mission of the church to the world "is to make available for successive generations of mankind the particular boon of salvation. It must keep clear its sole purpose of perpetuating the work begun by its Founder, whose body it is for our times in as real a fashion as human flesh and blood were his body for the days of his mortality." As such the mission of the church is anywhere and everywhere: in South Boston and in the Philippines, in the quest for social and international justice and in the struggle for the reunion of the churches. We have witnessed in these pages remarkable instances of Christians engaged in Christ's mission. St. Paul spreading the Gospel from Jerusalem to Rome, St. Boniface in the eighth century going from Britain to south Germany converting the barbarians, Francis Xavier among the fisher folk of South India in the sixteenth century, and the flood of missionaries (by 1914 half of them women) taking the Gospel during the nineteenth and early twentieth centuries to every part of the world. But we have also confronted instances, the medieval Crusades and modern colonialism, for instance, where the church has betrayed Christ's mission and witnessed to its own idolatry and faithlessness. It was to such betrayal that Brent referred when he wrote, "The idea of the Church has become so identified with the agencies and instruments in its employ that its essential character is lost to view." For the mission to proceed as it must, reform is necessary and the recovery of the essential nature of the church is called for. It was called for in the past and will be called for time and again in the future.

Indeed, Bishop Brent's reflections on the mission of the church pull together all of our themes and raise once more all of our issues, for mission involves the church in its essential nature, reformed so that it is not a mere tool of the world to which it is sent but the agent of God's justice and mercy for the transformation of the world, the restoration of the world to its true being in God. The truth is that our four themes go together and are separated only for the sake of examination.

Four Themes and One Person: Janani Luwum

The themes and issues come together forcefully in the martyrdom of Janani Luwum, Archbishop of Uganda, Rwanda, Burundi, and Boga-Zaire in East Africa. Archbishop Luwum was the spiritual leader of more than three million Christians in a population of about eleven million Ugandans. His church, with at least as many members as the Episcopal Church in the United States, if not more, has been steadily and dramatically growing while Anglican churches elsewhere have been shrinking. This is due in part to the strong tradition of evangelism in East Africa, but also in part to the inspired leadership which has led to the forming of a church in which the people with a great variety of gifts have been engaged in the vital functions of the Christian community. In the diocese of Kigezi, for instance, there are more than 700 congregations but only fifty salaried priests. Basic to the church's operation are the lay ministers, trained on the basis of their discerned, individual gifts to be teachers, pastors, evangelists, prophets, healers, and who would not wish to receive money for their ministries. The church in East Africa has been likened to that of the Book of Acts, so full of the Spirit and so vibrant its members. East African Christians help to account for the fact that the majority of Anglicans in the world today are nonwhites.

In part the spirit of the East African church is derived from and contributes to the heroic witness of its members throughout its history. The martyrdom of Bishop James Hannington and his companions at the hands of King Mwanga in 1885 is remembered. Further martyrdoms occurred, involving both Roman Catholics and Anglicans. But the church's mission did not end. Indeed, "the blood of the martyrs" was "the seed of the church." Now there is a new ruler in Uganda and there are new martyrs, one of them being Janani Luwum.

As is true of most martyrdoms, the archbishop's resembles the passion of the Lord. First of all, he was falsely accused of conspiring to overthrow the government. In Janani's own words, written just days before his death:

At about 1:30 A.M. on Saturday morning [February 5, 1977] I heard the dog barking wildly and the fence being broken down, and I knew some people had come into the compound. I walked downstairs very quietly without switching any lights on and, as usual, I stopped at the door. I opened the curtain on the door on one side and I was able to observe one man standing straight in front of the door. He began calling "Archbishop, Archbishop, open! We have come!" This man was called Ben Ongom. Because he had some cuts on his face and I knew him in the past, I thought he was in some kind of danger needing help. So I opened the door and immediately three armed men who had been hiding sprang on me, cocking their rifles and shouting, "Archbishop, Archbishop, show us the arms!" I replied, "What arms?" They replied, "There are arms in this house." I said, "No." At this point their leader who was speaking in Arabic and wearing a red kaunda suit put his rifle in my stomach on the right hand side whilst another man searched me from head to foot. He pushed me with the rifle, shouting, "Walk! Run! Show us the arms! . . . ."[1]

Thus a night of terror began. No arms were found in the house or on the grounds. The archbishop had reason to believe that he was being associated with a political coup in which he was not involved and knew nothing about.

His Excellency Al-Hajji Field Marshall Dr. Idi Amin Dada,

life president of Uganda, with leaders from his own Kakwa tribe, had decided to eradicate his enemies in the Acholi and Langi tribes, both of which had ties with Amin's predecessor Milton Obote and with many of the country's intellectuals and clergy. Janani came from the Acholi tribe and was regarded as a possible if not actual enemy of the president. In addition, the archbishop and his bishops were neither radical revolutionaries nor passive followers of Amin. In their letter protesting the unlawful search of the archbishop's house, the bishops stated:

> Your excellency, our Church does not believe nor does it teach its members the use of destructive weapons. We believe in the Life-giving love of Christ, we proclaim that love to all without fear—as your Excellency knows. We speak publicly and in private against all evil, all corruption, all misuse of power, all maltreatment of human beings. We rejoice in the truth, because truth builds up a nation, but we are determined to refuse all falsehood, all false accusations which damage the lives of our people and spoil the image of our country.[2]

At the end of the letter, concerned for the tarnished image of their country brought on by recurrent bloodshed, they boldly said: "Our advice, Your Excellency, is that you put your Intelligence under strict laws in their work, restore authority to the Police, and let the law replace the gun—then the image will be restored."

At the next stage of the developing drama we find the archbishop on trial. For days the bishops sought for an audience with President Amin and for days were put off. Finally, on Tuesday, February 15, they were summoned with all religious leaders—including Roman Catholics and Muslims—to the Government Conference Center in Kampala. On the same day Radio Uganda reported that arms had been found near the archbishop's house. The next day, Wednesday, February 16, at 9:30 in the morning, the bishops arrived outside the Conference Center to find almost all of the Uganda army present—one source reports that there were 3,000 heavily armed troops there—with all government officials, excepting President Amin, and with all of those accused of conspiracy to overthrow the government.

Accusations were made again, arms were displayed, confessions were read out implicating the archbishop and two government officials in the supposed plot. As the archbishop's name was read he was seen to shake his head in disbelief and denial. The trial—for such it was—went on for hours, the crowd being harangued into a frenzy. Finally, the vice-president of Uganda, General Mustafa Adrisi, cried out, "What do you think? What should we do with these people?" The troops shouted, "Kill them! Kill them now!" A vote was taken and all the soldiers voted for death.

The bishops then entered the Conference Center expecting an audience with Amin, but all the religious leaders were dismissed, with the exception of the archbishop, who was detained. Other sources say that Janani was arrested by Muslim Military Police and driven off to the Nakasero lodge for his meeting with the president. This was the last that Festo Kivingere, bishop of Kigezi saw of Janani.[3]

The third act in the drama concerns Archbishop Luwum's death by execution. We cannot be absolutely certain concerning the specific details of his death, except to say that the government's story was a lie. He and the two government officials accused with him were reported to have been killed in a car accident as they attempted to overpower the driver. But the car pictured by the Ugandan press was recognized as one involved in an accident two weeks earlier. Furthermore, witnesses came forward to testify to seeing the archbishop's body riddled with bullet holes. One eyewitness account has been given by Janani's driver, who managed to escape across the border into Tanzania.[4] The archbishop, we are informed, was brought handcuffed before President Amin at the Nakasero lodge. Janani was asked to sign a document confessing his part in the conspiracy. He refused. He was ordered to kneel before the president and beg forgiveness. Again he refused. Amin then sent for troops who pinned the archbishop to the floor, stripped him of his cassock and gold cross and then of all his clothes and whipped him. While he was being thus scourged Janani prayed. His prayers aroused the president who shouted obscenities at him and struck him. Once more he was ordered to sign the document and

beg for forgiveness, but Janani refused, now calm and stead-
fast. Amin then began to speak of his own greatness, telling
those present that God had given him power to warn the
archbishop and others. But they did not take his warnings
seriously and now, therefore, God would punish them for
their disobedience. When the punishment came to Janani
Luwum it was swift and violent. According to our source,
Amin pulled out his pistol and shot the archbishop several
times in the chest. He died at once and his body was secretly
disposed of, possibly dumped into Lake Victoria along with
others.

Bishop Kivingere remembers the last time Janani Luwum
spoke to his bishops, leading them in their devotions on the
day of his death. He appeared to them as one "full of the
Lord" and spoke to them of Jesus on the mountain alone,
praying, when he saw his disciples on a journey, "making
headway painfully." Janani remarked that in the last two or
three days the Lord had seen an archbishop making headway
painfully. "But I see the road very clear. . . ." The road was
the road of discipleship, the road which the Lord had
traveled before. It was the road of justice and truth.

In Janani Luwum we have seen the Church Catholic embodied, the bishop leading the church, the focus of its unity
and integrity. This does not mean that he was a pompous,
obviously powerful figure. He was not. And yet the power
was there. As Bishop Kivingere has pointed out, he was "full
of the Lord." And the church which he led possessed the
essentials of Scripture, creeds, sacraments and episcopal
ministry, but it possessed them in a creative and life-giving
manner. The church which the archbishop led was not bound
to past customs, as is apparent when we take into account the
variety of lay ministries which are so vital to that church and
provide for so much of its enthusiasm to witness.

In the archbishop we see one who by his courageous life
and heroic death recalls the church everywhere to its essential
being in Christ. Gothic cathedrals, smooth-running parishes,
good looking clergy—all pale in the light of Janani's death,
which illumines the death of the Lord, now risen to make all
things new. Nonessentials can have value, but only in rela-

tion to that which is essential. In order to remember this the church must constantly be reformed and its people renewed.

Janani Luwum loved his country and it was partly because of that love that he spoke out against the evils which were destroying it. He could have acquiesced to pressure and become the government's pawn, but he did not. He kept his distance from an evil government and did not cease his efforts to transform its president, recalling him to his true being in God. Therefore he, with his bishops, advised Amin to "let the law replace the gun"—only thus could the good and true image of the nation be restored.

Finally, Janani Luwum not only understood Christ's mission, he was that mission, representing Christ to the world. The Christ revealed in Janani's martyrdom stands for justice and truth, for renewal and reform, empowering his followers with grace and mercy to be his body in the world.

Notes

CHAPTER ONE

1. John Donne, *Devotions upon Emergent Occasions* (Meditation 17) (Ann Arbor, Mich.: University of Michigan Press, 1959), pp. 108–9.

2. Charles Henry Brent, *The Commonwealth: Its Foundations and Pillars* (New York: Appleton, 1930), p. 22.

3. John Booty, *John Jewel as Apologist of the Church of England* (London: S.P.C.K., 1963), pp. 93–94.

4. Richard Church, *Pascal and Other Sermons* (London: Macmillan, 1895), pp. 91–92; quoting Lancelot Andrewes, *Private Devotions*, Second Day, 4. Intercession.

5. Richard Hooker, *Of the Laws of Ecclesiastical Polity*, II. i. 4.

CHAPTER TWO

1. *Philadelphians* VIII; *The Apostolic Fathers*, trans. Kirsopp Lake, Loeb Classical Library (Cambridge, Mass.,: Harvard University Press, 1945), I:247.

2. *Magnesians* XI; ibid., p. 209.

3. *Trallians* IX; ibid., p. 221.

4. *Philadelphians* IX; ibid., p. 249.

5. *Ephesians* XIV; ibid., p. 189.

6. *Smyrnaeans* VI; ibid., p. 259.

7. *Smyrnaeans* VII; ibid.

8. *Philadelphians* IV; ibid., p. 243.

9. *Ephesians* X; ibid., p. 185.

10. *Romans* IV; ibid., p. 231.

11. *Ephesians* XI; ibid.; p. 185.

12. William Reed Huntington, *The Church-Idea: An Essay Toward Unity* (New York: E. P. Dutton and Co., 1870), pp. 155–56.

13. *The Lambeth Conferences (1867–1948)* (London: S.P.C.K., 1948), p. 39.

14. Ibid., p. 297.

15. C. H. Dodd, *The Apostolic Preaching* (New York: Harper, 1944), pp. 21–22.

16. J. Stevenson, ed., *A New Eusebius: Documents Illustrative of the History of the Church to A.D. 377* (London: S.P.C.K., 1957), pp. 144–47.

17. Ibid.

18. *Adv. Haer.* 4. 53. 2; translation in R. P. C. Hanson, *Tradition in the Early Church* (London: SCM Press, 1962), p. 95.

19. *Adv. Haer.* 1. 10. 2; translation based on text edited by W. Wigan Harvey, Tom. I (Cantabrigiae: Typis Academicis, 1857), pp. 90–91.

20. Hippolytus, *The Apostolic Tradition*, ed. B. S. Easton (Cambridge University Press, 1934), pp. 46–47; translation altered by editor.

21. Socrates, *Hist. Eccles.* 1. 8; translation in J. N. D. Kelly, *Early Christian Creeds*, 2nd ed. (New York: David McKay Co., 1960), pp. 215–16.

22. Theodoret, *Hist. Eccles.* 1. 5; translation in *A History of the Church by Theodoret and Euagrius*, Bohn's Ecclesiastical Library (London: Bohn, 1854), p. 28.

23. Socrates, *Hist. Eccles.* 1. 8; translation in Kelly, *Early Christian Creeds*, p. 216.

24. Translation in E. R. Hardy, *Christology of the Later Fathers*, Library of Christian Classics 3 (Philadelphia, Westminster, 1954), p. 373.

25. Richard Hooker, *Of the Laws of Ecclesiastical Polity*, V. liv. 10.

26. Augustine, *Enarr. in Psalm* 127:3; translation in J. N. D. Kelly, *Early Christian Doctrines* (New York: Harper, 1958), p. 413.

27. *Apostolic Fathers*, Loeb, I, p. 324.

28. Irenaeus, *Adv. Haer.* 3. 3. 2; translation in R. P. C. Hanson, *Tradition in the Early Church* (London: SCM, 1962), p. 145.

29. Anonymous account in Eusebius, *Hist. Eccles.* 5. 16. 6f; translation in J. Stevenson, ed., *A New Eusebius* (London: S.P.C.K., 1957), pp. 108–9.

30. Epiphanius, *Haer.* 48, 49; Eusebius, *Hist. Eccles.* 5. 16. 17; translation in Stevenson, *New Eusebius,* p. 113.

31. Cyprian, Epistle 63:14; translation in Henry Bettenson, *Documents of the Christian Church* (Oxford University Press, 1943), p. 108.

32. Cyprian, *On the Unity of the Catholic Church,* 4–6; translation in Stevenson, *New Eusebius,* p. 244.

33. Hippolytus, *The Apostolic Tradition,* pp. 54–56.

34. 1 Tim 4:13–14.

35. Hippolytus, *Apostolic Tradition* 4; translation based on text in Hippolyte de Rome, *La Tradition Apostolique,* ed. Dom B. Botte, Sources Chretiennes (Paris: Les Editions du Cerf, 1946), p. 33.

36. *The Disciplinary Decrees of the General Councils,* trans. H. J. Schroeder (St. Louis: Herder, 1937), pp. 237–39.

37. Ibid.

38. *De Divina Natura,* Book 5; translation in George H. Tavard, *Holy Writ or Holy Church* (New York: Harper, 1959), pp. 12–13.

39. *Commentary on the Sentences,* Art.10, q.1, n.10; translation in Tavard, *Holy Writ or Holy Church,* p. 24.

40. Quoted in Joseph A. Jungmann, S. J., *The Mass of the Roman Rite,* trans. Francis A. Brunner, C.S.S.R. (New York: Benziger, 1951), I:121.

41. Amédée Hallier, O.C.S.O., *The Monastic Theology of Aelred of Rievaulx,* trans. Columban Heaney, O.C.S.O. (Shannon, Ireland: Irish University Press, 1969), p. 102.

42. Ibid., p. 103.

43. As quoted in John Booty, *John Jewel as Apologist of the Church of England* (London: S.P.C.K., 1963), p. 29.

44. This and other quotations here are cited from *Articles* (London: Richard Jugge and John Cawood, 1571). Spelling modernized.

45. Cited from Booty, *John Jewel,* p. 23.

46. Hooker, *Of the Laws of Ecclesiastical Polity,* V. lxvii. 12.

47. *The Private Devotions of Lancelot Andrewes,* trans. John Henry Newman (New York and Nashville: Abingdon-Cokesbury, 1950), p. 62.

48. William White, *The Case of the Episcopal Churches in the United States Considered* (Philadelphia: Claypoole, 1782), p. 8.

49. Ibid., p. 18.

50. Quoted in E. Clowes Chorley, *Men and Movements in the American Episcopal Church* (New York: Charles Scribner's, 1946), p. 215.

51. Ibid., p. 292.

52. James Thayer Addison, *The Episcopal Church in the United States* (New York: Charles Scribner's, 1951), p. 252.

53. William Meade, *Reasons for Loving the Episcopal Church* (Philadelphia: King and Baird, 1852), pp. 41–42.

CHAPTER THREE

1. *Narratives of the Days of the Reformation*, ed. J. G. Nichols, Camden Society 77 (London, 1859), p. 240.

2. Ibid., p. 219.

3. *The First and Second Prayer Books of Edward VI*, Everyman's Library 488 (London: Dent, 1910), p. 3.

4. *Certain Sermons or Homilies* (London: S.P.C.K., 1852), p. 20.

5. Ibid., p. 22.

6. Ibid., pp. 30–31.

7. Ibid., pp. 58–59.

8. See *Narratives of the Days of the Reformation*, pp. 232–33.

9. Gregory of Nyssa, *De Virginitate*, 12, 13; translation in Gerhart B. Ladner, *The Idea of Reform* (Cambridge, Mass.: Harvard University Press, 1959), pp. 76–77.

10. *The Reformation Writings of Martin Luther*, trans. and ed. Bertram Lee Woolf (New York: Philosophical Library, 1956), p. 155.

11. *The Apostolic Fathers*, trans. Kirsopp Lake, Loeb Classical Library (Cambridge, Mass.,: Harvard University Press, 1945), 2:21.

12. Letter 22, *Ad Eustochium; Letters*, trans. C. C. Mierow, Ancient Christian Writers 33 (Westminster, Md.: Newman Press, 1963), p. 163.

13. *Vita S. Ant.*, 3; translation in *Nicene and Post-Nicene Fathers*, 2nd ser., 4:196.

14. *Praef. in regulam S. Pachomii*, 5, 6; trans. B. J. Kidd, *Documents Illustrative of the History of the Church* (London: S.P.C.K., 1923), 2:191.

15. *Regulae Fusius Tractatae*; translation in J. Stevenson, *Creeds, Sources Chretiennes (Paris: Les Éditions du Cerf, 1946)*, p. 33.

16. *Confess.* VIII. xii. 28; translation in J. Stevenson, *Creeds, Councils, and Controversies* (New York: Seabury, 1966) pp. 199–200.

17. *City of God*, X. 6; translation in Gerhart B. Ladner, *The Idea of Reform* (Cambridge, Mass.: Harvard University Press, 1959), pp. 280–81.

18. Translation by James Bruce Ross and Mary Martin McLaughlin, *The Portable Medieval Reader* (New York: Viking, 1949), pp. 78–79.

19. O. J. Thatcher and E. H. McNeal, trans., *A Source Book of Medieval History* (New York: Charles Scribner's, 1905), pp. 134–35.

20. Paschal Robinson, trans., *The Writings of Saint Francis of Assisi* (Philadelphia: Dolphin Press, 1906), pp. 81f.

21. Quoted in Ernest Gilliat-Smith, *Saint Clare of Assisi: Her Life and Legislation* (London and Toronto: J. M. Dent, 1914), pp. 281–82.

22. Quoted in J. M. Perrin, O. P., *Catherine of Siena*, trans. Paul Barret (Westminster, Maryland: Newman Press, 1965), pp. 32–33.

23. Ibid., pp. 199–200.

24. Ibid., p. 201.

25. Quoted in Preserved Smith, *The Age of Reformation* (New York: Holt, 1920), pp. 58–59.

26. Gordon Rupp, *The Righteousness of God: Luther Studies* (London: Hodder and Stoughton, 1953), p. 105.

27. Steven E. Ozment, "Homo Viator: Luther and Late Medieval Theology," in *The Reformation in Medieval Perspective*, ed. S. E. Ozment (Chicago: University of Chicago Press, 1974), p. 150.

28. Martin Luther, *Bondage of the Will*, trans. J. I. Packer and O. R. Johnston (London: James Clarke, 1957), pp. 307–8.

29. *Erasmus-Luther: Discourse on Free Will*, trans. E. F. Winter (New York: Unger, 1961), p. 92.

30. Ibid., pp. 92–93.

31. H. R. Trevor Roper, *Historical Essays* (London: Macmillan, 1957), p. 49.

32. Anon., *A treatyse provynge by the Kynges Lawes* [1538], Sig. Bii^v.

33. Pierre Jannelle, *Obedience in Church and State* (Cambridge University Press, 1930), p. 95.

34. In A. L. Rowse, *The England of Elizabeth* (New York: Collier, 1966), p. 432.

35. In J. P. Hodges, *The Nature of the Lion* (London: Faith Press, 1962), p. 74.

36. J. E. Neale, *Elizabeth I and Her Parliaments, 1559–1581* (London: Cape, 1953), p. 191.

37. John D. Walsh, "Origins of the Evangelical Revival," in *Essays in Modern Church History*, ed. G. V. Bennett and J. D. Walsh (London: Black, 1961), p. 143.

38. William Wilberforce, *Practical View of the Prevailing Religious Conceptions of Professed Christians in the Higher and Middle Classes in This Country Contrasted with Real Christianity* (Boston: Crocker and Brewater, 1829), p. 138.

39. In Horton Davies, *Worship and Theology in England: From Watts and Wesley to Maurice, 1690–1850* (Princeton, N.J.: Princeton University Press, 1961), p. 148.

40. In Eugene Fairweather, ed., *The Oxford Movement* (New York: Oxford University Press, 1964), p. 44.

41. *Tracts for the Times* (London: Rivington, 1834), 1:13–14.

42. Quoted in Clifton E. Olmstead, *History of Religion in the United States* (Englewood Cliffs, N.J.: Prentice-Hall, 1960), p. 164.

43. E. Clowes Chorley, *Men and Movements in the American Episcopal Church* (New York: Charles Scribner's, 1946), p. 144.

44. Ibid., p. 31.

45. Ibid., p. 23.

46. Ibid., pp. 317–18.

47. Ibid., p. 311.

CHAPTER FOUR

1. Quoted by Derek Beales, *From Casterleagh to Gladstone 1815–1885* (New York: Norton, 1969), p. 99.

2. Frank Mauldin McClain, *Maurice: Man and Moralist* (London: S.P.C.K., 1972), p. 73.

3. Frederick Maurice, *The Life of Frederick Denison Maurice* (New York: Charles Scribner's, 1884), 1:155.

4. F. D. Maurice, *Theological Essays* (London: James Clarke, 1957), pp. 276–77.

5. F. D. Maurice, *Sermons Preached in Lincoln's Inn Chapel* (London: 1891), 1:251.

6. Maurice, *Life,* 2:8–9.

7. Charles Kingsley, *Alton Locke* (New York: J. F. Taylor and Co., 1899), pp. 95–96.

8. Maurice, *Life,* 2:32.

9. F. D. Maurice, *Religions of the World,* 4th ed. (London: Macmillan, 1861), p. 63.

10. Maurice, *Life,* 2:285n.

11. Ibid., 2:641.

12. H. Richard Niebuhr, *Christ and Culture* (New York: Harper, 1951), p. 32.

13. Ibid., p. 229.

14. Quoted in Alan Butler, *The Lives of the Fathers, Martyrs, and Other Principal Saints* (New York: Kenedy, 1896), 3:533–39.

15. Pliny, Ep. X. 97; translation in J. Stevenson, ed., *A New Eusebius* (London: S.P.C.K., 1957), p. 16.

16. Tertullian, *Apol.,* I. 12–13; *New Eusebius,* p. 168.

17. Eusebius, *Hist. Eccles.,* VII. 13; *New Eusebius,* p. 267.

18. Eusebius, *Oration on the Tricennalia of Constantine*, 336; translation in J. Stevenson, ed., *New Eusebius* (London, S.P.C.K, 1957), p. 391.

19. Athanasius, *History of the Arians*, 33, 34, 39, 44, 51–53; translation in S. L. Greenslade, *Church and State from Constantine to Theodosius* (London: S.C.M., 1954), p. 49.

20. J. Stevenson, *Creeds, Councils, and Controversies* (New York: Seabury, 1966), p. 38.

21. Charles Norris Cochrane, *Christianity and Classical Culture* (London: Oxford University Press, 1944), p. 347.

22. *Ecloga*, Pref.; trans. J. M. Hussey, *The Byzantine World* (London: Hutchinson, 1957), pp. 85–86.

23. *Unam Sanctam;* translation in Henry Bettenson, *Documents of the Christian Church* (London: Oxford University Press, 1943), p. 160.

24. Harold Lamb, *Charlemagne* (Garden City, New York: Doubleday, 1954), p. 235.

25. Henri Daniel-Rops, *Cathedral and Crusade* (London: J. M. Dent, 1957), p. 186.

26. Innocentus III, *Selected Letters concerning England*, C. R. Cheney and W. H. Semple, eds. (London: Nelson, 1953), p. x.

27. Ibid., p. 89.

28. Ibid., pp. 149–50.

29. Amédée Hallier, O.C.S.O., *The Monastic Theology of Aelred of Rievaulx*, trans. Columban Heaney, O.C.S.O. (Shannon, Ireland: Irish University Press, 1969), p. 142.

30. Ibid., p. 146.

31. Ibid., p. 140.

32. Quoted in J. E. Neale, *Elizabeth I and Her Parliaments, 1584–1601* (New York: St. Martin's Press, 1958), p. 389.

33. Hooker, *Of the Laws of Ecclesiastical Polity*, VIII. i. 2.

34. Ibid., VIII. ii. 12.

35. Quoted in John Whitgift, *Works,* Parker Society (Cambridge University Press, 1851–1853), 3:189.

36. Luther, *Secular Authority* (1523); trans. John Dillenberg, *Martin Luther,* Anchor Books (Garden City, New York: Doubleday, 1961), pp. 368–69.

37. Copernicus, *de Revolutionibus*, I, 9; translation in J. H. Randall, *The Career of Philosophy* (New York: Columbia University Press, 1962), p. 313.

38. Quoted in Anson Phelps Stokes, *Church and State in the United States* (New York: Harper and Brothers, 1950), 1:393–94.

39. Karl Barth, *Church Dogmatics*, IV:2, trans. G. W. Bromiley (Edinburgh: T. & T. Clark, 1958), p. 692.

40. William Rainsford, *Story of a Varied Life* (Garden City, New York: Doubleday, 1922), p. 215.

41. Harry Emerson Fosdick, ed., *A Rauschenbusch Reader* (New York: Harper, 1957), pp. xiv–xv.

42. Quoted in Charles Howard Hopkins, *The Rise of the. Social Gospel* (New Haven: Yale University Press, 1957), p. 229.

43. Ibid., p. 230.

44. See Reinhold Niebuhr, *The Nature and Destiny of Man* (New York: Charles Scribner's Sons, 1951), especially 1:18–25; 2:157–212.

CHAPTER FIVE

1. Alexander Clinton Zabriskie, *Bishop Brent, Crusader for Christian Unity* (Philadelphia: Westminster, 1948), pp. 36–37.

2. Ibid., p. 49.

3. Ibid., p. 53.

4. Ibid., pp. 117–18.

5. Ibid., p. 169.

6. Charles Henry Brent, *The Commonwealth: Its Foundation and Pillars* (New York, London: Appleton, 1930), p. 14.

7. Ibid., p. 2.

8. Ibid., p. 3.

9. Ibid., p. 43.

10. Ibid., p. 88.

11. Ibid., pp. 89–90.

12. Zabriskie, *Bishop Brent*, pp. 169–170.

13. Charles Henry Brent, *Things That Matter*, ed. F. W. Kates (New York: Harper and Brothers, 1949), pp. 131–132.

14. Wilhelm Andersen, "Further Toward a Theology of Mission," *The Theology of Christian Mission*, Gerald H. Anderson, ed. (New York: McGraw-Hill, 1961), p. 301.

15. Ibid., p. 302.

16. Stephen Neill, *A History of Christian Missions* (Grand Rapids, Mich.: Eerdmans, 1965), pp. 39–40.

17. Ibid., p. 45.

18. J. Stevenson, *A New Eusebius* (London: S.P.C.K., 1957), p. 64.

19. Ibid.

20. Peter Brown, *Augustine of Hippo* (Berkeley and Los Angeles: University of California Press, 1969), pp. 297–98.

21. *The Hymnal of the Protestant Episcopal Church* (New York: Church Pension Fund, 1940), Hymn #268.

22. The Venerable Bede, *Historia Ecclesiastica*, i. 27.

23. H. O. Taylor, *The Medieval Mind* (Cambridge, Mass.: Harvard University Press, 1949), 1:552.

24. Neill, *A History of Christian Missions,* p. 137.

25. Bartholomew de Las Casas, *In Defense of the Indians,* Stafford Poole, ed. (De Kalb, Ill.: Northern Illinois University Press, 1974), pp. 43–44.

26. Quoted by Lewis Hanke, "Pope Paul III and the American Indian," *Harvard Theological Review,* April 1973, XXX (2):72.

27. In H. Shelton Smith, Robert T. Handy, Lefferts A. Loetscher, *American Christianity* (New York: Charles Scribner's Sons, 1960), 1:46–47.

28. Smith, Handy, and Loetscher, *American Christianity* 1:550.

29. Neill, *A History of Christian Missions,* pp. 394–395.

30. Geoffrey Moorhouse, *The Missionaries* (Philadelphia and New York: Lippincott, 1973), p. 308.

31. Ibid., p. 328.

32. Quoted in John V. Taylor, *For All the World: The Christian Mission in the Modern Age* (Philadelphia: Westminster, 1966), pp. 50–51.

33. Ibid., p. 186.

34. Ibid., pp. 180–81.

35. Ibid., p. 117.

36. Stephen F. Bayne, Jr., ed., *Mutual Responsibility and Interdependence in the Body of Christ: With Related Background Documents* (New York: Seabury, 1963), p. 18.

37. Ibid., pp. 23–24.

38. James W. Kennedy, collator-editor, *Partners in Mission: The Louisville Consultation,* 1977 (Cincinnati: Forward Movement, 1977), p. 91.

39. Ruth Rouse and Stephen Neill, eds., *A History of the Ecumenical Movement, 1517–1948* (London: S.P.C.K., 1954), p. 341.

40. Ibid., p. 720.

41. John Alexander Hutchison, *We Are Not Divided* (New York: Round Table Press, 1941), p. 33.

42. Robert Lee, *Social Sources of Church Unity* (New York: Abingdon, 1960), p. 123.

43. *A Plan of Union for the Church of Christ Uniting* (Princeton, N.J.: Consultation on Church Union, 1970), p. 9.

44. Albert C. Outler, *The Christian Tradition and the Unity We Seek* (London: Oxford University Press, 1958), pp. vii–viii.

45. *Modern Eucharistic Agreement* (London: S.P.C.K., 1973), p. vi.

46. William Temple, *Readings in St. John's Gospel* (London: Macmillan, 1949), p. 319.

47. Ibid., p. 320.

CHAPTER SIX

1. Quoted from a typed manuscript entitled, "Report of a very serious incident at the Archbishop's House in the early hours of Saturday, 5th February 1977," p. 1.

2. Quoted from a typed manuscript entitled, "A Prepared Response of the House of Bishops of the C.O.U.-Rwanda-Burundi and Boga Zaire to his Excellency on Wednesday 16th February 1977, at the Conference Centre in Kampala," pp. 1–2.

3. For this account I am dependent upon the eye witness report by Bishop Kivingere provided to me on tape by the Rev. George Woodard of Trinity Church, New York City.

4. The source for this account by the archbishop's former driver is Joseph Adero Ngala reporting from the Tanzania-Uganda border for the *National Catholic Reporter*, March 25, 1977, p. 5. The report was corroborated in its main point by Henry Kyemba, former Ugandan Minister of Health: *New York Times*, June 6, 1977. See also, *Newsweek*, February 28, 1977, p. 35; and *Time*, March 7, 1977, pp. 19–29.

A Table of Significant Dates

c. 30   Crucifixion of Christ.

c. 44   Paul and Barnabas in Antioch.

49   Apostolic Council in Jerusalem.

64   Rome burns; Emperor Nero persecutes Christians; possible date of Paul's death at Rome.

90ff.   Apostolic Fathers, I Clement, Didache, Ignatius of Antioch, Shepherd of Hermas, etc.

c. 110–17   Ignatius of Antioch, journey to Rome and death.

112   Pliny in Bithynia writes to emperor about Christians.

140   Basileides, Gnostic teacher.

c. 144   Marcion excommunicated.

165   Justin Martyr's death.

c. 170   Montanism.

178   Irenaeus, Bishop of Lyons.

c. 190   Muratorian Fragment lists New Testament Books.

193   Clement teaches at Alexandria.

197   Tertullian's *Apology* in defence of Christians.

202   Perpetua and her companions martyred.

c. 217   Hippolytus's *Apostolic Tradition*.

249   Decius, emperor, first general persecution; Fabian, Bishop of Rome martyred.

254   Origen of Alexandria dies.

258   Valerian persecution; Cyprian of Carthage martyred.

260   Gallienus, emperor; Edict of Toleration.

280   Conversion of Tidrates, King of Armenia.

303   Diocletian persecution.

271

313   Constantine and Licinius, emperors; so-called Edict of Milan and recognition for Christians; Eusebius, Bishop of Caesarea.

323   Pachomius founds "monastery" at Tabennisi.

325   Nicaea, the first General Council; condemns Arius.

328   Athanasius, Bishop of Alexandria.

340–383   Ulfilas, mission to the Goths.

347   Donatism, North Africa.

356   Antony dies.

361   Julian, emperor, favors pagans.

370–2   Cappadocian Fathers: Gregory of Nyssa, Basil of Caesarea, Gregory of Nazianzus, made bishops; Martin, bishop of Tours.

381   Constantinople, the second General Council; Arians and Apollinarians comdemned.

388–90   Clash between Emperor Theodosius and Ambrose, bishop of Milan.

395   Augustine, bishop of Hippo Regius.

410   Fall of Rome; Alaric, king of the Goths.

420   Jerome dies.

430   Augustine dies.

431   Ephesus, the third General Council; Nestorius condemned.

440   Pope Leo I, papal theory develops.

441   Patrick begins missionary work in Ireland.

451   Chalcedon, the fourth General Council; Eutyches condemned; Chalcedonian Definition.

496   Clovis, king of the Franks, baptized.

527   Justinian, emperor.

540   Benedict of Nursia issues monastic rule.

563   Columba to Iona off Scotland.

590   Pope Gregory the Great.

597   Augustine of Canterbury arrives in England.

632   Death of Mohammed; Muslim conquest begun.

651   Aidan of Lindisfarne dies.

663–4   Synod of Whitby; clash between Celtic and Roman missions; Hilda, Abbess of Whitby.

669   Theodore of Tarsus, archbishop of Canterbury, organizes English Church.

690   Willibrord of Ripon, mission to Frisia, Denmark, Hesse, Bavaria, and Thuringia.

718   Boniface, or Wynfrith, joins Willibrord and in 732 becomes archbishop of Mainz.

732	Defeat of Muslims at Tours and Poitiers by Charles Martel.
782	Benedict of Aniane, monastic reformer.
800	Coronation of Charlemagne as emperor by Pope Leo III.
817	Council of Aachen.
850	Viking conquests of England.
910	Cluny, monastic reform.
950	Age of feudalism and the manorial system in Europe.
1054	Schism between East and West.
1077	Emperor Henry IV humiliated by Pope Gregory VII (Hildebrand) at Canossa.
1084	Carthusians begin.
1095	Crusades to recover Holy Land begin.
1098	Cistercians begin.
1099	Jerusalem taken by Crusaders.
1109	Anselm, archbishop of Canterbury, dies.
1122	Concordat of Worms; end of investiture controversy.
1142	Abelard, theologian, dies.
1147	Ailred, abbot of Rievaulx.
1164	Heloise, French abbess, dies.
1179	College of Cardinals.
1204	Fourth Crusade, sack of Constantinople.
1208	England, under King John, under interdict.
1215	Fourth Lateran Council; Pope Innocent III.
1221	Dominic, founder of Dominican Order, dies.
1223	Francis of Assisi, rule approved, for Franciscan Order.
1253	Clare of Assisi dies.
1274	Thomas Aquinas dies.
1291	Last Crusader territory in Holy Land lost.
1293	John of Monte Corvino reaches Khanbalik (Peking), China.
1302	Pope Boniface VIII; *Unam Sanctam*.
1309	Avignon papacy.
1311–21	Dante's *Divine Comedy*.
1347	Black Death begins.
1378	Papal schism; Conciliarism.
1380	Catherine of Siena dies.
1384	John Wyclif of Oxford dies; Lollards continue his reform ideas.
1414–18	Council of Constance; John Hus, Bohemian reformer, burned 1415.

1445	Gutenberg, printing with movable metal type.
1487	Bartholomew Diaz rounds Cape of Good Hope.
1492	Columbus lands at San Salvador in the New World.
1493–4	Pope Alexander VI divides newly discovered lands between Portugal and Spain.
1509	Henry VIII, king of England.
1513	Machivelli, *The Prince;* Balboa reaches Pacific Ocean.
1516	Erasmus of Rotterdam, Greek New Testament.
1517	Martin Luther, Ninety-Five Theses.
1519	Cortez begins conquest of Mexico.
1526	William Tyndale, English New Testament.
1529	Fall of Cardinal Wolsey, England.
1533	Thomas Cranmer, Archbishop of Canterbury.
1534	Royal supremacy enacted by law in England.
1535	Thomas More, executed.
1539	The Great Bible.
1540	Jesuits founded by Ignatius of Loyola, recognized by papacy.
1541	Calvin organizes the Genevan Church.
1543	Nicholas Copernicus dies.
1547	Edward VI, King of England.
1549	First Book of Common Prayer; Francis Xavier, Jesuit missionary in Japan.
1552	Second Book of Common Prayer.
1553	Mary, Queen of England.
1555	Hugh Latimer, bishop of Worchester, and Nicholas Ridley, bishop of London, executed.
1556	Thomas Cranmer executed.
1558	Elizabeth I, queen of England.
1562	John Jewel, bishop of Salisbury, *Apology of the Church of England.*
1565	Puritanism rising.
1571	Thirty-Nine Articles of Religion.
1588	Spanish Armada.
1592	Michel de Montaigne dies.
1593	Richard Hooker, *Of the Laws of Ecclesiastical Polity.*
1604	Hampton Court Conference; King James I.
1607	Jamestown, Virginia, colonized.
1608	Samuel Champlain at Quebec.
1611	King James version of the Bible.
1618	Thirty Years War begun.

1621   John Donne, dean of St. Paul's Cathedral, London.

1626   Lancelot Andrewes, bishop of Winchester, dies.

1632   George Herbert, priest and poet, dies.

1633   William Laud, archbishop of Canterbury.

1642   Civil War in England.

1648   Peace of Westphalia ends Thirty Years War.

1649   Charles I, king of England, executed.

1658   Oliver Cromwell dies.

1660   Restoration of monarchy and church in England.

1661   Savoy Conference.

1688   Bloodless revolution in England.

1690   John Eliot, missionary to American Indians, dies.

1698   Society for Promoting Christian Knowledge (S.P.C.K.).

1701   Society for the Propagation of the Gospel (S.P.G.).

1714   Religious revival in Wales; beginning of Evangelical revival.

1729   John and Charles Wesley, the Holy Club at Oxford.

1734   First Great Awakening in America; Jonathan Edwards.

1739   George Whitfield preaching.

1752   Joseph Butler, bishop of Durham, author of *Analogy of Religion*, dies.

1776   American Revolution; James Madison; Virginia Bill of Rights; religious freedom.

1782   William White's *Case of the Episcopal Church Considered*.

1784   Samuel Seabury consecrated bishop in Scotland.

1785   Thomas Jefferson's Bill for Establishing Religious Freedom.

1789   Founding convention of the Episcopal Church in the U.S.A.

1791   Selina, countess of Huntingdon, dies.

1793   William Carey, Baptist missionary to India; century of Protestant missions begun.

1795   Methodist Church; London Missionary Society.

1799   Church Missionary Society, John Venn, Evangelical.

1801   Second Great Awakening; Deveraux Jarrat dies.

1805   Henry Martyn, Anglican missionary to India.

1811   John Henry Hobart, bishop of New York.

1812   American Board sends Adoniram Judson and others to Orient.

1820   Domestic and Foreign Missionary Society.

1826   American Home Missionary Society.

1833 John Keble's Assize Sermon, beginning of Oxford Movement, *Tracts for the Times;* Hannah More and William Wilberforce die.

1836 Charles Simeon dies; mission to Liberia begins.

1841 William Meade, bishop of Virginia.

1844 William Boone, first overseas missionary bishop of the Episcopal Church.

1845 J. H. Newman converted to Roman Catholic Church.

1848 Christian Socialism begins, F. D. Maurice, J. M. Ludlow, Charles Kingsley, leaders

1850 John Payne, bishop of Liberia.

1855 Ritualist Controversy in England, first court case.

1861 James T. Holly begins mission to Haiti.

1865 Society of St. John the Evangelist, R. M. Benson.

1867 First Lambeth Conference of Anglican bishops.

1870 William Reed Huntington, *The Church Idea.*

1874 Church Congress, U.S.A.

1880 Racist persecution of Samuel Crowther, ex-slave, bishop of the Niger Territories during this decade.

1882 Edward Bouverie Pusey, Anglo-Catholic leader, dies; William Rainsford, institutional church in New York City.

1883 Frederick C. Ewer, Tractarian leader in America, dies.

1887 Church Association for the Advancement of the Interests of Labor (C.A.I.L.).

1888 Chicago-Lambeth Quadrilateral.

1891 Philips Brooks, bishop of Massachusetts; Christian Social Union.

1895 Student Christian Federation, John R. Mott.

1908 Federal Council of Churches in U.S.A.

1910 First World Missionary Conference, Edinburgh; Theodore Munger, "New Theology," dies.

1912 V. S. Azariah, bishop of Dornakal in India.

1914 World War I.

1917 Russian revolution.

1919 National Council of the Episcopal Church; Church League for Social and Industrial Democracy.

1920 Lambeth appeal for reunion, "To All Christian People."

1921 International Missionary Council.

1925 Universal Conference of Life and Work, Stockholm, Sweden.

1927   Faith and Order Conference, Lausanne, Switzerland, Charles Henry Brent.

1935   Jane Addams, founder of Hull House in Chicago, dies.

1938   International Missionary Council, Tambaram, India, missionary church heard.

1939   World War II.

1942   William Temple, archbishop of Canterbury.

1947   British withdraw from India; Church of South India.

1948   First meeting of World Council of Churches, Amsterdam.

1950   National Council of Churches, U.S.A.

1951   H. Richard Niebuhr, *Christ and Culture*.

1960   Geoffrey Francis Fisher, archbishop of Canterbury meets with Pope John XXIII; Anglican-Roman Catholic International Committee results.

1961   Consultation on Church Union (COCU) begins.

1963   Vatican II, Pope John XXIII; Anglican Congress, Toronto, Canada, *Mutual Responsibility and Interdependence*.

1965   Paul Tillich, Protestant theologian, dies.

1970   *Plan of Union* for the Churches of Christ Uniting; Reinhold Niebuhr dies.

1973   Anglican Consultative Council, Dublin, Ireland, "Partners in Mission."

1976   Proposed Book of Common Prayer and ordination of women priests in Episcopal Church.

1977   Janani Luwum, archbishop of Uganda, martyred; partners in Mission Consultation in U.S.A.

Suggestions for Further Reading

In addition to the books cited in full in the notes accompanying the text of the foregoing chapters, the following books may be of interest and assistance to the reader.

COMPREHENSIVE OVERVIEWS AND SURVEYS

The conventional mode of presenting history, in a chronological and sequential narration, has been used countless times to tell the story of the Christian enterprise. Williston Walker's *A History of the Christian Church*, first published in 1918 and revised and brought up to date by Cyril C. Richardson, Wilhelm Pauck, and Robert T. Handy (New York, 1959) has long served as a standard text book, a comprehensive overview from a Protestant perspective. *The Pelican History of the Church* is a six-volume series, each volume with its own author. The authors and titles of the first five volumes, which constitute a sequential history of the church from its beginnings to the present, are: Henry Chadwick, *The Early Church*; R. W. Southern, *Western Society and the Church in the Middle Ages*; Owen Chadwick, *The Reformation*; Gerald R. Cragg, *The Church in the Age of Reason 1648–1789*; and A. R. Vidler, *The Church in an Age of Revolution*. The sixth volume, which has been noted in chapter five, is Stephen Neill's

A History of Christian Missions. Not so much a conventional, chronological history as an extended essay on the history of the church is the account by British novelist Charles Williams, *The Descent of the Dove: A Short History of the Holy Spirit in the Church* (Grand Rapids, 1972).

A striking visual approach to the history of the church is *The Horizon History of Christianity* (New York, 1964); its rich illustrations are embellished by the lively running text by Roland H. Bainton, professor emeritus at Yale. The text alone of this volume, together with black and white drawings and photographs, has been published separately in two paperback Torchbooks: Roland H. Bainton, *Christendom* (New York, 1966).

Atlases are visual starting points for surveying history, and a fine example appropriate to this listing is provided by Frederic van der Meer, *Atlas of the Early Christian World* (London, 1958). The maps and plans are clear, concise, and sequentially arranged, and are accompanied by carefully annotated photographs selected for the significance of the persons and places depicted and for their illustrative usefulness. The successor volume to this atlas, Frederic van der Meer's *Atlas of Western Civilization,* 2nd ed. rev. (Princeton, 1960), continues the story down to the twentieth century and has a compass broader than the church alone. Franklin H. Littell, *The Macmillan Atlas History of Christianity* (New York, 1976) is a single-volume presentation, with connecting commentary, of the emergence of Christianity and its spread throughout the world, with especially helpful reference to the Third World in the present century.

A very useful encyclopedic volume is *The Oxford Dictionary of the Christian Church,* 2nd ed., edited by F. L. Cross and E. A. Livingstone (London, 1974). Its historical and biographical information is easily gotten at, and its individual articles include valuable bibliographical listings. Another manageable one-volume compendium, which has been noted in chapter two, is Henry Bettenson's *Documents of the Christian Church* (New York, 1943). It is noted again as a modestly priced and remarkably inclusive companion to any survey of the history of the church.

THE CHRISTIAN COMMUNITY

A great deal of church history has been written from the perspective of and with focus on the church's clerical leadership. Consequently, it is often difficult to catch sight of the life of lay people in the church. An attempt to correct this limited view is a volume of essays, *The Layman in Christian History* (London, 1963), prepared for the World Council of Churches Department of the Laity by Stephen Neill and Hans-Ruedi Weber, editors. Massey H. Shepherd's *At All Times and in All Places* (Greenwich, Ct., 1953) provides some view of lay people in a collection of vignettes of the church gathered in worship at six points during its history. Virginia Corwin's *St. Ignatius and Christianity in Antioch* (New Haven, 1960) is valuable not only as a biography of Ignatius but as a broad view of what it was like to be a Christian in that time and place. Bernard Manning's *The People's Faith in the Time of Wycliffe* (reprinted, Totowa, N.J., 1975) is a specific look at the fourteenth century.

One consequence of not having the laity as a focal point of historical writing, is that the contribution of women in the life of the church is often neglected. Women are included in great numbers in compilations of lives of the saints, and their sanctity during the course of the centuries was often a mode of real power in the church. Women have contributed other kinds of leadership as well. Edith Deen's *Great Women of the Christian Faith* (New York, 1959) presents brief sketches of over one hundred women, from the first century to the nineteenth, who in a variety of ways exercised leadership in the Christian community, often as pioneer agents of social change. Roland H. Bainton's two volumes on the sixteenth-century, *Women of the Reformation in France and England* (Minneapolis, 1973) and *Women of the Reformation in Germany and Italy* (Minneapolis, 1971), study the role of women in that crucial century of the church's history. Chapter 7 of R. W. Southern's *Western Society and the Church in the Middle Ages* (noted above as volume 2 of *The Pelican History of the Church*) discusses the effective role of women in the medieval church both within the religious orders and outside the established communities. Not yet published but forthcoming is a shared study by a theologian and an historian: Rosemary R. Reuther and Eleanor L. McLaughlin, *Women of Spirit.*

Two important studies of the churches in the New World are Sydney E. Ahlstrom's *A Religious History of the American People* (New Haven, 1972) and Robert T. Handy's *A History of the Churches in the United States and Canada* (Oxford, 1976). Of more specified interest in the history of the Episcopal Church are: Clara O. Loveland's *The Critical Years* (Greenwich, Ct., 1956), which traces the difficulties of American Anglicanism's survival in and adaptation to the newly founded United States, and George Freeman Bragg's *History of the Afro-American Group of the Episcopal Church* (reprinted New York, 1968), which brings to the fore an all too often overlooked aspect of the history of the Episcopal Church.

RENEWAL AND REFORM

The living out of the ascetic ideal in Christianity, in both its eremitic and conventual patterns, has had a profound influence upon the spread and development of the church, its renewal and its reform, and has generated an enormous amount of biographical, historical, and analytical writing. This long and wide-ranging story is effectively compressed and handsomely illustrated in David Knowles's *Christian Monasticism* (New York, 1969).

In specific regard to the reform of the church in England, T. M. Parker's *The English Reformation to 1558,* 2nd ed. (London, 1966), sets the events of the sixteenth century in the continuum of what preceded them but stops short of Elizabethan and seventeenth-century developments. Gordon Rupp's *Six Makers of English Religion 1500–1700* (London, 1957) approaches English Protestant development in terms of its literature: Bible translation (William Tyndale), liturgy (Thomas Cranmer), biography (John Foxe), and poetry (John Milton, John Bunyan, Isaac Watts). Albert Frederick Pollard's *Thomas Cranmer and the English Reformation, 1489–1556* (reprinted Hamden, Ct., 1965), which first appeared in 1905, has long been the standard biography of this controversial figure;

Jasper Ridley's *Thomas Cranmer* (Oxford, 1962) is a more recent assessment.

John R. H. Moorman's *The History of the Church in England*, 3rd ed. (London, 1973), is an overview of the origins and development of Anglicanism which pays some attention to its descendants outside the British Isles. In looking at the historical and liturgical processes which resulted in the Episcopal Church's Book of Common Prayer, Massey H. Shepherd's *The Oxford American Prayer Book Commentary* (New York, 1950) provides a wealth of historical material about the American church, supplementing such overviews as James T. Addison's *History of the Episcopal Church*, noted in chapter one.

CHURCH AND CULTURE

The first five volumes of *The Pelican History of the Church*, listed above under "Comprehensive Overviews and Surveys," are especially useful in surveying the history of the church with attention to its social, political, and cultural involvements with the world. The standard comprehensive treatment of the issues arising from these involvements is Ernst Troeltsch's *Social Teachings of the Christian Churches* (New York, 1931), a monumental, two-volume work. There are many other studies of the matter devoted to specific time periods or themes, for example: Bede Jarrett's *Social Theories of the Middle Ages 1200–1500* (Westminster, Md., 1942); R. H. Tawney's *Religion and the Rise of Capitalism* (New York, 1926); and Anson Phelps Stokes's *Church and State in the United States* (New York, 1950, 3 volumes; New York, 1964, revised one-volume edition).

THE MISSION OF THE CHRISTIAN COMMUNITY

Stephen Neill's *A History of Christian Missions*, noted above as volume 6 in *The Pelican History of the Church*, is a comprehensive, historical overview. Of more specific historical focus are James Thayer Addison's *The Medieval Missionary: A Study of the Conversion of Northern Europe* A.D. *500–1300* (New

York, 1936), and G. J. Cuming, editor, *The Mission of the Church and the Propagation of the Faith* (Cambridge, Eng., 1970). Both Addison's book and the essays edited by Cuming set the missionary activity of the church in the context of the social and political circumstances of the times. Max Warren, a priest of the Church of England, has addressed Anglican missionary movements in modern times in two works: *Missionary Movements from Britain in Modern History* (London, 1965) and its companion volume, *Social History and Christian Mission* (London, 1967).

Present-day missionary endeavors have contributed to an understanding of the need for the Christian churches to achieve interdependent cooperation (comity) in their activities and the merging of their organizational structures (unity) in both the parent churches and the younger churches which have emerged out of missionary activity. This matter has been treated historically in R. Pierce Beaver's *Ecumenical Beginnings in Protestant World Mission* (New York, 1962).

A comprehensive overview of the history of ecumenism and of the ecumenical movement is provided in a two-volume collection of essays from various hands: volume 1, Ruth Rouse and Stephen Neill, editors, *A History of the Ecumenical Movement, 1517–1948,* 2nd ed. (Philadelphia, 1957); and volume 2, Harold E. Fey, editor, *A History of the Ecumenical Movement, 1948–1968* (Philadelphia, 1970). George K. A. Bell's *The Kingship of Christ: The Story of the World Council of Churches* (Baltimore, 1954) deals with ecumenism among Protestant, Orthodox, and Anglican churches; and Robert McAfee Brown's *The Ecumenical Revolution: An Interpretation of the Catholic-Protestant Dialogue* (Garden City, N.Y., 1967) continues the historical account in light of Vatican Council II.

The Early Church

Europe in the Middle Ages and the Reformation Era

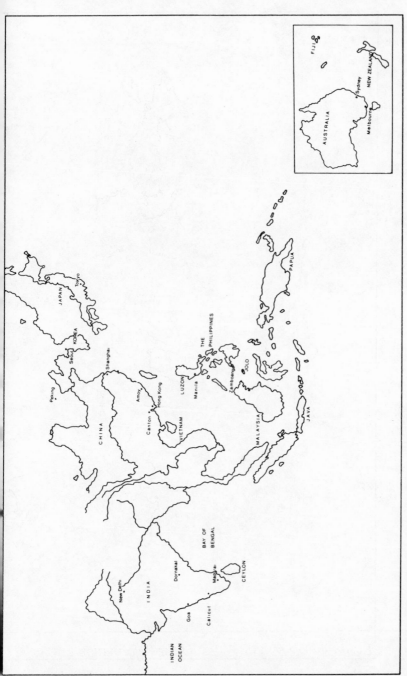

The Christian Mission in the Far East

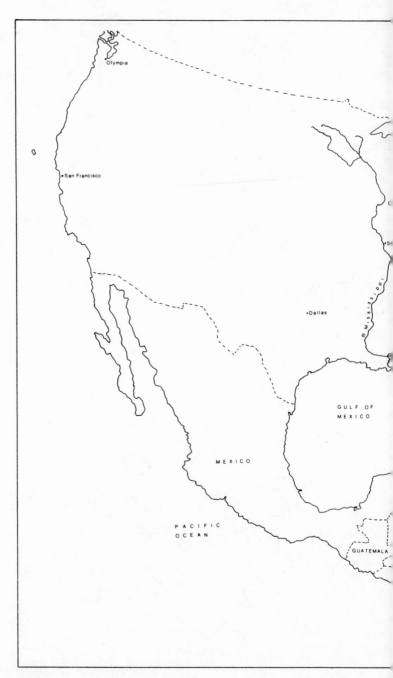

North America in the Modern Era

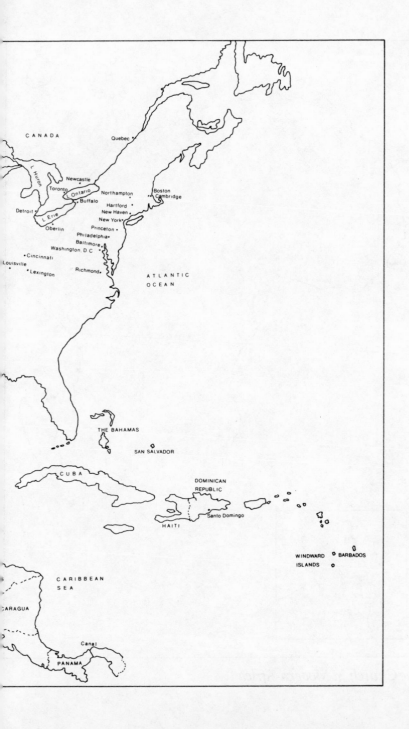

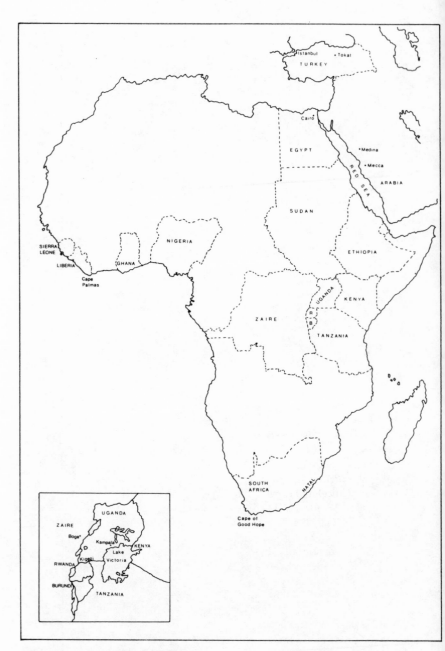

The Church in Modern Africa

Index